JORDAN COOPER

A Contemporary Protestant Scholastic Theology: Prolegomena

First published by The Weidner Institute: A Division of Just and Sinner 2020

Copyright © 2020 by Jordan Cooper

All rights reserved. No part of this publication may be reproduced, stored or transmitted in any form or by any means, electronic, mechanical, photocopying, recording, scanning, or otherwise without written permission from the publisher. It is illegal to copy this book, post it to a website, or distribute it by any other means without permission.

www.JSPublishing.org

First edition

ISBN: 978-1-952295-25-6

This book was professionally typeset on Reedsy. Find out more at reedsy.com

Contents

Acknowledgement	iv
Proposed Volumes in this Series	v
Endorsements	vi
1 Introduction	1
2 Current Scholarship on Theological Method	13
3 Theological and Philosophical Foundations	83
4 A Defense of the Scholastic Method	197
5 Implications for Contemporary Issues	284
Bibliography	333

Acknowledgement

Thank you to everyone who made this work possible, including my doctoral advisor Dan Lioy, and the South African Theological Seminary for granting me permission to publish this dissertation. I also want to give thanks to my wife, Lisa, who always encourages me throughout my writing.

Proposed Volumes in this Series

I. Prolegomena: A Defense of the Scholastic Method

II. The Doctrine of God: A Defense of Classical Christian Theism

III. Theological Anthropology: An Augustinian Approach

IV. Christology: Jesus's Person and Work

V. Justification: Salvation as Forensic Declaration

VI. Union with Christ: Salvation as Participation

VII. Law and Gospel: In Scripture, History, and Contemporary Theology

VIII. The Church and Sacraments

IX. Eschatology

Endorsements

"Privileged to have been a friend of Robert Preus, I know that he would have greeted this book with a broad smile. Through his labors as well as Richard Muller's, at least two generations have now rediscovered the exceptionally fertile gardens of Lutheran and Reformed orthodoxy. I heartily commend this work and expect it to contribute significantly to this trend."

Michael Horton
J. Gresham Machen Professor of Systematic Theology and Apologetics, Westminster Seminary California

"By placing its idiosyncratic redefinition of justification by faith at the center of its theology, Radical Lutheranism has garnered followers from both ELCA and the LCMS, church bodies which are irreparably divided on biblical interpretation and church practice. Jordan Cooper identifies the foundations of Radical Lutheranism in existentialism and linguistic philosophy and shows its incompatibility with the Lutheran Orthodoxy of Martin Chemnitz and Johann Gerhard. Special attention is given to Gerhard Forde and Oswald Bayer both of whose views have been appropriated by the literarily productive Steven Paulson in their articles in the *Lutheran Quarterly* and books. Law is defined by what it does rather than what it is and so it is existentially regarded as a function without a prior reality in God. This leads to placing the act of atonement not within God or in the past event of Golgotha but in the hearers' faith which is the existential moment when in hearing the gospel the believer is justified. Readers will find here an easy to read clarification of a movement whose claims to authentically represent Luther's theology cannot be substantiated."

David P. Scaer

Professor of Biblical and Systematic Theology, Concordia Theological Seminary, Fort Wayne, Indiana

1

Introduction

Introductory Thoughts

Scholasticism is often derided in church history courses as a bygone era of theologizing which relied on pagan Greek thought and overly systematic thinking. It is common for seminary-trained pastors to be unaware of the fact that such a thing as a Protestant scholasticism even existed in the immediate post-Reformation era, as such a project is identified solely with medieval Catholicism. However, I want to argue that rather than being simply the relic of an outdated worldview, the scholastic theological method is one that can and should be used in the modern era. In the last few centuries, since the rise of modern philosophy through Descartes and the Enlightenment following him, theologians have attempted to use various other philosophical systems to explain theological truths. But the fact is that none has such explanatory value as those philosophical convictions which guided the church throughout the medieval period. Thus, I contend that it needs to be revived.

This project arose from my doctoral dissertation, which is both a defense of the scholastic method and a critique of the movement known as Radical Lutheranism. I soon realized, however, that the scope of this work is beyond a critique of one particular theological school which has existed only for the last fifty years. As I began to read various other criticisms of scholastic thought from both the Lutheran and Reformed traditions, it became clear that the primary arguments given by the Radical Lutheran authors broadly echo those of other traditions who are similarly critical. Thus, while this work does engage extensively with those authors who are part of the Radical Lutheran movement,[1] this emphasis should not put off readers who are unfamiliar with these thinkers, as the criticisms extend far beyond this particular group of Lutheran theologians. This book stands primarily as a defense of the older theological method, which has roots in both the medieval and Reformation eras.

It should be noted that this work is self-consciously Lutheran, though the title simply describes itself as a *Protestant* scholastic theology. In the seventeenth century, the scholastic tradition generally divided itself into two distinctive schools of thought: the Lutheran and the Reformed.[2] One could not just be a Protestant scholastic in some general sense, as the goal of this theological method is precision, and the attempt to argue in such precise categories cannot

---

[1] The primary three figures dealt with here are Gerhard Forde, Oswald Bayer, and Steven Paulson.

[2] It is true that some Arminian and Socinian theologians also used a similar method.

ignore the differences between these two branches of the Reformation. Thus, I place myself firmly within the Lutheran orthodox tradition, holding to a *quia*[3] subscription to the confessional writings of the Evangelical church as contained in *the Book of Concord*. However, despite the differences that remain between the Lutheran and Reformed churches, both retain a common heritage in the scholastic approach to doing theology in the seventeenth century. Both held to similar philosophical convictions, using the categories developed by Plato and Aristotle while affirming the primacy of Scripture over human reason and tradition. Despite the popularity of Cornelius Van Til in contemporary Reformed thought,[4] as well as the total rejection of apologetics by some modern Lutherans,[5] these two historic traditions also both held to a strong natural theology, as well as a defense of the notion of natural law. Thus, while the particulars of various doctrines differ, the method itself is one used by the broader Protestant tradition throughout the seventeenth century. This work, then, is intended as a defense of the scholastic method as a whole, thus speaking to both the Lutheran and Reformed communities.

---

[3] The word *quia* denotes a complete acceptance of the teachings of the confessions "because" they agree with Holy Scripture. This is differentiated from the *quatenus* approach, which argues that these documents are to be accepted "insofar as" they affirm the teachings of Scripture.

[4] His method of presuppositional apologetics contains a strong denial of Thomistic thought, in favor of a transcendental argument for God's existence. I contend that this is a strongly Kantian move, but such a discussion is beyond the scope of this work.

[5] This is discussed in the final chapter.

A final note to be given here is that this dissertation was originally written to stand alone, but as I began to work through some of the implications of the scholastic method, it became clear that all of the desired topics could not be covered in a single volume. Out of this realization came the idea to develop the ideas addressed here in relation to particular doctrinal topics. These texts are not merely historical in scope, as a summary of the doctrines taught in the seventeenth century. Both Robert Preus and Richard Muller have done this in a more thorough way than this systematician possibly could. These volumes are an attempt to bring the work of those thinkers and apply them to contemporary debates in both theology and philosophy. This is not a pure repristination of older thinkers, as modern developments inform and develop these ideas for the modern world. The discussion begins here with an explanation of the shift in nineteenth and twentieth century Lutheran thought away from scholasticism.

Background

In order to understand the basic differences between various theological systems, one must first comprehend the various philosophical and methodological presuppositions which guide these systems. Traditional prolegomena texts outline the basic differences between theological schools, such as those between the Lutheran, Reformed, and Roman Catholic traditions.[6] Within the Lutheran tradition, there has been

---

[6] See the first volume in Johannes Quenstedt's system of theology, available in English as Quenstedt, *Nature of Theology*. Also see Lindberg, *Christian Dogmatics*, 20–33.

an extensive amount of discussion surrounding these issues, especially as writers have been critical of the developments in seventeenth-century Lutheran scholasticism. Several writers have argued that Greek metaphysical convictions underlie the theology of Lutheran writers following the 1580 Book of Concord, and they have for that reason abandoned the theology of Martin Luther himself.[7] In order for the differences among Lutherans to be properly explicated, such methodological presuppositions and philosophical starting-points must be outlined and examined.

The criticisms of Lutheran orthodoxy began in the nineteenth century through the rise of Protestant Liberalism, which greatly impacted the German church. In particular, Albrecht Ritschl influenced later Lutheranism through his contention that there is a great theological divide between Luther and the later Protestant tradition.[8] This development is based in a significant manner not upon particular theological convictions, but upon the development of Kantian philosophy. Prior to Kant, traditional metaphysical categories were generally adopted by Christian theologians, being rooted in either the Platonic or the Aristotelian tradition. Kant revolutionized Western thought through his division of reality between the noumenal and phenomenal realms. For Kant, only the phenomenal realm is accessible to the human subject. One can know a thing only insofar as that thing impacts the human creature, and it is thus known subjectively. One does not have access to the noumenal realm, or the thing-in-itself. Christian theology consequently was impacted by this

---

[7] See Ritschl, *Three Essays*, 149–218 and Forde, *Law-Gospel*, 3–11.

[8] See the discussion of this in Lotz, *Ritschl and Luther*.

shift and began to speak not about God as he is in himself, but the practical import of the Christian faith as it affects the individual believer. It was Ritschl who combined Kant's basic presuppositions with Luther's thought, and in doing so, shifted the emphasis of theology from the objective study of God to the cultivation of morality through the Christian community.[9]

Throughout the twenty-first century, a new philosophical school was popularized, commonly known as existentialism. While differing from Kant on a number of significant points, existentialism affirms the fact that a thing is to be known by its effects upon the human subject. In existentialist writers, existence precedes essence, and act is prioritized over being. This movement influenced a variety of theologians—most notably, Rudolph Bultmann, who based his theology in part on the philosophy of Heidegger.[10] The Radical Lutheran school of thought, following Gerhard Forde, emphasizes many of these same ideas, while attempting to formulate an approach to Lutheran theology that is focused not on metaphysics, but upon God's act toward the sinner.

In his *Theology Is for Proclamation* (1990), Forde develops a system of theology that is dependent upon the act of proclamation rather than traditional categories of substance and essence. He distinguishes between two modes of discourse: primary and secondary. Primary discourse is language that speaks directly to a human subject, addressing the individual in the second person. An example is the statement "I love you." Secondary discourse is language which speaks *about*

---

[9] Ritschl, *Justification and Reconciliation*.

[10] See Macquarrie, *Existentialist Theology*.

something. The emphasis in Christian theology should always be on primary discourse, rather than secondary. Traditional theological systems, especially those influenced by Aristotle, are wrongly focused on secondary discourse (and not even the correct kind, according to Forde) and privilege the essence of various theological categories over their acts within history. This emphasis leads to a redefinition of the entire theological system, especially through Forde's contention that the law is defined not as an eternal standard, but as that which functions in an accusatory manner. Forde similarly redefines the doctrine of God, Christology, and other dogmas in light of this revision.

Four years after Forde published his work, Oswald Bayer released his book *Theologie*, in which he presents a theological prolegomenon through his study of Luther. Published in English in 2007 under the title *Theology the Lutheran Way*, this work delivers a systematic presentation of the theological task from a perspective similar to that of Forde. Like Forde, Bayer is critical of traditional metaphysical approaches to Christian theology, and he continually rejects the use of Aristotle as a valid theological source. He presents a theology which is dependent on the acts of God upon the human subject, but emphasizes the linguistic aspects of God's work. Lutheran theology for Bayer is focused not upon virtue or metaphysics, but upon God's word of promise—or *promissio*—given to the sinner. Theology is, at heart, a dialogue between God and man. Bayer's system results in a revision of several essential doctrines, such as justification and the nature of God.

The most extensive study of the classical Lutheran scholastic methodology is Robert Preus's *The Theology of Post-Reformation Lutheranism* (1970, 1972). This two-volume

A CONTEMPORARY PROTESTANT SCHOLASTIC THEOLOGY: PROLEGOMENA

set explains the history and methodology of the seventeenth-century writers. Preus contends that Protestant scholasticism remains a viable theological tradition, and argues that modern theologians are wrong for discarding these writers in favor of other theological and philosophical movements. He divides the Lutheran orthodox period into three separate times: the golden age, the high age, and the silver age. Preus favors the earlier writers, as he remains critical of the overuse of Aristotelian categories in some later writers. In this way, Preus defends a moderated form of Protestant scholasticism. Throughout these two volumes, Preus exposits traditional Lutheran prolegomena and the doctrine of God.

The most prolific contemporary proponent of the Protestant scholastic method is the Reformed theologian Richard Muller. Though Muller is not Lutheran, his work remains invaluable in this area, as he exposits the various tenets of Protestant scholasticism—many of which coincide with the Lutheran approach. In his four-volume *Post-Reformation Reformed Dogmatics* (2003),[11] Muller gives an account of the various Reformed scholastic writers and explains the development of various theological ideas in their thought. Like Preus, Muller contends that the seventeenth century remains an essential and productive time of theological discourse. He argues that Protestant scholasticism remains relevant in the contemporary world, as the various developments in the seventeenth century led to the contemporary theological landscape—whether their influence is recognized or not.

Two divergent approaches to Christian theology are presented here. Some follow in the tradition of Lutheran exis-

---

[11] A new edition is currently being worked on.

tentialism and reject the scholastic theological methodology for various reasons.[12] These writers are not unified in each element of their particular systems, but all prefer to speak in categories of act (whether linguistic or otherwise) over being. From the other perspective, there are theologians who argue for the validity of the traditional dogmatic system presented in seventeenth-century Protestant orthodoxy.[13] Again, there is a divergence among theologians regarding the usefulness of the extensive application of Aristotelian language, among other particulars. However, despite these differences, these theologians hold to a general agreement that the basic methodology of the Lutheran orthodox remains a beneficial way to exposit Christian theology.

Objectives of This Work

The overarching idea to be addressed in this work is the superiority of the classical Protestant scholastic method over contemporary proposals. Following this primary goal, the following four chapters address these topics: the current state of scholarship on theological method within the Lutheran tradition; the theological and philosophical foundations of the Lutheran scholastic method; a defense of this method in response to criticisms of contemporary authors; and the practical implications of the loss of the scholastic approach. Each of these topics confronts the rejection of traditional Protestant scholastic categories by the Radical Lutheran au-

---

[12] As examples, see Forde, *Where God Meets Man*, and Paulson, *Lutheran Theology*.

[13] See the above works from Preus and Muller.

thors, and the consequences of such a neglect for theology and the church. This evaluation includes authors who identify explicitly with the Radical Lutheran title, such as Gerhard Forde, Oswald Bayer, and Steven Paulson, who reject scholasticism and affirm a contemporary theological method impacted by existentialism and linguistic philosophy. The problems with other writers, such as Robert Kolb and William Schumacher, who attempt to combine elements of the Radical Lutheran method with theological convictions inherent in Lutheran scholasticism (while simultaneously rejecting the metaphysical convictions of scholasticism), are also addressed, in order to defend the scholastic approach.

It is the contention of this work that traditional essentialist categories, as defended by Lutheran scholastics, are necessary for the theological task. While the seventeenth-century writers are not immune to criticism from modern authors, their general theological and metaphysical convictions provide a more beneficial framework for theological discourse than do contemporary systems.

A revival of Lutheran scholasticism in contrast to Radical Lutheranism and other modern approaches is beneficial to the church for a variety of reasons. First, this method allows for more productive theological and ecumenical discourse among Christians. The Radical Lutheran system is one which differentiates itself foundationally from other Christian traditions, and thus makes dialogue with other traditions exceedingly difficult. The scholastic method provides several commonalities between the Lutheran, Roman Catholic, and Reformed traditions which—historically at least—have general agreement on various aspects of the theological method and philosophical presuppositions. Second, this method allows for a clear exposition of various doctrinal points in a manner which is not possible through contemporary systems. Several areas of theology become conflated with one another or confused when modern categories are applied to the theological task, as is the case in Radical Lutheranism. Third, the scholastic method provides for closer continuity with the historic church. The categories proposed by the seventeenth-century Lutheran writers are an extension of both patristic and medieval dogmatic theology, whereas Radical Lutherans function on categories that either are present only in Luther (often not significantly so) or are modern constructions. This latter tendency threatens the catholicity of the Lutheran Reformation.

Conclusion

The primary themes and concerns of the present study have been outlined. Twentieth-century Lutheran thought gradually shifted from the scholastic method under the influence of thinkers like Werner Elert[14] and Rudolph Bultmann. Existentialism led to a different mode of discourse than those which utilized more traditional Greek metaphysical categories. This led to the formation of the Radical Lutheran theological movement which is prominent today and includes thinkers such as Gerhard Forde, Steven Paulson, and Oswald Bayer. In this work, a critique of these thinkers is offered with the attempt to defend the older scholastic method in theological discourse within the Lutheran church.

In opposition to Radical Lutheranism, the following chap-

---

[14] Elert, *Structure of Lutheranism*.

ters propose a theological model which is in accord with classical metaphysics as modified by scholastic thinkers such as Martin Chemnitz and Johann Gerhard. This is done through addressing the fundamental research objective alongside the four subsidiary topics. At work in this study is a mixture of theological disciplines, including historical, systematic, and exegetical theology. All of these areas of study lead to practical application for pastoral theology in the contemporary church.

In the following chapter, the first objective, regarding contemporary theological methodology within Lutheranism, is addressed. This is done through a literature review which examines authors from the Radical Lutheran movement, along with those who defend the Protestant scholastic method and authors who utilize aspects of both theological schools. This then leads to a study of the methodological presuppositions of the Lutheran scholastic writers in the following chapter.

2

Current Scholarship on Theological Method

Introduction

As the general research question, "How is the scholastic method a more sufficient one than other modern theological approaches?" is answered, it is imperative that the general field of theological prolegomena within Lutheran thought be examined, especially in view of contemporary developments. Everyone engaged in the theological task has a variety of both methodological and philosophical presuppositions, whether explained clearly or not, which guide one's writing and thought. In this chapter, the following question is answered: *What is the current state of scholarship concerning theological methodology within the Lutheran tradition?* This discussion serves as a basis for expounding upon the differing perspectives on these issues in further chapters.

As a review of all literature on this particular subject would be impossible, representative texts have been chosen in order to evaluate theological methodology in contemporary scholarship. These texts are divided into three categories. First, there are those texts from a Radical Lutheran perspective. The three authors evaluated here are Gerhard Forde, Oswald Bayer, and Steven Paulson. These writers disagree on various points, but they share a common theological conviction surrounding the importance of the divine speech-act as formative for a proper Christian theology, and a general rejection of traditional scholastic categories, especially those that arise from Aristotle. The second category of authors are those from the confessional Lutheran tradition who combine traditional confessional theology with some of the changes in the field made by Gerhard Forde and Oswald Bayer. This is a mediating view between the older scholastic perspective and modern rejections of the older methodology. The authors examined in this section are Charles Arand, Robert Kolb, and William S. Schumacher. Finally, scholars who promote a traditional scholastic methodology are discussed. The two authors used here are Robert Preus and Richard Muller. Both of these figures have written extensively on Protestant scholasticism and have produced significant writings on its theological methodology in comparison with modern approaches. Throughout this review, each of these contributions is compared to other developments in the field.

Radical Lutheran Authors

The field of scholarship within the broader category of Radical Lutheranism is somewhat varied. These authors are unified by some common methodological concerns, and a conviction that justification is the central tenet and theme of all Christian theological discourse, though they differ on other points.[15] These writers are examined individually, so that their unique contributions to the development of Lutheran theology in the twentieth and twenty-first centuries are clearly explained. Gerhard Forde is the father of this theological school, and thus his work serves as a basis for further exploration of theological prolegomena from a Radical Lutheran perspective. Oswald Bayer shares many commonalities with Forde, but he has developed his own somewhat independent theological system with the concept of divine speech at the center. In many ways, Bayer is more favorable to traditional theological categories than Forde. Finally, Steven Paulson is evaluated. Paulson began his theological career after both Forde and Bayer, and draws upon both figures in his own approach to Christian doctrine.

Gerhard Forde

Gerhard Forde is the founder of Radical Lutheranism, as he coined this term in an essay of that title first published in the 1987 inaugural issue of *Lutheran Quarterly*. In this article, Forde contends that in order to move forward as a theological tradition, the Lutheran church must proclaim the centrality of justification by faith even more boldly than before, and thus must be "radically" Lutheran.[16] This centrality of the doctrine of justification frames the entirety of Forde's career. It is to be

---

[15] As will be demonstrated, what they mean by the term "justification" differs from the scholastic definition commonly accepted within Protestant theology.

[16] Forde, *More Radical Gospel*, 7.

noted, however, that the idea of justification for Forde is not exactly the same as that of the confessional Lutheran tradition. While the scholastics argued that justification is a forensic declaration based on the imputation of Christ's merit to the sinner, Forde contends that justification refers to the acts of killing and making alive through God's declarative word.[17] Justification is identified with the act of proclamation given by a preacher. This is done in opposition to the law, which according to Forde is not the eternal will of God, but God's act of accusation toward the sinner. This central thesis guides Forde's theological system.

In light of his specific theological contentions, Forde constructs a unique system of Christian doctrine in his book *Theology Is for Proclamation*. While his theological method can be exposited from his other writings, this work in particular highlights the uniqueness of his theological method. Forde begins this work by expositing a distinction between two different modes of theological discourse.[18] The first is *primary* discourse, and the latter is *secondary*. Primary discourse is language which speaks directly to an individual, whereas secondary discourse merely speaks *about* a thing. Forde uses the example of love. Primary discourse is the lover saying to the beloved, "I love you." Secondary discourse involves the lover simply talking *about* love, either through an exposition of what love is or by making general statements that he loves people.[19] According to Forde, traditional Christian theology has generally emphasized secondary discourse to

---

[17] Forde, *Justification by Faith*, 3.

[18] Forde, *Theology Is for Proclamation*, 1–9.

[19] Forde, *Preached God*, 49.

the neglect of primary. This primary discourse Forde further labels "proclamation," or "kerygma."[20] For Forde, this proclamation is to be at the center of one's theology. In this manner, Forde rejects the traditional Lutheran scholastic approach to Christian theology, since this twofold distinction is not characteristic of earlier theology, which privileged secondary discourse over primary. He views the history of the Lutheran church as one of discontinuity with Luther's own thought.[21] In Forde's view, the evangelical church must abandon the scholastic method and instead look to Luther's own theology, which he contends is centered on primary theological discourse.

In light of his argument that proclamation is the central element of Christian thought, Forde then constructs a basic system of theology consistent with this contention. The division of theology into these two modes of discourse is not merely an attempt to include a "for you" proclamation of forgiveness within the constructs of traditional Lutheran doctrine. In Forde's view, secondary discourse has been misunderstood as that which is purely theoretical, or which is concerned with something in the realm of ideas. In contrast to this, Forde argues that secondary discourse should simply be "the kind of reflection that takes place between yesterday's and today's proclamation."[22] In other words, theological discourse must always be based upon proclamation, and it is only relevant insofar as it fosters proclamation. Because the Lutheran scholastics did not function on the basis of

---

[20] Forde, *Theology Is for Proclamation*, 1.

[21] Ibid., 6.

[22] Ibid., 4.

such a distinction, there was no conscious attempt to do this. The majority of the theological textbooks, then, according to Forde's argument, are inconsistent with the centrality of proclamation. Therefore, the central tenets of Lutheran orthodox teaching should be discarded.

The central problem with Lutheran orthodoxy, according to Forde, is the adoption of a "static-ontological" concept of the divine law.[23] This idea is developed especially in his book *The Law-Gospel Debate*, but this contention stands behind his theological method as developed in *Theology Is for Proclamation*. I have argued for Forde's incompatibility with traditional Lutheran thought in *Lex Aeterna*.[24] For the Lutheran orthodox, the law is defined as an eternal standard that coheres with God's own nature and character. It is both eternal and unchanging. This definition then, according to Forde, informs the orthodox writers' perspectives on almost every other topic. Since the law is a set of static propositions, the gospel to is reduced to the same. Similarly, the doctrine of God in Lutheran orthodoxy is mistaken, because the law is identified with God's nature.[25] In his desire to reject the traditional conception of God's commandments, Forde argues that theology should not be based upon the category of "substance" but of "act."[26] I have labeled this an "existential," rather than "essentialist," approach to Christian theology.[27] While the basic outlines of this move were outlined in my

---

[23] Forde, *Law-Gospel Debate*, 4.

[24] See Cooper, *Lex Aeterna*.

[25] Forde, *Law-Gospel Debate*, 8–9.

[26] Forde, *Theology Is for Proclamation*, 105.

[27] Cooper *Lex Aeterna*, 4.

previous work, the details of each philosophical system had not been explored as they will be in the present work. In his book *Theology Is for Proclamation*, Forde attempts a revision of each primary Christian doctrine in light of his existential convictions, including sin, Scripture, Christology, and the doctrine of God. This leads to a vastly different set of beliefs than is found in Lutheran orthodoxy.

Theological prolegomena, for Forde, are founded on the distinction he makes between "God preached" and "God not preached."[28] This fundamental paradigm allows for his reconstruction of doctrine. Forde identifies "God not preached" with the hidden God of wrath and abstraction. Another term for this is the "naked God." This is the God that is sought by philosophers, wherein God is viewed as some kind of unifying force or timeless principle, through which meaning is given to all of reality. This God is placed in the realm of timelessness, and is inaccessible to the human creature. Forde further identifies this God with law, and contends that this God is "hardly distinguishable from Satan."[29] Forde is not merely rejecting the abstractions of pagan philosophers, but he identifies the majority of approaches to the construction of Christian theology as attempts to explain God apart from the act of proclamation. By making such a claim, Forde rejects the scholastic method altogether, as he is particularly critical of Aristotle and Thomas Aquinas. The Lutheran scholastics, such as Johann Gerhard, construct a traditional doctrine of God through an exposition of his nature and attributes, agreeing

---

[28] Forde, *Preached God*, 33–55.

[29] Forde, *Theology Is for Proclamation*, 16.

with Aquinas that God is *actus purus*.³⁰ This, in Forde's view, is merely timeless abstraction, and is inconsistent with Luther's approach to Christian doctrine.

The abstract ideas inherent in traditional Lutheran doctrine are, for Forde, transferred to the realm of concrete action upon the individual. The prime example of a mistaken approach to theology, for Forde, is the orthodox doctrine of vicarious atonement.³¹ For the seventeenth-century dogmaticians, the atonement is placed into a logical scheme according to God's attributes. God is just, and sin is an infinite affront to God's justice and honor. God, then, must atone for sin through the satisfaction of his own justice. Christ does this through his death on the cross. For Forde, this takes the gospel away from its immediacy and direct nature to the sinner, and places it into the realm of the abstract and theoretical. Instead, Forde argues that Christian theology is centered on a confrontation between the sinner and God not preached. When encountering this hidden God, the believer is under existential duress in confrontation with God's wrath. In this dilemma, the revealed God, or "God preached," arrives in order that the one hearing the word of proclamation might be saved from the God of abstraction.³² One is on a constant flight from God-not-preached to God-preached. This dialectic shapes the nature and content of Christian theology.³³

---

[30] See, for example, the treatment of God's essence and attributes in Gerhard, *Nature of God*.

[31] Forde, *Where God Meets Man*, 34.

[32] Forde, *Preached God*, 48.

[33] For a further explanation of both the traditional orthodox view of the law and Forde's criticism of it, see Scott Murray, *Living God*.

Forde presents a theological method which is radically different from all other Christian theology. The Lutheran orthodox construct a theology on the basis of various theological concepts which are explained and defended in their essence, and they then consequently present practical application of these concepts to the individual. Forde, instead, begins with the application of doctrine to the individual through the act of proclamation, and then consequently expounds upon theology in relation to this proclamation. According to Forde, the scholastics subordinated proclamation to discourse *about* God, and in doing so, neglected the New Testament *kerygma*. He contends that Christian theology must change this methodology, and it can only do so through the adoption of his two primary distinctions between primary and secondary discourse, and that between God-not-preached and God-preached.

Oswald Bayer

Of those theologians who criticize the traditional scholastic approach to theology in contemporary Lutheranism, Oswald Bayer provides the most in-depth and philosophically informed critiques. Bayer is a professor of systematic theology at Tübingen and an influential Luther scholar. Throughout his writings, Bayer contends that the systems of traditional and contemporary systematic theologians are insufficient due to their neglect of the linguistic element of theological discourse. Bayer promotes a theology based upon linguistic philosophy, especially as influenced by John Austin and Johann Georg Hamman. In Bayer's view, these authors help to give proper categories in which one can rightly exposit Luther's theology of the *promissio* given to the sinner in Christ. These ideas are present throughout Bayer's theological career, but the two works which most clearly exposit his methodology are *Theology the Lutheran Way* and *Martin Luther's Theology: A Contemporary Interpretation*. The first is a theological prolegomenon, in which Bayer sets Luther's doctrinal approach in contrast to various other theological methods and philosophical systems. The second, which is Bayer's most extensive contribution to Luther scholarship, is a treatment of his own unique approach to the reformer.

Bayer's *Theology the Lutheran Way* is divided into two primary sections. First, he overviews Luther's theological methodology; second, he places this understanding of theology in the context of modern problems and gives a thorough critique of theological systems developed since the time of Kant. He begins this work with the premise that there is a problem in identifying theology strictly with either metaphysics or ethics.[34] The metaphysical approach to theology begins with Plato; he seeks to explain God as a unifying element to all of existence.[35] There are two fundamental axioms which drive metaphysical theology as formulated in Plato and developed in the later Greek and Christian traditions. First, God is the cause only of that which is good; he is not the direct cause of evil. Second, God is completely unchangeable in both character and essence. This leads to an understanding of God as timeless. Plato does not, however, completely disregard myth as an essential element of theology, as he combines mythology and metaphysical

---

[34] Bayer, *Theology the Lutheran Way*, 9.

[35] Ibid., 4–6.

questions. In Aristotle, however, the metaphysical element completely overtakes the mythological or historical, so that theology is based purely on abstract ideas, identified with a timeless and separate God.[36] The criticisms of Bayer here echo those of Forde, who is similarly critical of Greek metaphysics, and consequently its adoption by Christian theologians.[37]

While Bayer is not willing to argue that early Christian theology blindly adapted Greek philosophy to Christian truths, he purports that some of the problematic elements of the older view of God corrupted the nature of Christian truth, especially in the Middle Ages. This is evident through various divisions which developed in theological discourse, such as that between meditation and disputation. The divide between scholasticism and mystical piety unfortunately separated theological disputation from the spiritual life, and also, the practice of piety from rigorous theology.[38] This divide impacts not only medieval thinkers, but the Lutheran scholastics as well. Bayer is critical, for example, of Johann Gerhard's separation of writings between those which are devotional and those which consist in *disputatio*.[39] The beginnings of this separation in Gerhard eventually culminate in the theology of Johann Semler and Rudolph Bultmann, wherein either the moral or existential element of Christian truth is completely divorced from doctrinal explication. In view of these

---

[36] Ibid., 7.

[37] Criticisms of classical metaphysics have been common in German theology since the rise of nineteenth-century Liberalism. Adolf von Harnack, who argues for a strong differentiation between Hebraic and Hellenistic thought in his *History of Dogma*, is a classic example of this.

[38] Bayer, *Theology the Lutheran Way*, 11.

[39] Ibid., 12.

criticisms, Bayer argues that Luther's theological method offers a third alternative to these common conceptions of Christian doctrine. It is in this third methodology that Bayer echoes Forde's contention that the theological method must be redefined in light of Luther's evangelical discovery.

For Bayer, theology should not be placed in the realm of the speculative, or in that of the subjective experience. Theology, instead, is in essence a dialogue between God and man. God is not to be studied in the abstract, according to his nature and attributes. Instead, Bayer argues that the specific content of theology is the *justifying* God and the *sinful* human.[40] This position separates Bayer from the Lutheran scholastic tradition, wherein the particular essence of God and that of man are evaluated and discussed. For Bayer, this older methodology has essentially the same problems as that of older Greek thinkers. It seeks to find a kind of justification for reality through some unifying concept, which is then identified as God.[41] For Bayer, as for Forde, God is not identified with any particular theory or idea, nor with a timeless and unchangeable being, but with justification. For the theologian, God is identified as the one who justifies through his word.[42] Bayer does not negate the usefulness of essentialist categories altogether, as he acknowledges that they may have their place in the secular sphere. Yet these essences are not the concern of the theologian.[43] A dialogical approach to theology, according to Bayer, overcomes the

---

[40] Ibid., 18.

[41] Ibid., 26.

[42] Ibid., 27.

[43] Ibid., 19.

division between the practical and speculative approaches. This communicative approach to Christian theology is similar to the contention of Forde that it is primary discourse which guides the theologian, rather than secondary or speculative. Rather than speaking of "primary discourse," Bayer uses the language of a "performative speech-act."[44] The two ideas are synonymous.

One of the most important contributions of Luther's thought, according to Bayer, is the manner in which he overcomes the Aristotelian distinction between theory and praxis. This divide is exemplified in the medieval debates surrounding the story of Mary and Martha, wherein the *vita activa* and the *vita contemplativa* are presented as two divergent aspects of the Christian life.[45] For Bayer, these are not alternatives at all, but the theologian instead follows the unifying idea of the *vita receptiva*. For Luther, the Christian life finds its essence in its passivity *coram Deo*. This is the way of faith, wherein one does not live in order to reconcile all things in a metaphysical system (what Bayer refers to as "justifying thinking") or through an attempt at self-actualization through the ethical life (what Bayer calls "justifying doing"), but through a continual reception of God's gifts.[46] Faith is a third element standing at the center, through which both ethics and contemplation are to be engaged. Through his formulation of a theology based on reception, Luther has a fundamental disagreement with medieval scholasticism. According to Bayer, Aquinas attempts to do just the kind of

---

[44] Ibid., 126.

[45] Ibid., 108.

[46] Ibid., 25.

justifying thinking that Luther so radically opposes. Thomas views theology as a science, concerned primarily with the realm of ideas. For Luther, in contrast, theology deals with history and experience. God is not to be dealt with abstractly as a unifying concept of all reality. Such a conception, according to Bayer, is a *theologia gloriae* which stands in opposition to Luther's *theologia crucis*. Luther, for Bayer, destroys the radical divide between eternity and time as two divergent realms that separate God and man.[47] The perception of a timeless God arises from Plato's fundamental axiom about what constitutes divinity, rather than from Scripture. In Luther's theology, God himself is radically historicized. Bayer contends that, like creation, God himself experiences "history, time, change, and suffering."[48] While Bayer does not explicitly engage with the Lutheran scholastics in this critique, it is apparent that the same criticisms leveled against Aquinas would apply to seventeenth-century Lutheran orthodoxy. Like Aquinas, some of the Lutheran scholastics define theology as a science,[49] and the later analytical theologians clearly explain God as a unifying concept of all theology and existence generally. Classical theistic concepts are utilized by all of the scholastics as well, with the conviction that God is timeless

---

[47] Ibid., 30.

[48] Ibid., 31. This is a common theme in both contemporary philosophy and contemporary theology, which challenge the notion of timelessness. Examples include the theology of hope as promoted by Wolfhart Pannenberg and Jürgen Moltmann, as well as in writings of Reformed philosopher Nicholas Wolterstorff.

[49] Though this is often highly qualified in contrast to Aquinas, as theology (in its most proper sense) is an aptitude. However, in its exposition into various loci, it is exposited scientifically.

and immutable.

Since Bayer rejects the utilization of traditional systematic categories, including that of the doctrine of God, in his exposition of the Christian faith, he approaches the nature of doctrine in a different manner. The unifying principle of his theology, if he can be said to have one at all, is the distinction between law and gospel. These are viewed not as abstract doctrinal ideals, but as direct words of address from God to man.[50] Here, Bayer again echoes Forde's concerns. For Forde, the law is not defined by what it is in essence, but by what it does. Bayer argues similarly, but emphasizes the linguistic aspect of both the law and God's *promissio*. The only type of metaphysic that Bayer employs in this context is a "relational ontology."[51] The human creature does not live in himself, but ecstatically in Christ. The category of relation has precedence over that of essence for the theologian. The law and the gospel, then, are not to be explained in categories of essence, but in terms of their relation to the sinner through their linguistic application.

The central doctrine of the Christian faith for Bayer is justification. This doctrine is not explained in traditional dogmatic categories, but is identified as a performative word. Bayer draws upon the philosophy of J. L. Austin to explain that there are two fundamentally different forms of speech: constative and performative.[52] For Bayer, earlier linguistic theory largely relied on the division between the *signum* and *res*. Language points one to ideas elsewhere, and does not

---

[50] Ibid., 30.

[51] Ibid., 53.

[52] Ibid., 127.

then give or do anything directly. This understanding was applied to the sacraments by St. Augustine and continued to be the general understanding of the Western tradition. Baptism, the Lord's Supper, and absolution were all then viewed as mere "signs" which point to something that is signified, to be received elsewhere.[53] For Luther, this division between sign and thing signified was broken, as he came to understand that the absolution is speech that does what it says. In Austin's language, it is a performative speech-act. This performative speech-act is what Gerhard Forde refers to as "primary discourse." This is language which does what it says, similar to God's words "let there be," which effected creation *ex nihilo*. This linguistic act constitutes the essence of Christian theology.

This linguistic turn in Christian theology is promoted in opposition to a variety of other theological methods. Bayer criticizes earlier theology for its emphasis on metaphysical questions that seek a unified theory in the nature of God.[54] This criticism applies to much pre-Reformation theology, as well as to the Protestant scholastics. Bayer is similarly critical of various modern theological movements. The divide between theory and praxis remains in much modern theology. For Kant and Ritschl, the moral aspect of existence replaces the theoretical or speculative, making the early divide between ethics and theology complete.[55] For Friedrich Schleiermacher, this division takes a purely subjective turn, as faith itself is

---

[53] Ibid., 129.

[54] In the language of James Dolezal, Bayer promotes theistic mutualism, also identified as theistic personalism. See Dolezal, *All That Is in God*.

[55] Bayer, *Theology the Lutheran Way*, 142–44.

reflected upon as a feeling of absolute dependence.[56] Existential theologians similarly emphasize the purely subjective impact of Christian truth upon the individual. Hegel, and other modern theologians like Wolfhart Pannenberg, have fallen into the same mistake as the ancient Greeks through an attempt at explaining all of reality through a theological metaphysic. Linguistic theology does not only overcome the divide between theory and praxis, but also between subjective and objective. All of these various theological schools, according to Bayer, have made the mistake of pitting the objective and subjective realities of Christian theology against one another. The performative speech-act avoids a pure objectification of Christian theology in that this declarative word does not simply represent some truth found elsewhere, as is the Aristotelian tendency; nor does the speech-act base theology upon the human response to or experience of a divine act. Instead, theology is centered upon the act itself.

Throughout his book *Martin Luther's Theology: A Contemporary Interpretation*, Bayer expounds upon many of the themes addressed in the previous work. This volume is divided into two sections: "Prolegomena" and "Individual Themes." For present purposes, only the first section is discussed as directly related to the topic at hand.[57] The exposition of various topics in the latter section is dealt with in later chapters as the conclusions of Bayer's theological methodology are examined in light of Lutheran scholastic thought. The prolegomena here are an exposition of Luther's theological method and concerns, and thus echo much of the previous book.

---

[56] Ibid., 152.

[57] Bayer, *Martin Luther's Theology*, 1–92.

For Bayer, Luther's writings remain relevant in the modern theological milieu. In particular, Luther's theological method serves as a foundation upon which the contemporary writer is able to properly engage with modern theological trends. Bayer does not attempt in this work simply to exposit Luther's historical understanding of doctrine within a sixteenth-century context, but this work is an attempt to relate his concerns to modern debates and concerns. Two themes, in particular, that arise from Luther's theology are emphasized in Bayer's work: his idea of the hidden God, and his emphasis on the divine *promissio* given to the sinner through the word of the gospel.

The first essential topic here is the idea of the hidden God as exposited by Luther.[58] It might appear, at first, that this idea is simply the contention that God cannot be fully known in his essence by the human creature. This much would be affirmed by nearly the entire Christian tradition, from Pseudo-Dionysius' apophaticism through the scholastic distinction between archetypal and ectypal theology. The concept of the hidden God, however, goes far beyond this. For Luther, God is at work in all things, through both creation and providence. This includes good and evil, so that God often appears to us as the devil himself.[59] In Bayer's thought, this concept helps guard against modern conceptions of theology, as well as the theodicy problem, such as in theologies which posit love as a kind of unifying principle, or which try to separate God from the effects of sin in the world.[60] The attempt to separate God from evil ultimately leads to the Aristotelian contention

---

[58] Ibid., 4.

[59] Ibid., 4.

[60] Ibid., 31.

that God stands as one totally other than creation, one who is completely ahistoricized. He spends eternity contemplating himself, with no concern for the historical acts in the world.[61] For Bayer, God is a historical being, who is providentially present in all things which occur.

The idea of the hidden God, for Bayer, is a third essential element of theological discourse alongside the traditional Lutheran distinction between law and gospel.[62] God's hiddenness is *not* identified with the law, as it seems to be at times in Forde's writing. This hiddenness terrifies the human creature and leads to an experience of existential dread before the God who appears to be Satan himself.[63] Bayer is fond of posing the story of Jacob wrestling with God (Gen 32:26) as analogous to the general human experience of encountering God. In faith, the believer flees from the hidden God to the God who reveals himself in Christ.[64] This dialectic shapes the Christian experience, so that it is not *only* the law which drives one to the gospel. The distinction Bayer makes here between the hidden and revealed God is similar to Forde's distinction between God-preached and God-not-preached. Like Bayer, Forde emphasizes the historical nature of the gospel message, so that the metaphysically abstract ideas of a supreme being lead one to the preached God as given in Christ. Bayer's exposition of the hidden God is the most existential area of his thought, and it is essential for understanding the

---

[61] Ibid., 32.

[62] Ibid., 42.

[63] These same themes appear earlier throughout the writings of Werner Elert. See, for example, *Structure of Lutheranism*.

[64] Bayer, *Martin Luther's Theology*, 40.

nature and purpose of theology from a Lutheran perspective.

The second major theological distinctive outlined by Bayer as part of Luther's theological method is his emphasis on the linguistic nature of theological discourse.[65] In contrast to a subjectivist understanding of faith, wherein theology simply studies the religious experience of individuals or communities, Christianity is founded upon the word of address that precedes religious experience. Faith is given through the word, and the word stands apart from it, as the foundational principle of belief.[66] For Luther, according to Bayer, theology is not a scientific enterprise, but a linguistic one. It is not merely the scholar who is a theologian, then, but anyone who is addressed by God and called to respond. This divine address is universal. The theological task is constituted by address and response, rather than theoretical study or proposition.[67] Therefore, the central task of the theologian is to hear the address of God and consequently respond in praise and thanksgiving. This linguistic approach is liturgical in nature, as it mirrors the function of a worship service that is based upon speech which extends from God through the pastor, and then back to God through the congregation.[68]

For Bayer, the theological task is tied together with human identity. In his view, the identity of a creature is determined by the address of God's word.[69] In this way, Bayer, like Forde, differentiates himself from earlier scholastic methods. While

---

[65] Ibid., 50.

[66] Ibid., 53.

[67] Ibid., 41.

[68] Ibid., 16.

[69] Ibid., 55.

scholastic theologians, both medieval and Protestant, speak in essentialist categories in relation to the human creature, Bayer prefers the language of address and relation as definitional to a Christian ontology. Human nature (at least in a theological sense) is to be understood in relation to God's speech-act, through which man is created, and recreated by the gospel.[70] God's word of address gives value to the human subject and constitutes one's place in the world. This dependence upon God's word runs in opposition to the human desire for a kind of self-actualization, wherein one is constituted by personal decision, works, or anything else. The speech-act of God radically destroys any sense of human autonomy.

For Bayer, faith, justification, metaphysics, and the doctrine of God are all radically historicized. One does not encounter any of these truths in the realm of the theoretical and abstract, but through human experience.[71] In this way, Bayer echoes Forde's concern for God's word in act over its objective being and content. Unlike Forde, however, Bayer spends more space nuancing his position, discussing the importance of traditional scholastic disciplines as an essential part of the theological task. He notes, for example, Luther's continuity with medieval thought in his use of the trivium and quadrivium. Grammar, logic, and rhetoric are all essential elements of theological discussion on an academic level.[72] In this way, Bayer does not completely reject the definition of a theologian as one who theorizes about various doctrines through an exposition of the biblical text. His approach is similar to

---

[70] Ibid., 37.

[71] Ibid., 53.

[72] Bayer, *Theology the Lutheran Way*, 81.

Forde's in his emphasis upon act over being, yet his focus on the linguistic elements of theology, through the nuances he makes throughout this work, differentiate him from Forde, who is more explicit in his rejection of traditional theological methodology.

In these two writings, Oswald Bayer promotes a unique approach to Christian theology which is centered on linguistic analysis rather than metaphysical speculation. Though he does not use the specific language of primary and secondary discourse, Bayer comes to many of the same conclusions as Forde, while remaining similarly critical of the scholastic method. This theological method is not completely discordant with the seventeenth-century Lutheran dogmaticians, but it remains critical of them.

Steven Paulson

In his book *Lutheran Theology* in T&T Clark's Doing Theology series, Steven D. Paulson explains Lutheran thought and theological method using the book of Romans as a rough guideline. Throughout this work, Paulson explains similar themes to those previously explored in both Forde's and Bayer's writings. Paulson is a professor of systematic theology at Luther Seminary in Saint Paul, Minnesota, and an influential voice in contemporary Lutheranism. He is a frequently published author in *Lutheran Quarterly* and other Lutheran periodicals. This book is the most succinct and complete treatment of Paulson's unique approach to Lutheran theology, which is heavily influenced by both Forde and Bayer. Though it is not a book on prolegomena in a direct manner, as are the works of the previous two authors, Paulson deals throughout this text with material related to theological method and consistently criticizes Lutheran orthodoxy.

Affirming the primary contention of Forde's *Theology Is for Proclamation*, Paulson purports that all theology should arise from preaching. He argues that Lutheranism can best be understood not as a branch of the church catholic, but as a preaching movement. More than anything else, Luther sought to revitalize and reform the preaching task within the medieval church. In light of this emphasis on preaching, Paulson argues that the distinction between God-preached and God-not-preached is "the most important distinction Lutheran theology makes."[73] This particular distinction is not one that is found in historic Lutheran sources, but arises from Luther's *Bondage of the Will*.[74] Forde revitalized this theme, and Paulson uses it as an undergirding theme of the entirety of all of his theology. At one point, Paulson argues that there are no prolegomena to theology at all other than preaching.[75] Paulson's category of "God not preached" is similar to Bayer's emphasis on the hiddenness of God. This is God apart from the proclamation of Christ, in the abstract. This is the "naked God," or the God who is the one sought for by metaphysicians. This God only brings wrath, as he works through both good and evil. One is set free from God-not-preached only through God-preached in the gospel.

When speaking about God-preached, Paulson identifies this

---

[73] Paulson, *Lutheran Theology*, 23.

[74] See Packer and Johnston's translation for a good modern edition of *The Bondage of the Will*.

[75] Paulson, *Lutheran Theology*, 62.

preaching with "for you" gospel proclamation.[76] In other words, he argues that preaching is to involve primary discourse first and foremost, rather than secondary discourse.[77] In Bayer's language, Lutheran theology is centered on the divine speech-act which creates faith. Like Forde and Bayer, Paulson prioritizes act over being. Preaching, the law, the gospel, justification, and the doctrine of God are described in categories of act upon the individual, rather than as separate independent doctrinal ideas which stand alone. This is clear in Paulson's affirmation of Bultmann's thought in opposition to Lutheran orthodoxy.[78] Paulson argues that Bultmann rightly understood the personalistic-eschatological nature of Christian theology (though he disagrees on Bultmann's idea of personal existential decision). Theology deals with that which impacts the sinner directly, instead of themes within some out-there realm of ideas. In Paulson's view, Lutheran orthodoxy—especially in the seventeenth century—misunderstood the true nature of the biblical message and retreated to a medieval approach to Christian theology much different from Luther's own.[79]

The primary error that Paulson identifies in previous theological methods, including that of scholastic Lutheranism, is what he identifies as the "legal scheme."[80] This legal scheme is similar to what Forde often labels the "*theologia gloriae*," or in other places, the "ladder scheme." In this scheme,

---

[76] Ibid., 31.

[77] Ibid., 25.

[78] Ibid., 32.

[79] Ibid., 12.

[80] Ibid., 2.

God's law is described as eternal, and it inheres within his own nature. This law serves as the structure of all further doctrine, including sin, salvation, and Christology. God's law is a standard that merits entrance into eternal glory.[81] Sin, then, is viewed as a violation of this standard. Salvation involves Christ actively and passively obeying this law as a substitute. Justification is identified with the application of this legal merit acquired by Christ to the sinner through a purely forensic verdict. In Paulson's perspective, this legal scheme was rejected by Luther and early Melanchthon. Throughout Lutheran history, and especially through the writings of Calov and Quenstedt, the law was reintroduced into Lutheran thought as the backbone of the theological system.[82] This, according to Paulson, was done to defend God's own honor and justice in relation to the forgiveness of sins. The scholastics contended that God must satisfy his divine justice in order to grant the verdict of justification to his people. This is done through the contention of a vicarious atonement in which the penalty of the law is paid by Christ as a substitute for the human race. In Paulson's view, this perspective does not significantly depart from medieval scholasticism and is in error.[83]

Like Forde and Bayer, Paulson is highly critical of Aristotle's influence upon Christian theology—especially in medieval and Protestant scholasticism. Throughout this book, Paulson repeatedly mentions the Aristotelian distortion of various biblical doctrines. One idea that he is particularly critical of

---

[81] Ibid., 11.

[82] Ibid., 12.

[83] Ibid., 107.

is the *ordo salutis*.[84] In the later Lutheran scholastics—most notably Calov, Hollaz, and Quenstedt—the idea was formulated that there is a precise order of events whereby the Holy Spirit applies salvation to the individual. One is called by the gospel, regenerated by the Spirit, comes to repentance and faith, is justified, receives mystical union with God, and lives a life of sanctification, all culminating with one's entrance into eternal glory.[85] This, according to Paulson, is dependent upon a logical scheme of cause and effect that is drawn from Aristotle.[86] This idea is also dependent upon a doctrine of God's unity, which is inconsistent with Luther's distinction between law and gospel.[87] In Paulson's view, there is no ultimate unity of law and gospel, even within God himself. The *ordo salutis* and the contention of a *lex aeterna* in Lutheran orthodoxy, in contrast to Luther, were attempts to place law and gospel into a larger logical scheme and ultimately to arrive at an ultimate unity of the two. In Paulson's perspective, these ideas have more in common with Aquinas than with Luther.[88]

One of the most important sections of Paulson's book is a short one titled "Lutheran Method," wherein Paulson differentiates the Lutheran theological methodology from that of scholasticism.[89] He places Melanchthon's first edition of the *Loci Communes* in opposition to the foundational texts of both Eastern and Western theology in the medieval period.

---

[84] Ibid., 12.

[85] Schmid, *Doctrinal Theology*, 407–10.

[86] Paulson, *Lutheran Theology*, 60

[87] Ibid., 25.

[88] Ibid., 128.

[89] Ibid., 28–34.

He criticizes John of Damascus as utilizing a Neoplatonic metaphysic to guide his theological conclusions rather than Scripture itself. He also critiques Peter Lombard as merely setting forth a number of human opinions in a rabbinical manner, rather than engaging the text directly. These two figures set the foundation for the scholastic theological method in which various doctrines are exposited topic by topic, beginning with the doctrine of God. For Paulson, it is a mistake to begin one's doctrinal system with an exposition of the nature of God—including his attributes, existence, unity, and triunity. These ideas, apart from the foundational task of preaching, are abstract. Paulson affirms Forde's critique of previous Christian thought, that the fundamental distinction between secondary and primary discourse has been neglected, and that this has resulted in a flawed theological method. This sets Paulson apart from the majority of Christian theologians in history.

Another aspect of Aristotelian thought that Paulson is critical of is the concept of virtue.[90] For Paulson, Aristotle and Luther present opposing perspectives on the virtuous life. Aristotle emphasizes human effort, whereby one is habituated into various virtues. In Luther's thought, the gospel puts an end to the search for virtue. Both the medieval scholastics and the Lutheran orthodox sought to view redemption as a path from vice to virtue, but Paulson argues that the search for virtue itself constitutes the human problem.[91] One must not be saved *unto* virtue, but *from* virtue. The re-imposition of virtue ethics into Lutheran thought is largely connected to

---

[90] Ibid., 4.

[91] Ibid., 32.

the scholastic belief that the law has a third use that follows the gospel. For Paulson, the gospel puts an end to the law altogether.[92] The *ordo salutis* was built in order to put an emphasis on virtue and to allow the legal scheme to take over in the Christian life. Sanctification is called an effect of justification, so that justification is always leading to something beyond itself.[93] This contradicts Luther's justification-centric theological approach.

Paulson presents an approach to Christian theology that draws heavily from the thought of Gerhard Forde and Oswald Bayer. Throughout his work, Paulson synthesizes the ideas of these two authors and offers several of his own unique developments on this basis. What he offers, ultimately, is a theological method that is fundamentally opposed to both medieval and Protestant scholasticism. For Paulson, theology does not consist in the exposition of doctrinal ideas organized around various loci, from prolegomena through eschatology. Instead, theology is based in proclamation, having at its heart the fundamental distinction between God-preached and God-not-preached.

Radical Lutheranism: Critical Analysis

Though the school of thought under the rubric of Radical Lutheranism is broader than the figures mentioned here, three of the most influential writers within this theological movement have been examined in regard to their most popular writings. Each writer criticizes the Lutheran scholastic

---

[92] Ibid., 119.

[93] Ibid., 125.

method as taught by the seventeenth-century Lutheran orthodox theologians. Gerhard Forde, Oswald Bayer, and Steven Paulson all disagree on some particulars of their theological systems, but they have a unified criticism of the scholastic method, and all generally prioritize categories of act over those of being.

Lutheran scholasticism, all three authors argue, constitutes a static approach to theology, which relies upon supposedly abstract ideas as heavily influenced by Greek philosophy, and is thus incompatible with the biblical message. Instead, they purport that Luther functioned on the basis of linguistics rather than ontology. For Forde, theology must emphasize the primary discourse act of proclaiming the gospel directly to the sinner. Forde contends that the scholastics misunderstood the nature of both primary and secondary discourse by emphasizing God's nature along with a supposed static-ontological concept of the divine law. In light of this, for Forde, the "for you" proclamation of the gospel is neglected, constituting a departure from Luther's thought. This is what I have previously labeled Forde's "personalized-eschatological" approach, wherein God's act of justifying the sinner, thus putting the old self to death, constitutes the most fundamental theological category.[94] These ideas are placed in opposition to the traditional method of seventeenth-century orthodoxy.

For Bayer, who shares many of the same criticisms as Forde, the central element of theology is the divine speech-act which creates faith and righteousness. Theology is primarily discourse, not *about* God, but between God and man. In this way,

---

94 Cooper, *Lex Aeterna*, 84.

Bayer shares a common concern with Forde for linguistics over metaphysics. Yet Bayer's approach is somewhat different than that of Forde. Rather than using the categories of primary and secondary discourse, Bayer uses the terminology of twentieth-century linguistic philosophy. In particular, he draws from John L. Austin's book *How to Do Things with Words* to elucidate the gospel as a speech-act of God the Father. Bayer's work is more substantive in that he engages philosophy more critically than Forde and gives a stronger ideological grounding for his assertions regarding divine speech. Also, while Forde often simply rejects traditional metaphysics altogether, Bayer is more nuanced in his criticisms, and thus recognizes some value in metaphysical categories within the secular sphere, though neglecting their usefulness in theology. He also appears less impacted by Barth than is Forde, who sometimes appears to simply echo the ideas of the Swiss theologian with Lutheran terminology. It is perhaps for this reason that Forde's work appears more existential than that of Bayer.

In Steven Paulson, a synthesis is made between Forde and Bayer. Paulson is comfortable using both the primary-secondary discourse language of Forde and the speech-act language of Bayer. Like the previous two theologians, Paulson is also highly critical of Lutheran scholasticism, arguing that contemporary thinkers should attempt to replicate the purer theology of the reformer over that of his successors. Paulson's importance is not so much in his own original ideas, but in his efforts at synthesizing other thinkers and utilizing their ideas in interaction with other contemporary theological movements. Despite such efforts, however, Paulson is not as precise in his terminology as either of his predecessors, which sometimes leads him to make statements which many would find problematic, such as his assertion that Jesus sinned on the cross.[95] Yet Paulson's influence gives him an immense amount of importance in contemporary Lutheran thought.

As all three of these authors have been examined, their unified theological concerns can be summarized in three primary points. First, Lutheran scholasticism represents a departure from the theology of Martin Luther, especially as it uses the philosophy of Aristotle. Second, theology is to be described as a dynamic enterprise, emphasizing the impact of God upon the sinner, rather than descriptions of the essence and attributes of God. Third, linguistics provides a more beneficial theological category than that of being, and that theological development must be done in light of contemporary approaches to language. These convictions have an impact on those theologians who explicitly consider themselves part of the Radical Lutheran tradition, as well as thinkers who are generally considered confessionally-minded authors.

Confessional Writers Influenced by Radical Lutheranism

There are many writers within the confessional Lutheran tradition who are influenced in various ways by the Radical Lutheran theological method. Unlike Forde, Bayer, and Paulson, these authors have a firm adherence to the entirety of the Lutheran Confessions, including the Formula of Concord. Therefore, their perspectives on the atonement, the third use of the law, and other topics align more with the Lutheran

---

[95] Paulson, *Lutheran Theology*, 104–5.

scholastics than with modern theological schools. However, despite these differences, the criticisms of the scholastic method, and of classical metaphysics in particular, have been repeated by several confessional writers. It is worth noting that two of the three endorsements which appear on the back of Paulson's *Lutheran Theology* are from professors within the Lutheran Church—Missouri Synod. Though several sources could be examined in order to explain contemporary approaches to the theological method from these theologians, two texts have been chosen. The first is William W. Schumacher's critique of the Finnish approach to Luther, titled *Who Do I Say That You Are?* The second is *The Genius of Luther's Theology,* by Charles Arand and Robert Kolb. Each of these writings explains confessional Lutheran teaching while utilizing various insights from Radical Lutheran thought.

William W. Schumacher

William W. Schumacher's book, *Who Do I Say That You Are?: Anthropology and the Theology of Theosis in the Finnish School of Tuomo Mannermaa,* is an in-depth critique of the Finnish approach to Luther interpretation, as well as a treatise on Christian anthropology. While the Finnish approach to Luther is not directly relevant to the topic at hand, discussions surrounding this theological school often address the nature of theological method, as well as the relationship between theology and metaphysics.[96] Finnish scholars, in their defense of theosis as a valid extrapolation of Luther's thought,

---

[96] For an overview of the Finnish approach, see Braaten and Jenson, *Union with Christ*.

have argued for a type of essentialism, though perhaps more Neoplatonic than Aristotelian. In response to this theological movement, Schumacher argues that a strong substance metaphysical approach to the human person is flawed.[97] Instead, Schumacher purports that Luther functions on the basis of an ontology of the word.

Lutheran theology, according to Schumacher, has unfortunately neglected the importance of anthropology in its exposition of Christian theology. Francis Pieper, for example, spends less time discussing anthropology than he does the doctrine of angels.[98] In traditional dogmatics, the majority of space dedicated to exposing the human creature has been spent discussing the nature of sin, which seems to indicate that sin itself is definitive of the human creature. In opposition to this unfortunate neglect, Schumacher asserts that the field of anthropology is one in which the theologian must be engaged.[99] It is in this area that Schumacher explains his own approach to Lutheran theology, which borrows several insights from Radical Lutheran writers, and Oswald Bayer in particular. Schumacher addresses several criticisms of traditional Lutheranism from the Finnish interpretation of Luther, and uses this to promote his own theological methodology in order to explicate the nature of the human person in relation to God's efficacious word.

Tuomo Mannermaa, Simo Peura, and other Finnish writers argue that since the time of Ritschl, the subject of metaphysics

---

[97] Schumacher, *Who Do I Say*, 14–15.

[98] Ibid., 8.

[99] Ibid., 15.

has been neglected in Lutheran thought.[100] In Ritschl, the historical and ethical dimensions of the gospel took precedence over those related to medieval debates surrounding the nature of being.[101] This is largely due to the influence of Kant's noumenal-phenomenal divide upon various philosophers and theologians, in which the thing-in-itself remains inaccessible. These authors contend that metaphysical issues must once again become a prominent point of discussion within Lutheran theology. While one might assume then that these writers seek to retreat back to the Lutheran scholastic era, they (like the Radical Lutheran writers) view a strong Aristotelian essentialism as inadequate.[102] Instead, they argue for a more Neoplatonic Eastern version of theological metaphysics. For the Finnish writers, while Luther utilizes Aristotelian language, he is committed to a more dynamic and relational metaphysic that is drawn from the movement of the Trinity through the *ad intra* works of eternal generation and spiration.[103] In other words, while Aristotle emphasizes being, Mannermaa and Peura emphasize becoming, as the human person participates in the divine nature.

The primary problem in these approaches to Luther, according to Schumacher, is that they neglect Luther's word-centric theology. Schumacher argues, through a utilization of Bayer, that the human creature is constituted and defined by a word of address. He purports that Bayer's catechetical

---

[100] Mannermaa, *Christ Present in Faith*, 2.

[101] Ritschl, *Three Essays*, 149–218.

[102] Schumacher, *Who Do I Say*, 31.

[103] Ibid., 31.

systematics[104]—through which theology is defined by address and response—gives a more confessional anthropology than that of Peura and Mannermaa. Schumacher's anthropology is essentially summarized by this statement: "To be, and to be human, is to be addressed by God's word."[105] He affirms Bayer's dialogical approach to Christian theology, and thus argues that linguistics serves as a more basic theological foundation than metaphysics. While the medieval scholastics spoke about the human essence, Luther (according to Schumacher) emphasized one's being in relation to the dynamic speech-act of God. Schumacher is concerned that any discussion of a human essence apart from God's creative word gives room to human autonomy, especially as developed in Cartesian and post-enlightenment philosophy.[106]

For Schumacher, theology is defined by the relationship between the justifying God and the sinful human creature. This separates him from the earlier Lutheran scholastic tradition, as is apparent in his discussions about particular theological topics. He argues, for example, that questions of the "how" and "why" of God's act of creation are irrelevant from a Lutheran theological perspective.[107] He associates questions about the particulars of the creation event with Calvinism and fundamentalism. In contrast to Schumacher's claim, the seventeenth-century scholastics spent a large amount of space discussing the specifics about the nature and purpose

---

[104] Ibid., 149.

[105] Ibid., 149.

[106] Ibid., 150.

[107] Ibid., 153.

of God's creational act.[108] Further, Schumacher argues that there is no essential differentiation between creation and preservation; the scholastics, in contrast, treated these as two related, though separate, loci.[109] For Schumacher, man is discussed only theologically, in relation to God, not in terms of a general essence that inheres within the human person. He calls this a "radically theological" anthropology.[110] The questions about a historical Adam and Eve are not the most relevant questions from this perspective, because the real concern in the doctrine of creation is for the relationship between the individual as creation, and the Creator who addresses him. This radically theological anthropology is deeply imbedded in creation. God addresses man through man's fellow creatures, who serve as his masks through which we are addressed and preserved. God creates and preserves mediately, so that humanity is defined largely by the various human relationships in which one is involved.

The primary problem in the Finnish approach, according to Schumacher, is that this word-centric approach to reality is ignored. Mannermaa and Peura place humanity's value in one's union with God that brings one *beyond* creatureliness.[111] For Luther, however, man is defined precisely *as* a creation of God—not as one who is divine.[112] God's word constitutes man's place in the world as a creature, and one's life as a creature continues through the divine work of

---

[108] Schmid, *Doctrinal Theology*, 159–70.

[109] Ibid., 170–76.

[110] Schumacher, *Who Do I Say*, 152.

[111] Ibid., 61.

[112] Ibid., 149.

preservation, wherein God continues to speak through his creation as a mask.[113] In essence, Schumacher proposes an entire theological methodology defined by justification. In justification, God declares that one is righteous, and this declaration actually makes one righteous. This reality is connected to creation, wherein God's word similarly does what it says. It is an efficacious word.[114] Regeneration is also connected to the declaration of the justifying word spoken to the sinner, wherein new life is created *ex nihilo*. In the Lutheran scholastics, however, regeneration is defined as the *donatio fidei* which precedes justification.[115] Preservation, for Schumacher, is similarly connected with God's speech-act which occurs through other creatures. While Schumacher does not outright reject essentialist categories altogether (he acknowledges that God's essence dwells in the human creature), there is essentially no place for such language in his theological system.[116] In a particularly bold statement which summarizes his argument, Schumacher writes, "no other definition of 'reality' is to be sought than this word addressed by the Creator to his fallen creatures."[117] Ultimately, according to this and other statements, there is no place for essentialist metaphysics whatsoever in the theological task.

Schumacher's work shares many similarities with that of writers previously addressed within the Radical Lutheran movement. Schumacher has an approach to theology which

---

[113] Ibid., 157.

[114] Ibid., 164.

[115] Schmid, *Doctrinal Theology*, 459.

[116] Schumacher, *Who Do I Say*, 176.

[117] Ibid., 181.

is essentially anti-metaphysical. Like Bayer, Forde, and Paulson, he argues that theology is a linguistic enterprise, centered upon God's word of address to the human creature. He utilizes the language of divine speech-act in particular to define the human creature's identity, and this is similar to Forde's language of primary theological discourse. Unlike the Radical Lutheran writers, Schumacher is fully committed to the entirety of the Lutheran Confessions, and thus affirms the mystical union of the believers with God and other ideas that are not discussed by the previous writers. In this way, Schumacher combines some of the theology of Lutheran scholasticism with a theological methodology drawn from Radical Lutheranism rather than Lutheran orthodoxy.

Kolb and Arand

In *The Genius of Luther's Theology: A Wittenberg Way of Thinking for the Contemporary Church*, Robert Kolb and Charles Arand present a theological methodology on the basis of Luther's writings. This book, written by two professors at Concordia Seminary in St. Louis, Missouri, is a theological prolegomenon which draws upon both Luther's thought and contemporary interpretations of Lutheranism. Though Kolb and Arand remain committed to the Lutheran Confessions, they draw heavily upon modern writers such as Bayer and Forde. Like Schumacher, they argue for a Lutheran confessionalism which is critical of Aristotelian essentialism, based instead on a linguistic interpretation of reality and a relational ontology.

Kolb and Arand argue that there are two fundamental theological matrixes which frame Luther's theology. These ideas are presented as relevant to the church today as Luther's own theological method is revitalized. The first of these is the theme of the two kinds of righteousness, and the second is Luther's theology of the efficacious word. This book is divided into two sections that deal with these two topics respectively. Each of these ideas is discussed here in connection with the previous authors examined, with a view to explaining the differences between Kolb and Arand's theological methodology and that of earlier Lutheran theologians.

Like Schumacher, Kolb and Arand argue that theological anthropology is a neglected discipline in the history of Lutheran thought. They contend that Luther's two-kinds-of-righteousness distinction serves as the proper model for explaining what it is to be human in a contemporary context.[118] This is the "nervous system" of Reformation theology, which lies at the core of Luther and Melanchthon's thinking.[119] This theme, taken from Luther's sermon "Two Kinds of Righteousness," distinguishes between the passive and active righteousness which both belong to the Christian. These two types of righteousness define the identity of the human creature in two different spheres: before God, and before the world. Humanity is defined not by a static essence as in Aristotelian thought, but by one's relationships with God and the world. *Coram Deo*, one is defined solely by the righteousness of Christ as received in faith. This is one's "core identity."[120] *Coram mundo*, one is defined by active righteousness in connection with one's earthly responsibilities and relationships.

---

[118] The best contemporary treatment of the two kinds of righteousness is Biermann, *Case for Character*. See also Cooper, *Hands of Faith*.

[119] Kolb, *Genius of Luther's Theology*, 25.

[120] Ibid., 26.

The most definitive aspect of humanity is one's relatedness to God. This is addressed in reference to Luther's great Reformation discovery, that righteousness *coram Deo* is a divine gift rather than a human work. As that which receives this righteousness, faith is not merely accidental to the human creature, but it "lies at the core of human existence."[121] Kolb and Arand repeatedly note that this righteousness is not the righteousness of the divine nature as it indwells the Christian. This idea would rely on a Neoplatonic substance metaphysic, which they reject. Like Schumacher, they argue that righteousness must always remain *extra nos*. In light of this conviction, these writers affirm a relational ontology, as does Bayer, wherein the being of God's creatures is constituted by their relatedness to one outside of them, and identity is not found within the subjects themselves. At the core of this relatedness to God is a recognition that one is a creature. God's creative word constitutes one's identity, not as divine, but as distinctively human. To seek some kind of divinity, such as in the Eastern approach to theosis, is to negate creatureliness as a gift.

According to Kolb and Arand, creation is an essential aspect of Christian theology which has been neglected by many theological systems. Drawing upon the work of Gustaf Wingren, they argue that there is a strong link between God's declarative word, creation, and preservation.[122] At the moment of creation, God spoke, and *ex nihilo*, the world came into existence. God's creative act did not then cease, but divine providence is identified as *creatio continua*, whereby creation

---

[121] Ibid., 38.

[122] See Wingren, *Creation and Law*.

is upheld through the creative word. As Schumacher argues, God's creatures serve as *larvae dei*, through which his word is continually communicated to human persons. Justification is tied to this same reality, because in God's declarative statement "I forgive you," the word does precisely what it says. New life is created. This word is mediated through God's creatures (namely, the pastor, in this instance), and God uses this word to uphold and constitute reality. There is an overarching relational ontology here, whereby everything is defined as that which is related to God or others in one way or another. Kolb and Arand do not speak about God creating a human "essence," but of the relation between a creature as one who is spoken to, and God as the one who speaks. This relational ontology extends through creation, preservation, and redemption. In this manner, Kolb and Arand affirm the basic convictions of Oswald Bayer, and neglect some of the essential aspects of the Lutheran scholastic method, which does not exclusively speak in language of relation, but is favorable toward Aristotelian essentialism.

A prime example of how Kolb and Arand's theology is impacted by their strong adherence to a relational ontology is in their treatment of the relationship between justification and sanctification. Like Schumacher, these writers are critical of Mannermaa and the Finnish Luther interpreters. In particular, they criticize what they call a "Platonic, spiritualizing frame of reference" which stands behind Eastern views of theosis.[123] Because Luther's philosophical foundation is relational rather than essentialist, one cannot speak of any sort of ontological or substantial change within the believer through a process

---

[123] Kolb, *Genius of Luther's Theology*, 48.

of sanctification. In justification, one is already fully and perfectly related to God through the righteousness of Christ. Thus, there can be no percentages in sanctification. This understanding leads to a unique approach to sanctification in which it is simply the partial manifestation of an already perfected work. In contrast to this, in an Aristotelian framework (such as that of the scholastics), there is allowance for talk about ontological change in relation to one's accidental qualities of sin and righteousness.

The second section of Kolb and Arand's book expands upon Luther's theology of the efficacious word. According to these authors, Luther's theology is, at its heart, one of the word. God is identified primarily as the one who creates and re-creates.[124] Like Bayer and Forde, Kolb and Arand are critical of the ancient distinction between *signum* and *res*. A purely symbolic approach to human language led to several of the errors in the medieval church, as well as in contemporary Protestantism. At worst, this leads to a dualism, wherein the words of Scripture point one away from oneself to otherworldly Platonic realities. For Luther, however, words are not mere symbols. Instead, they are effective realities. Kolb and Arand draw on Austin's theory of speech-acts, following Bayer. When God speaks, he does not do so descriptively, but in a performative manner. All of creation is constituted by God's speech-acts, and is preserved in the same way. Speech is not merely *one* way that God acts but is definitive of who God is.[125] The Christian's life day to day also takes on this liturgical structure, wherein God speaks his word to the creature, and the human person

---

[124] Ibid., 130.

[125] Ibid., 136.

responds with words of praise and thanksgiving. Kolb and Arand share a fundamental agreement with Forde, Paulson, and Bayer, that theology is essentially a linguistic enterprise.

Along with defining creation, preservation, and redemption by God's speech, Kolb and Arand similarly define sin in the same manner. The breaking of communication between God and his creatures is called "the essence of sin."[126] The problem of sin as the breach of communication is fixed through the declarative and re-creative word of justification which creates faith as its response. God himself is defined by this promise that he gives to sinners, and the receptive hearer is also defined by his relationship to that promise. Kolb and Arand argue that the primary aspect of what it means to be human is to be in communication with God.[127] This communication occurs through the twofold message of law and gospel, through which God both kills and makes alive. These words, while they have objective content attached to them, are defined primarily in terms of their impact upon the hearer.

Kolb and Arand share several of the same fundamental convictions as Bayer, Paulson, and Forde. In agreement with these latter writers, they argue that traditional Aristotelian and Platonic substance language is inadequate for an expression of Lutheran theology. Instead, theology is to be exposited through linguistics, and speech-act theory in particular. The human creature is defined not by a created essence, but by one's relationships—to God and the neighbor. As in Forde's thought, there is a general preference for categories of act over those of being, though it is not nearly as extensive as in Forde's

---

[126] Ibid., 138.

[127] Ibid., 141.

writings, as Kolb and Arand are confessional Lutherans. Kolb and Arand also agree with Schumacher on their fundamental theological convictions in response to the Finnish approach to Luther, by emphasizing dynamic language over ontology. In this way, these writers combine confessional Lutheran convictions with insights from Bayer, Forde, and Paulson.

Confessional Writers Influenced by Radical Lutheranism: Critical Analysis

In Schumacher, Kolb, and Arand, there is a combination of elements of the Radical Lutheran theological method alongside the doctrinal convictions of Lutheran scholasticism. Schumacher, Kolb, and Arand are unified in their rejection of certain elements of the theological systems of Forde, Paulson, and Bayer. These authors contend for an inerrantist view of the scriptural text, the vicarious atonement of Christ, and the third function of God's law. All of these ideas are inconsistent with those of Radical Lutheranism. Yet, despite disagreements on these particulars, the underlying methodological convictions of Radical Lutheran thought remain untouched.

One place where the metaphysical convictions of these authors is particularly clear is in their dispute with Tuomo Mannermaa and the Finnish interpretation of Luther, which is discussed in both texts mentioned above. Why this is particularly important is that the claims Mannermaa makes are largely metaphysical, and thus an author's response to this movement demonstrates his own convictions on these matters. Schumacher, Kolb, and Arand all point to the inadequacy of Greek metaphysics, and of Plato's thought in particular. Theosis is an inherently metaphysical concept, since it relates to one's being as transformed by the presence of God. Rather than simply discussing the issue as regards the relationship between justification and transformation, these figures reject the entire ontological category through which theosis is explicated. In contrast, I have argued for the compatibility of Lutheran thought and theosis in *Christification: A Lutheran Approach to Theosis*.[128] At the center of the critique offered by Schumacher, Kolb, and Arand is a rejection of essentialist categories altogether, as are defended by the Lutheran scholastics. Here, there is agreement with Forde and Paulson, who similarly argue against these ideas.

Along with a rejection of Platonism, these authors all propose, like the Radical Lutherans, that linguistic philosophy provides a basis through which reality is to be explained. Justification is described not simply as a judicial act of pardon, but as a divine speech-act delivered through the words of a preacher. In some ways, justification becomes a metaphysic in itself, as it is given as a manner in which to explicate the being of man, as well as that of God. The dialogical approach to Christian thought as taught by Bayer is utilized by all of these authors. Similarly, all three use Forde's distinction between primary and secondary discourse. These distinctions result in a general priority of act over being in these authors, just as is made by Forde, Bayer, and Paulson. One particularly clear example of this is Schumacher's treatment of the fall as explained above. The historical questions concerning Adam and Eve, the creation week, and other ideas are simply ignored as irrelevant to the theological task, which is simply not concerned with such questions, as they are not directly related

---

[128] Cooper, *Christification*.

to God's speech to man in the act of proclamation. While disagreement exists among theologians as to how the early chapters of Genesis are to be read, there is at least agreement among most that such a discussion is important. In these ways, some of the programmatic elements of the Radical Lutheran system are affirmed by these writers.

Another element of agreement among the writers discussed above is the adequacy of relational ontology to explain questions which have been traditionally explicated by way of essentialist metaphysics. In contrast to Mannermaa's emphasis on Christ's indwelling, Schumacher argues that the human being is defined by one who lives *extra nos*. Identity is not found inside an individual, but through one's ecstatic connection to Christ in faith. Kolb and Arand frame their convictions regarding the two kinds of righteousness in the same manner. The human creature is defined by relationship, and these relations are twofold: to God, and to the neighbor. Rather than viewing such relatedness as an outgrowth of a created human essence, identity is connected to the relations themselves. This is why Schumacher can speak of faith as being of the essence of the human person, rather than an accidental quality.

All of these writers brings forth several important aspects of Luther's theology in their treatments. However, it is apparent that certain methodological concepts as derived from Radical Lutheranism impact their understanding of such ideas. Even though they differ with Forde, Paulson, and Bayer on some doctrinal topics, they have adopted the philosophical framework through which these authors operate.

The Scholastic Method

There is, unfortunately, not an abundance of literature published which exposits the Protestant scholastic theology developed in the seventeenth century. At the time of the enlightenment, the kind of scholastic methodology expressed previously in Christian theology faced challenges from various philosophical movements. Specifically, after the time of Kant, Christian theologians were faced with certain theological concerns which did not previously dominate theological discussions. Conversations drifted from metaphysics to epistemology, and this greatly reshaped all academic disciplines. Through the writings of Ritschl, Hofmann, Dorner, and others, Protestant scholastic theology was derided as incapable of answering contemporary questions, and theologians rejected that methodology for others. Scholasticism did see a revival from the mid-nineteenth through early twentieth centuries, but through the influence of existentialism and Neo-orthodoxy, it was once again viewed as inadequate for addressing questions of the modern world.

Some scholars today have recognized that the dismissals of scholasticism have not been fair, and that these works deserve reexamination. Some Roman Catholic authors, such as Edward Feser[129] and Thomas Weinandy,[130] have argued that Thomistic philosophy remains relevant, and that scholasticism is in need of revival in the contemporary church. There have been some contemporary Reformed authors, such as Carl

---

[129] Feser, *Scholastic Metaphysics*.

[130] See Weinandy, *Does God Change*.

Trueman[131] and James Dolezal,[132] who have revived various ideas from the seventeenth-century Protestant scholastic tradition. Within the Lutheran tradition, however, there has not been as much of a widespread defense of scholastic ideas, though there is a conscious attempt to get several Lutheran scholastic sources back into print, and these scholastic ideas are apparent at times in various authors. There are two authors who have written more than any others in recent years on Protestant scholastic thought: Robert Preus and Richard Muller. Preus published a two-volume set titled *The Theology of Post-Reformation Lutheranism*, in which he sets forth the usefulness of the Lutheran scholastics for the contemporary church through an examination of their theological method and doctrine of God. He also explains Lutheran scholastic thought in a number of published articles. Following Preus, Richard Muller has taken on a similar project from a Reformed perspective through the publication of his four-volume *Post-Reformation Reformed Dogmatics*, in which he gives an extensive exposition of Reformed scholastic thought. Each of these authors is discussed below.

Robert Preus

Robert Preus is one of the most influential confessional Lutheran theologians of the twentieth century. A professor in the Lutheran Church—Missouri Synod, Preus fought against encroaching liberalism in the church and argued for a strict form of confessionalism in accord with the fathers of the

---

[131] Trueman, *Protestant Scholasticism*.
[132] Dolezal, *God Without Parts*.

Missouri Synod—most notably, C. F. W. Walther and Francis Pieper. Along with these nineteenth-century theologians, Preus argued for a recovery of the Lutheran dogmatic heritage as exposited in the seventeenth century. Throughout several essays and a few influential books, Preus demonstrated the relevance of scholastic Lutheran thought for the contemporary church. The most important works in this regard are Preus's two volumes on post-Reformation Lutheran theology titled *The Theology of Post-Reformation Lutheranism*. This two-volume work is the now standard treatment of Lutheran theology in the era immediately following the Reformation. In the first volume, Preus discusses theological prolegomena, and in the second, he exposits the doctrines of God and man. The first volume is most important for the present work, since Preus explains the scholastic method and addresses various criticisms.

Preus notes that there are a number of important characteristics of the scholastic theologians that unite these various writers, despite their differences from one another. The first is that these writers were conservative in their methodology. The purpose was not to depart from Luther and create their own theological system, as Paulson alleges.[133] These authors were much less willing to break from their own theological forebears than Luther was with previous church tradition. Luther himself formulated several of the basic categories upon which these authors functioned, and when going beyond Luther, they were cautious in their exposition. A second characteristic of Lutheran scholasticism is that these writers had a special concern for the purity of doctrine, especially

---

[133] Preus, *Theology of Post-Reformation Lutheranism*, 28.

as relates to the gospel. This much is apparent as well in scholasticism's detractors, who criticize these writers for an overemphasis on correct teaching over the pastoral impact of law and gospel. Preus views this as a positive aspect of their thought, especially in relation to the fact that he does not believe that such orthodoxy was privileged over practical application. Another aspect of seventeenth-century Lutheran writers that Preus notes is their adherence to both confessionalism and catholicity.[134] He argues that the scholastics were not concerned simply to reiterate the statements of the confessional documents themselves, but spent the majority of their time defending their views from Scripture and the church fathers. In this way, the scholastic writers spoke so as to communicate with Christians in other traditions (often polemically). Such a catholic approach to Christian thought stands over against the writings of Paulson and Forde, wherein much of historical Christian thought is derided as neglecting the central theological tenet of the two types of linguistic discourse.

One of the most common criticisms of the Protestant scholastics is that they represent a significant departure from the foundational writers of both the Lutheran and Reformed traditions. This rift has created a "Luther versus the Lutherans,"[135] and a "Calvin versus the Calvinists"[136] thesis, wherein the writers following in the tradition of these

---

[134] Ibid., 35.

[135] This was promoted heavily by the Luther Renaissance of Karl Holl.

[136] See Kandall, "Calvin and English Calvinism," which popularized this notion. Paul Helm responded to this essay with a book, *Calvin and the Calvinists*.

reformers represent an abandonment of the fundamental principles of their respective reformations. This trend is apparent throughout twentieth-century Luther scholarship, wherein the reformer is studied apart from those theologians who carried his name in the following centuries. In the nineteenth century, Albrecht Ritschl argued that Luther is a purer example of Christian faith and life than the scholastics, and through his influence, such an approach became predominant. Among those writers who argued similarly in the twentieth century are Werner Elert, Rudolph Bultmann, and Gustaf Wingren. Elert in particular was influential in his criticisms of Lutheran orthodoxy, especially in relation to the orthodox contention that the law has a positive function in the life of the Christian. For Elert, this teaching represents a synthesis of Lutheran and Reformed ideas that came through Melanchthon. Such criticisms are repeated by contemporary Radical Lutheran theologians.

Preus answers these charges cautiously. He notes that there is a clear difference in the mode of presentation between Luther and someone like Quenstedt. Luther wrote in the midst of existential struggle and spiritual battle. This leaves quite a different tone in his writings than one finds in an extensively systematic writing that is by nature impassionate. Preus observes that students who might be enraptured with Luther's own writing style might then be bored reading the later scholastics.[137] As he puts it, the "pulsating joy of discovery is no longer dominant" in those theologians who were acquainted with Luther's Reformation discovery since

---

[137] Preus, *Theology of Post-Reformation Lutheranism*, 40.

childhood.[138] However, despite such stylistic differences, Preus contends that there is a significant amount of continuity between Luther and the seventeenth-century writers who write in his name. This continuity is seen in Luther's own insistence on the purity of doctrine, which is never in conflict with his emphasis on the practical and pastoral nature of his theological concerns. This zeal for doctrinal purity, then, is an extension of Luther, not a departure from him. Also, the Lutheran scholastics, though their actual style of writing might appear to be dry and unattached for the modern reader, were immensely practical in intent. Preus cites Gerhard and Calov as examples of theologians whose piety and concern for spiritual life is apparent in their writings.[139]

One of the most significant areas of departure (perhaps *the* most significant) of the scholastics from Luther's method is in their use of philosophy. Preus is somewhat critical of the later scholastics for what he sees as an overuse of philosophical categories. He notes that Luther himself would likely be "repelled and disappointed" by such a development.[140] However, despite his reservations, Preus argues that the use of pagan philosophical writers by the Protestant scholastics has been overstated. These writers did not simply adopt reason as some kind of neutral force unaffected by sin, wherein theological conclusions could be reached outside of Scripture. The scholastics repeated Luther's distinction between the ministerial and magisterial use of reason, wherein even regenerate reason is not able to come to theological conclusions

---

[138] Ibid., 40.

[139] Ibid., 40.

[140] Ibid., 41.

outside of God's direct revelation in the inspired text. Preus also argues that Luther himself was not always critical of the use of reason and philosophy, but of its *misuse* in the medieval scholastic tradition.[141] In summary, Preus argues that "There is no cleavage between the period of the Reformation and the period of Lutheran orthodoxy."[142] Scholastic theology is the natural development of Luther's theology, despite differences in the employment of philosophical categories.

Preus categorizes the Lutheran scholastic period into three distinct eras.[143] First is the "golden age of orthodoxy," which follows the immediate period after the writing of the Formula of Concord (1580) through the beginning of the seventeenth century. In his view, as is apparent in his use of the phrase "golden age," this represents the best period of Lutheran thought and development. The most important figure in this era is Martin Chemnitz, who began the process of systematizing Luther's thought following Melanchthon. These authors follow a loci method, wherein topics are treated individually in relation to the biblical text and to one another. The second period described by Preus is "high orthodoxy," which is the era of the Thirty Years' War. In this time, Johann Gerhard is the most significant figure. During this time, a greater emphasis was placed on polemical theology, as Lutheran theologians were in conversation with those of the Reformed and Roman Catholic traditions. It is in this era that Aristotelian terminology is once again introduced into the theological task, though not overwhelmingly so. The third period outlined by

---

[141] Ibid., 41–42.

[142] Ibid., 42.

[143] Ibid., 45–47.

Preus is what he labels the "silver age" of Lutheran orthodoxy, extending from the end of the Thirty Years' War to the end of the orthodox period in the early eighteenth century. The most important writers of this period were Quenstedt, Calov, and Hollaz. Preus views the writings of this era as rigid and dry in presentation, and argues that an overuse of philosophy led to the decline of scholasticism in this era. This is not to say, however, that Preus's view of these writers is entirely negative. He argues that there is much to be commended in these authors, such as their adherence to an attempt to present all theology as a unit through the analytic method.[144] He also notes that though the theological textbooks might appear dry upon a first read, these authors were immensely concerned with practical piety. Through this overview, Preus is in agreement with *some* of the criticisms given by Bayer, Forde, and Paulson. In his view, there is a divide between Luther and the latest orthodox writers, especially in their utilization of Aristotle. However, he is still favorable toward the scholastic method in general, though more in line with Chemnitz and Gerhard than later writers.

Throughout his work, Preus treats the Lutheran scholastic era from a sympathetic perspective. He contends that the large divide between Luther and later writers put forward by some modern scholars is an inaccurate portrayal of the orthodox period. Though he acknowledges some discontinuity, especially in methodology, he argues that the general trend is one of continuity between Luther and orthodox writers. Like the writers examined above from both the Radical Lutheran and confessional traditions, Preus has reservations about the

---

[144] Ibid., 46.

utilization of Aristotle in later scholastics. This present work is more sympathetic toward the later scholastic tradition than is Preus. However, Preus does ultimately demonstrate that scholasticism remains a viable theological method which is consistent with Luther's Reformation.

Richard Muller

Of all writers engaged with the seventeenth-century scholastic method, Richard Muller is the most prolific and influential. Muller is a Reformed scholar and professor of historical theology at Calvin Theological Seminary in Grand Rapids, Michigan. He has authored numerous articles and books, all on various aspects of Reformed theology from Calvin through the scholastic era. The most important of Muller's works for the present purposes is his four-volume series *Post-Reformation Reformed Dogmatics: The Rise and Development of Reformed Orthodoxy, ca. 1520 to ca. 1725*. This series is an extensive overview of scholastic theology within the Reformed tradition and is similar to Preus's work on post-Reformation Lutheranism. Like older scholastic texts, Muller's work overviews doctrines topically and exposits the development and discussions surrounding those particular doctrines with reference to post-Reformation Calvinist writers. The first volume covers theological prolegomena and is most relevant to this discussion. Most particularly, the introductory section of this text is explained here, wherein Muller addresses various criticisms of Protestant scholasticism in defense of that theological method.

Prior to engaging the actual content of this text, something must be said about the examination of a Reformed text in a work on the Lutheran theological method. While Muller deals to a small extent with Lutheran theologians in his work, he is himself a Reformed writer, and thus most often exposits Reformed rather than Lutheran scholasticism. There are three reason why Muller is included in the discussion here. First, though these two traditions differ on specific doctrines, there is a unified Protestant scholastic tradition which underlies Lutheran and Reformed authors in the post-Reformation era. The theological method of writers from both Reformation traditions is largely consistent, although some minor differences appear (just as they do among the Lutheran scholastics themselves). Second, Muller is simply the most important writer on Protestant scholasticism in the modern era. To neglect his contributions to the field simply due to his ecclesiastical affiliation would be an unfortunate gap in the research necessary for this text. This present work, though from a Lutheran perspective, deals with issues of theological methodology that impact the church at large, including the Reformed tradition. Finally, Muller addresses various criticisms of Reformed scholasticism which echo those offered by contemporary Lutheran authors toward the Lutheran scholastic theologians. For these reasons, Muller is engaged here and throughout this work.

Muller writes his work as a historical theological treatment of post-Reformation dogmatics, not only as an unbiased historical study, but partially in response to several criticisms leveled at Protestant scholastic thought and method. In this way, his work echoes some of the themes of Preus's volumes. There are two types of criticisms that Muller is especially concerned with. First, he engages the common misconception that scholastic theology represents a departure from the

Reformation into Greek thought, as opposed to the more biblical orientation of the reformers. Second, Muller argues against the common notion that the earlier reformers—most notably Calvin and Luther—represent an entirely different theological tradition than those who fell back into the oddities and rationalistic tenets of medieval scholastic theology as drawn from Aquinas.[145]

The prominent liberal theologian Adolf von Harnack argued in his monumental *Lehrbuch der Dogmengeschichte* (*History of Dogma*) that in the first three centuries of the church, the gospel was gradually dominated by Greek thinking that is foreign to the New Testament text. In the Reformation, Harnack argues, the original gospel message was recovered, but it was soon once again buried under various Greek philosophical ideas in the Protestant scholastic tradition. For Harnack, therefore, the Protestant theologian must look for the message of Christ in the Gospels apart from the theological categories which distorted Christ's teaching in later church history.[146] Although they do not adhere to the entirety of Harnack's argument, Bayer, Forde, and Paulson argue for a similar shift following Luther's Reformation. In Bayer's language, a search for a justifying metaphysic dominated the post-Reformation era, which led to an overuse of Aristotelian philosophy in opposition to the gospel-centric approach of Luther. Muller criticizes this approach as anachronistic and simplistic.[147] There were a number of historical and theological factors which led to the development of the scholastic

---

[145] Muller, *Post-Reformation Reformed Dogmatics*, 38.
[146] Ibid., 41.
[147] Ibid., 41.

method—many of which come from the Reformation itself. Furthermore, the scholastics did not simply adopt Greek metaphysical categories with no modification or attention to the biblical text.[148] Far from being rationalistic, this approach was a tool used by later scholastics to fight encroaching rationalism in the church.

The second criticism that receives prominent attention in Muller's work is the common argument that both Luther and Calvin represent a different type of Christian theology than the one developed in their respective names. This conviction is demonstrated through Paulson's writing in *Lutheran Theology*. One of the major methodological problems in several authors who argue in this manner is that they function upon the conviction that the Protestant scholastics formulated their theology on the basis of a central dogma which was determinative for all other beliefs.[149] In this view, the later Reformed tradition made the doctrine of predestination *the* primary theological conviction, and Lutherans did the same with the doctrine of justification. Muller demonstrates that this is simply not the case, as the loci method developed in the earlier Protestant scholastic authors seeks to explore each doctrinal topic, both on its own merits and in relation to all other doctrine. Another flaw in these arguments, according to Muller, is that there is an inherent assumption that theological method determines doctrinal content. The fact that the writing of Luther and Calvin differs from that of Quenstedt and Musculus is apparent even upon the most basic read of the relevant materials. However, Muller argues that they differ

---

[148] Ibid., 40.

[149] Ibid., 39.

most in presentation, while retaining essentially the same substance.[150] This does not mean that the early reformers agree with the scholastics on every particular, but that the underlying theological convictions remain the same.

Another criticism countered by Muller is the notion that the post-Reformation scholastics revert to a pre-Reformation theological method as taught in the thirteenth-century scholastics. In order to understand Muller's response, the actual term "scholasticism" must be defined. Muller argues that though some have attempted to include certain doctrinal or philosophical convictions (such as a commitment to Aristotelian philosophy) within the definition of scholasticism, it is most properly defined as a theological method, rather than adherence to specific doctrinal beliefs.[151] When speaking of scholasticism, therefore, one is not necessarily asserting that the Protestant scholastics affirm the doctrinal particulars of Anselm, Aquinas, or other medieval writers. Muller notes that Protestant scholasticism draws from both the medieval theological method and the Renaissance *ad fontes* ideal. There is, then, a closer examination of the biblical text in post-Reformation scholastic authors and less of an inclination toward speculative philosophical questions. Muller points out that, in this way, the scholastics do not differ significantly from the reformers, who also drew from medieval theologians and Renaissance ideals.[152] The development of scholastic theology is not, then, a loss of Luther's original intention, as

---

[150] Ibid., 44.
[151] Ibid., 30.
[152] Ibid., 36.

Forde argues, but the logical development of Reformation thought.

One writer whom Muller spends extensive space interacting with is Gerhard Ebeling. This is especially significant, because the criticisms of Ebeling are repeated by Forde and Paulson in their rejection of scholastic theology. Ebeling views Luther as the Archimedean point of all theology. He represents a break with the past, and the post-Reformation theologians broke away from his theological uniqueness. At the heart of Ebeling's critique is his argument that for Luther, the Christian faith was a dynamic event of God's act and the human response of faith.[153] This existential character of Luther's thought is broken by the orthodox emphasis on correct doctrine. This shift moves the focus from concrete action to abstract truths. The criticism mentioned here by Muller is nearly identical to those given by Bayer, Forde, and Paulson. In response, Muller notes that this process of systematization was not foreign to the Reformation, but began in 1521 with the writings of Melanchthon (and importantly, Luther approved of such work). He also argues that this divide laid out by Ebeling misunderstands both the theology of the reformers and that of the scholastics. While the Protestant reformers emphasized dynamic preaching, they also argued for the purity of Christian doctrine. Also, while the scholastic theologians emphasized orthodox theology, they did not do so to the neglect of practical piety and preaching.[154]

While Muller does not offer explicit critiques of Bayer, Forde, or Paulson, the arguments that he presents in defense

---

[153] Ibid., 47.

[154] Ibid., 49.

of the Protestant scholastic method address their primary concerns. Throughout this work, Muller demonstrates that the large divide proposed between the reformers and later Protestant tradition does not accurately reflect the historical sources themselves. The reformers (especially Luther), though emphasizing the nature of preaching and one's existential encounter with God's word, were thoroughly steeped in the medieval scholastic tradition, and sought to systematize their own theological developments. The first edition of Melanchthon's *Loci Communes Rerum Theologicarum* was released only four years after the posting of the Ninety-five Theses.[155] Muller demonstrates that the roots of scholasticism lie in the Reformation, and particularly within their synthesis of earlier Christian thought and Renaissance ideals. Also, unlike the common caricature put forward by critics, the scholastics were immensely practical in intent and application.

Scholastic Writers: Critical Analysis

In this section, two writers from divergent Reformation traditions have been presented. Naturally, there are numerous differences between them relating to theological particulars, as Preus represents the Lutheran tradition, and Muller the Reformed. Yet, in spite of such theological differences, their general methodological concerns are remarkably similar. Both authors deal with criticisms of Protestant scholasticism and give answers that are consistent which each other in response. Preus confronts scholars who contend that scholasticism

---

[155] Ibid., 53.

represents a departure from the purer theology of Luther, and Muller does the same for those who argue for a broad divergence between John Calvin and later Calvinism. Both authors note that Protestant scholasticism is diverse, and is not simply a return to a medieval method and system. These ideas all contrast with the contentions of authors discussed above.

Preus defends the notion that the Lutheran scholastics had a moderated view of human reason. As Martin Luther distinguished between a ministerial and magisterial use of reason, so did the scholastics. While some of the later authors may have given too much credit to human rationality, Preus argues that they all consciously attempted to privilege the truths of Scripture over logical argumentation. Muller uses another argument to differentiate Protestant scholasticism from that of the Middle Ages. He notes that Protestant scholasticism melds together influences from medieval scholasticism, humanism, and exegetical theology. This differentiates the two traditions in that, in the Protestant scholastics, there is a greater emphasis on the biblical text over against Greek philosophy than is found in some medieval scholastics. Also, Muller defends the notion that scholasticism is not a theological system as such, but simply a method of theological presentation and argument. Therefore, the use of the scholastic method does not equate to an adoption of medieval theology. This is especially seen as one examines the medieval writers and the Protestant ones on the subject of the angels. While earlier authors engage in extensive speculation, the Lutheran and Reformed scholastics only discuss those aspects of the angelic world which are addressed in special revelation. The conclusion regarding continuity between the reformers and their progeny is in opposition to Paulson in particular, who derides the development of Lutheran thought after the Reformation.

Another commonality between Muller and Preus is their emphasis on doctrinal purity, and the importance of clarity in theological exposition. This idea, again, is not in opposition to either Luther or Calvin, who both contended for the importance of correct doctrine. In Forde, Paulson, and Bayer, the emphasis is not so much on doctrinal purity as it is on doctrinal application. To emphasize the precise formulation on various loci is to privilege secondary over primary discourse. This, again, demonstrates the difference between scholastic thought and Radical Lutheranism over the prioritization between act and being. For Forde, theology is to be proclaimed in a "for you" declaration of forgiveness. For Preus, it is to explained, defended, and preached. This is what Forde would refer to as preaching "*about* the gospel," rather than preaching the gospel. These ideas lead to vastly different theological conclusions.

The philosophical basis of the thought of these different sets of authors is apparent here. Bayer relies primarily on linguistic philosophy through the writings of Austin. Forde, while he does not rely heavily on any particular philosopher, speaks in a manner that is more consistent with existentialism. Paulson utilizes both linguistic and existential ideas. Muller and Preus both defend an Aristotelian metaphysic as an adequate system to explore Christian theology. Preus, however, is more skeptical than Muller on this subject. While he acknowledges the usefulness of Aristotelian categories, Preus prefers theologians who use Aristotle's thought less extensively. Nonetheless, both authors view Aristotle's metaphysics as a more adequate philosophical system than modern alternatives.

Preus and Muller offer an assessment of Protestant scholasticism which differs radically from that of its modern critics. Paulson, as probably the harshest critic of the scholastics discussed above, views the entire history of the Lutheran church as a movement away from Luther through various attempts to privilege the law in theological discourse. He generally regards Aristotelian philosophy, relating to both metaphysics and ethics, as an impediment to Christian proclamation.

Conclusion

This chapter began with the question, *What is the current state of scholarship concerning theological methodology within the Lutheran tradition, including that articulated by Radical Lutheran writers?* This question has been answered through the exposition of contemporary scholarship in various publications. Within the Lutheran theological milieu there are essentially three perspectives on theological method. First, there are those authors writing within the Radical Lutheran tradition who argue that the scholastic method that arose in the post-Reformation period is flawed. These include Gerhard Forde, Oswald Bayer, and Steven Paulson. Though differences remain between each writer, they share some common concerns surrounding theological method. Each of these writers argues that Aristotle should not heavily influence Christian theology, and that his impact has resulted in the use of essentialist categories to define God, man, and other doctrines, which they view as problematic. Instead, they argue that theology should be exposited from a linguistic perspective, through the law and gospel as words to the sinner and as instruments of death and life. They also view a strong divide between the theology of Luther and that developed throughout the seventeenth century. It is the duty of the theologian to return to Luther's own thought rather than the corrupted ideas of his theological descendants.

Second, some authors argue that Forde, Bayer, and Paulson are largely correct in their theological methodology, and that these insights can be combined with a Lutheran orthodox theology. Kolb, Arand, and Schumacher all argue that essentialist categories (though not rejected altogether) are an insufficient philosophical basis upon which one can exposit a theological system. Instead, they argue that Luther functions upon an ontology of the word, and that doctrine should be formulated from this perspective. They all view contemporary linguistic philosophy as useful as a means to exposit the proclamation of law and gospel, and they adopt Forde's distinction between primary and secondary discourse. Also, these writers all tend to view the human person through relation, which includes both a relationship to God and to other human persons. This is in opposition to a philosophical anthropology which explains identity by way of a human essence with particular characteristics, both essential and accidental. This is especially clear in their criticisms of the Finnish approach to Luther, which relies on a Platonic metaphysic. These thinkers all affirm some of the basic methodological presuppositions of the Radical Lutheran writers, but they also arrive at different doctrinal conclusions on specific loci.

Finally, some writers have argued that the scholastic method remains a viable approach to Christian theology, and that contemporary criticisms are based upon a misunderstanding of the seventeenth-century sources. Robert Preus is the most influential writer from this perspective, arguing that the theology and method of the earliest Lutheran orthodox writers—especially Chemnitz and Gerhard—remain viable in the contemporary church. Richard Muller, though a Reformed writer, argues alongside Preus that the Protestant scholastic method is a beneficial approach to theological discourse and development. These writers contend that the criticisms leveled at the scholastic approach often fail to consider both the theology of the reformers and that of the scholastic texts. When the reformers criticized the excesses of the medieval era and its use of philosophy, they did not reject philosophy altogether, but instead sought to place it in a subsidiary position to theology. Luther, Melanchthon, and Calvin all used Aristotelian language at different points in their theological careers. The Protestant scholastics, according to both Preus and Muller, are also not as philosophically indebted to Aristotle as they are often characterized to be. They all claimed to use reason only in a ministerial, rather than magisterial, sense, and thus defended the primacy of Scripture as a theological authority. For these authors, then, the scholastics are a relevant and important source of theology who speak to the contemporary church.

In this examination of contemporary literature, areas of both commonality and significant differences between these various perspectives are apparent. While the emphasis here is on divergence, it is noteworthy that there are places of agreement in engaging in the theological method. All writers discussed share a connection to Martin Luther and are consciously attempting to do theology in a manner similar to that of the reformer. Thus, due to this common heritage, there are important concepts that transcend these divides. All authors, for example, are aware of the limitations of human reason. It is the contention of Lutheran theologians from various backgrounds that in certain areas of medieval thought, Aristotle had been used in an improper manner, thus having a damaging effect upon the proclamation of the gospel. In particular, all of these authors contend that the application of Aristotle's ethical theory to the doctrine of justification is inconsistent with St. Paul's doctrine of justification, and thus should be rejected. Second, there is agreement among them regarding the centrality of Scripture in establishing one's theology. While differences remain surrounding the nature of biblical inerrancy in these authors, there is fundamental agreement over the prime importance of Scripture in establishing doctrine over against church tradition and Greek philosophy. With these commonalities in mind, one can then properly understand areas of divergence.

The most basic differentiating factor between the Radical Lutheran writers and Lutheran scholastics is that of philosophy. While all of the authors cited above consider themselves to be theologians rather than philosophers in the strict sense, there are fundamental metaphysical convictions which guide their understanding of Luther's theology. These are what I am labeling the *linguistic-existential* metaphysic and the *real-essentialist* metaphysic. These terms are used throughout the study. In reality, it is impossible to reject metaphysics altogether as a theologian, because everyone writing about God must take some kind of stance regarding his nature and existence. Thus, the question is not whether one holds to a metaphysical system or not, but what that system is and whether it is internally coherent. The linguistic-existential approach is that of Forde, Paulson, and Bayer, as well as that of Kolb, Arand, and Schumacher to a lesser extent. The phrase "linguistic-existential" arises out of two important philosophical schools of the twentieth century. The first is the linguistic philosophy of John Austin, alongside other philosophers of language such as Ferdinand de Saussure and Ludwig Wittgenstein. In spite of differences between these thinkers, all argue that philosophy should utilize language as a primary category for one's comprehension of reality. Rather than examining the world through the contemplation of Platonic ideals, reality is largely mediated by way of speech. These ideas are applied, in Lutheran writers, to the reformer's understanding of the efficacy of the divine word as proclaimed in the twofold manner of law and gospel. The second aspect of this phrase arises from the existential philosophy associated with Kierkegaard, Marcel, Sartre, and Heidegger. While, again, these philosophers have rather different ideas, they all hold to a common conviction that existence is a primary philosophical category over that of essence. While Forde, Bayer, and Paulson all reject the theme of human freedom that appears in existential thought, they utilize similar arguments against viewing reality through the lens of essence, and instead approach the world through the human struggle of inauthenticity and the inevitability of death.

The second approach, labeled the "real-essential," is that which follows in the tradition of Plato, Aristotle, and the medieval scholastic writers. This is that of the Protestant scholastics, and it is followed by proponents of that school of thought, including Muller and Preus. Essentialism is the conviction that there are distinct essences which unite things of a common kind together. They have real existence, whether in the Platonic forms or in the things themselves, as in Aristotle. These convictions have implications for the doctrines of God, man, and the law. An example of the application of these concepts is in divergent understandings of the law. The scholastics understood the law as something objective—a standard reflecting God's eternal nature.[156] It is defined, first, by its essence, and then its impact upon the sinner follows. In the existential approach of Forde, on the other hand, the law is defined by its impact upon the sinner, rather than its distinct essence.[157] Thus, like the existentialist concept of "existence," a thing is defined by its relation to the individual. The word "real" in this terminological construction is to distinguish an actual existing essence as opposed to a mere human construction as in nominalist thought, and also to distinguish this essentialism from that of contemporary philosophers of science, like Brian Ellis, who speak about a "scientific essentialism," which differs in some significant respects from more traditional formulations.[158]

In light of this analysis of the relevant literature addressed in this chapter, the scholastic theological method is examined in the following chapter in response to the question, *What are the theological and philosophical foundations of the Lutheran scholastic method?* These foundations are given through the historic Lutheran scholastic sources as well as in the thought of contemporary scholarship surrounding scholastic theology, including that of Preus and Muller. This includes a further detailed exposition of the nature of essentialism

---

[156] Cooper, *Lex Aeterna*, 109.

[157] Ibid., 108–9.

[158] Ellis, *Philosophy of Nature*.

and its different forms as taught by various theologians. A form of essentialist philosophy is proposed which arises from an examination of both Luther and the Lutheran scholastic thinkers of the seventeenth century. This also includes engagement with contemporary philosophical theologians in the Thomistic tradition. These methodological foundations are then exposited in light of various other approaches to the theological method within the Lutheran tradition.

3

Theological and Philosophical Foundations

Introduction

In the previous section, the question, *What is the current state of scholarship concerning theological methodology in Lutheranism?* was answered. Following this evaluation of the general field of modern approaches to this subject, the following question is addressed: *What are the theological and philosophical foundations of the Lutheran scholastic method?* These foundations are explored through the historic scholastic sources—especially Martin Chemnitz and Johann Gerhard. These two authors are generally considered the most significant Lutheran voices after the Reformation era. Along with these writers, theologians from the supposed "silver age" of orthodoxy as defined by Preus[159] are used. Sources include Johannes Quenstedt, Abraham Calov, and Heinrich Schmid's compendium of

---

[159] Preus, *Theology of Post-Reformation Lutheranism*, 45.

Lutheran orthodoxy, *The Doctrinal Theology of the Evangelical Lutheran Church*. The first two authors are the most systematic thinkers of the later era, and they have developed an extensive amount of material on theological method. The third source is important for its influence on the scholastic revival of the nineteenth century. Alongside seventeenth-century writers, scholastic authors from the late nineteenth and early twentieth centuries are utilized. The three most noteworthy authors in this regard are Revere Franklin Weidner, Adolf Hoenecke, and Conrad Emil Lindberg. These writers are perhaps the most scholastic of any figures writing during this later era. Robert Preus and Richard Muller—the two authors who have published most extensively on Protestant scholasticism in recent decades—and other modern scholars are used as secondary sources in expositing the theology and method of scholastic authors. The ideas developed in this chapter are also explored in light of contemporary theological developments and controversies.

This chapter begins with an overview of the historical development of the scholastic method within the Lutheran tradition. There is a particular emphasis on theological prolegomena in Lutheran thought, wherein the basic presuppositions for the study of theology are explicated. After this, the relationship between Plato, Aristotle, and theology is explored in light of common criticisms that scholastic thought is overly indebted to Greek philosophy. This is also explored in relation to Aristotle's impact on Thomistic theology—both medieval and modern. Here, the relationship between faith and reason as explained in Lutheran thinkers is also explored in a broader context than simply the reception of Aristotle. Following this discussion, the utilization of essentialist categories is discussed in relation to Lutheran scholastic sources, as is some commentary from contemporary Thomistic thinkers. In light of these Aristotelian distinctions, the relationship between cause and effect is explained, specifically with a view to exploring Aristotle's fourfold definition of causation. After the relationship between Aristotelianism and Lutheran scholasticism is exposited, the discussion moves to an explication of archetypal and ectypal theology in view of the debate between univocity and an analogical concept of being. Finally, the findings are synthesized into a scholastic metaphysical system which combines elements of both Plato and Aristotle's philosophies. These concepts formulate the theological method addressed by the current question under consideration, by demonstrating that Lutheran scholastic thinkers utilize classical essentialist philosophical categories as a subsidiary authority to Scripture in making theological determinations and formulating doctrinal concepts.

The Development and Characteristics of the Scholastic Method

Thus far, various sources that offer their unique approaches to Christian theology broadly, and scholasticism in particular, have been discussed. However, until this point, the term "scholasticism" itself has not actually been defined. For the present purposes, it is necessary that a working definition of scholasticism be proposed in order that further explication of the relative benefits of the scholastic method can be explored. Here, proposals for the definition of scholasticism are discussed, followed by a brief overview of the history of this method from the medieval period through the post-

Reformation era, with a special emphasis on the development of the Lutheran scholastic method in the seventeenth century.

In some older Protestant works, the term "scholasticism" is used almost entirely in a negative manner. For example, the church historian Philip Schaff, who addresses scholasticism exhaustively in his *History of the Christian Church*, categorizes scholasticism as a distinctive theological movement in the late Middle Ages, extending from the time of St. Anselm to the pre-Reformation era. He identifies the scholastic method by two primary realities. First, scholastic theologians functioned upon the basis of a combination of Aristotle's philosophical categories and St. Augustine's theology.[160] Second, they taught dogmas on the basis of church authority in contrast to the *sola Scriptura* principle of the Reformation, and gave reason an undue position as a basis whereby Christian doctrine is established. Though many would recognize such a characterization as simplistic and overly critical, such negative attitudes toward anything that might be associated with scholasticism still pervade the contemporary church, including Lutheran scholarship. Schaff's negative estimation of scholasticism is not far from Paulson's dismissals of the entire scholastic method (including that of the Lutheran scholastics) as opposed to Luther's gospel-centric theology.[161]

Another proposal for the definition of scholasticism is offered by Eugene R. Fairweather, in his introduction to *A Scholastic Miscellany: From Anselm to Ockham*. While recognizing the difficulty of giving a concrete definition of scholasticism at all, Fairweather identifies this term with the intel-

---

[160] Schaff, *Christian Church*, IV:589.

[161] Paulson, *Lutheran Theology*, 12.

lectual theological and philosophical movement of the later Middle Ages, leading up to the Renaissance and Reformation eras.[162] In using the term in this manner, Fairweather avoids the identification of scholasticism with a specific Aristotelian philosophy and theology, but limits scholasticism to a particular historical context, which would exclude the Protestant scholastic tradition. In more recent times, scholars have offered more positive and thorough definitions of scholasticism, which identify the movement not with a specific theology or historical period, but with a theological method. Richard Muller writes that scholasticism is an "academic style and method of discourse," rather than one "particular theology or philosophy."[163] This definition of scholasticism avoids problems in both Schaff's and Fairweather's explanations of the term. While older scholarship often identified the employment of Aristotle with scholasticism, this use only applies to the development of scholasticism following St. Thomas Aquinas. Abelard and Anselm are both generally considered scholastic thinkers, but neither shows a particularly strong Aristotelian influence in his writings. Aristotelian thought was brought into the West through the Islamic philosopher Averroes, who was born nearly twenty years after Anselm's death. The definition of Fairweather is flawed in its application of the term only to the pre-Reformation era. This definition neglects to include Protestant theological methods as genuine forms of scholasticism. Furthermore, it negates post-Reformation Catholic scholasticism, as well as the nineteenth-century neo-scholastic movement in Roman Catholic thought.

---

[162] Fairweather, *Scholastic Miscellany*, 18.

[163] Muller, *Post-Reformation Reformed Dogmatics*, 30.

For the present purposes, the approach of Muller is used, and scholasticism is roughly identified as a particular academic method of theology, wherein doctrines are studied systematically with the use of technical philosophical and theological terminology, and with an emphasis on the formation of various theses and refutations of various objections to these proposed theses. This definition accounts best for the data, as it avoids simplistic understandings of scholasticism which identify it with any single theological or philosophical schema. Even with such a definition, there is some difficulty in categorizing the exact theological method at work in scholasticism, as a variety of approaches can be categorized as scholastic. An examination of the writings of St. Anselm, Aquinas, and Quenstedt reveals three very different approaches to Christian theology, though they are united by some common methodological presuppositions. In his treatment of Puritan theology, *Unity in Diversity: English Puritans and the Puritan Reformation, 1603–1689*, Randall Pederson utilizes Wittgenstein's concept of *familienähnlichkeit* (family resemblance) to explain the connection between the various writers under the broad banner of Puritanism. There is no strict definition of what constitutes a Puritan writer, because for every characteristic of Puritanism, there is an exception. Instead, it is better to think of these writers as sharing a number of similar qualities, though individual qualities might be absent in particular figures. This mirrors the resemblance of members of a family who all share similar qualities, though distinctive physical characteristics might be absent in any one person. This concept can be helpfully applied to scholasticism as well. The advantage of the use of the concept of "family resemblance" is that it avoids the problems in characterizing scholasticism with any one aspect of the method. For every single identifying factor of the scholastic method, such as a heavy utilization of Aristotle, exceptions can be found in authors who are still labeled scholastic theologians. Thus, scholasticism is identified here by a variety of similar characteristics among theologians, though some of these characteristics might be absent in various writers. As the discussion proceeds, the nature of Lutheran scholasticism is explained with regard to the relationship between faith and reason in the thought of Luther and later writers.

The Relationship between Aristotle and Theology

The connection between Aristotle and Lutheran theology is complex. Luther himself often spoke disparagingly about the Greek philosopher, as if virtually nothing positive is to be gained from using Aristotelian categories and reason within theological discourse. In contrast to this, Aristotle is a favorite thinker of Johann Gerhard and the later scholastic authors. It is this divergence of opinion surrounding the Greek philosopher that has led to the thesis that a philosophical chasm separates Luther from the later thinkers of the Lutheran tradition. According to some Lutheran writers, the imposition of Aristotle upon Luther's earlier and purer theology led to the complete abandonment of the central theological principles of the Reformation.[164] The nature of this project does not allow

---

[164] Eric Gritsch, for example, writes that "Lutheran orthodoxy lifted Luther from his historical context and viewed him as a prophet of indisputable divine truth," which then led to a systematization of Luther's thought foreign to the first generation of reformers (Gritsch, *History of Lutheranism*, 113).

for an in-depth exposition of Luther's view of Aristotle, nor of an extensive overview of the published texts on the topic. Thus, some brief commentary on Luther's view of reason and Aristotle is given, followed by an evaluation of the use of this philosopher in later writers.

Aristotle and Aquinas in Luther

Luther was not an overly philosophical thinker, as he generally sought to use biblical and theological, rather than philosophical, categories when explaining his thought on various subjects. One cannot, then, find any particular text wherein Luther explains his own metaphysical system or epistemological presuppositions. This is not to say, however, that Luther had no understanding of philosophy. His grasp of the philosophical discussions in the sixteenth century is apparent throughout his works, and especially in his early writings. When determining Luther's view of Aristotle, reason, and related subjects, one must glean insights from his occasional statements on the subject, rather than examining one particular treatise or set of works. Thus, a determination of his exact philosophical foundations is somewhat difficult in contrast to defining those of the Lutheran scholastic writers, who lay out their views on the topic in theological prolegomena texts.

Much of the debate surrounding Luther's relationship to philosophy concerns his nominalist training. The question of the relationship between Luther and nominalism is an often-discussed topic. Luther scholar and historical theologian Heiko Oberman popularized the thesis that Luther was greatly influenced by nominalist thought. Through his works such as

A Harvest of Medieval Theology and various essays published together as *Dawn of the Reformation: Essays in Late Medieval and Early Reformation Thought*, Oberman contends that following his Reformation breakthrough, Luther retained several of the ideas taught to him by his nominalist teachers. In this view, while Luther distanced himself from Ockham and Biel in various ways, he retained their rejection of Thomistic realism as well as Ockham's emphasis on divine freedom. This stands in contrast to later theologians like Gerhard and Chemnitz, who do not write so favorably about the late medieval nominalist thinkers.

One example of Ockham's influence on Luther lies in the distinction made by the nominalist philosopher between the *potentia absoluta* (absolute power) and the *potentia ordinata* (ordained power) of God.[165] This distinction itself precedes Ockham, as it is found in Thomas and other medieval thinkers, but the manner in which such a distinction functions differs radically in later medieval thought. For Aquinas, God's ordained laws are a reflection of his own divine nature. Lying, for example, is inherently wrong not simply because God decreed it as such, but because it is inconsistent with God's own being. For Ockham, however, God could just as easily (according to the *potentia ordinata*) have decreed that lying is a virtuous trait and truth-telling a sin. This position, known as voluntarism, posits a radical freedom within the divine will and rejects an eternal standard of law and justice in accord with God's nature.[166] In this system, God does not *need* his justice to be satisfied in any sense in order for God to forgive sin. Such

---

[165] Oberman, *Harvest of the Reformation*, 473.

[166] Ockham, *Philosophical Writings*, xlix.

could be the case if God ordained it in such a manner, but God might ordain that he would simply overlook sin without justice being satisfied whatsoever. Some scholars contend that this voluntarism lies at the root of Luther's Reformation doctrine of justification.[167] In this view, God can impute the sinner as righteous apart from any actual righteousness within the individual simply because God decreed it as such according to the *potentia ordinata.*

There are several problems with the nominalist thesis, which has generally been rejected or at least modified in recent years. It is undeniable that Ockham had an impact on Luther, as he admits as much. However, Luther's own statements about his nominalist teachers are often quite critical. The theologians Luther cites most frequently in the medieval period are not scholastic at all—whether realist or nominalist—but mystics.[168] Bernard, Tauler, and the anonymous author of the *Theologia Germanica* are the most prominent influences upon his thought.[169] These writers, especially in drawing from the works of St. Augustine, use Neoplatonic language more than either Thomistic Aristotelianism or Ockhamist nominalism. This is not to say, however, that Luther simply adopts the metaphysical convictions of any particular mystical writer, either. Luther was rather eclectic in his influences; one might then wonder whether one should seek to find any consistent metaphysical system at all in Luther's writings. The present

---

[167] Howsare, *Balthazar and Protestantism*, 144.

[168] See Hoffman, *Theology of the Heart,* for an in-depth exposition of the role of mysticism in Luther's theology.

[169] For an exposition of the theology of these figures, see Clark, *Great German Mystics.*

writer is not convinced that this is possible. In order to explain the relationship between Luther and Aristotle, then, the best method of proceeding is not to give an exposition of Luther's philosophical system, but to examine two particular topics which appear as themes throughout Luther's career. First are the continual negative comments directed toward Aristotle, and second is Luther's view of the relationship between faith and reason.

Luther's attacks on Aristotle (and Aquinas) are most prominent from the years 1517 to 1522. A large portion of his polemical statements about the relationship between philosophy and theology appear in this era, though such ideas continue to be explained throughout his career, such as in the 1535 Galatians commentary. The roots of Luther's view of Aristotle can be found in his 1517 *Disputation Against Scholastic Theology*.[170] An examination of this text demonstrates that Luther's problem is not with Aristotle *as such*, but with the connection between Aristotle's ethics and a perceived neo-Pelagianism in the Middle Ages. The disputation begins as a defense of Augustinianism and a rejection of Pelagius. Luther is concerned that the scholastics deny the impact of sin upon the will in favor of a pure libertarianism. It is important to note that Luther specifically cites Biel and Scotus, rather than Aquinas, as proponents of this false idea (as in theses 10, 13, and 23). The thesis which is perhaps most relevant for the present discussion is thesis 50, in which it is stated that Aristotle's relation to theology is as "darkness is to light."[171] It is important, however, to note in what sense Luther rejects

---

[170] Luther, *Early Theological Works*.

[171] Ibid., 270.

the work of the philosopher. The first sense in which Luther rejects Aristotle is in the utilization of logical syllogism. For Luther, divine truth is to be accepted through revelation rather than through logical argumentation. He notes, for example, that such a use of logic as expositor of divine truth would negate even the dogma of the Trinity as a teaching of faith, instead placing it within the realm of natural reason (thesis 49). The second reason Luther rejects Aristotle is the use of his ethical writings. The reformer does not, however, reject Aristotle's ethical theory as such, but the imposition of virtue ethics into the category of justification *coram Deo* (thesis 40). While these ideas, if isolated from the rest of his writings, might imply a complete rejection of traditional Greek thought forms in Luther, there are two important considerations which negate such a conclusion. First, Luther's theology of faith and reason and the relationship between the two kingdoms demonstrates that logical categories are essential for the proper functioning of the human creature in society. Second, modern scholarship has demonstrated that the proposed gap between Luther and Aquinas is not quite as extensive as Luther himself seemed to think.

It is well known that Luther referred to reason as the "devil's whore," among other pejorative terms. One might then conclude that Luther was an irrationalist or a fideist. It is said that John Wesley, though at one point quite impressed with Luther, termed him an enemy of reason after reading his 1535 Galatians commentary.[172] Such caricatures continue to be propagated, though it must be acknowledged that some of the blame is to be laid on Luther himself, who was prone to

---

[172] Westerholm, *Lutheran Paul*, 64.

overstatement. Yet, Luther did at other times praise reason as a great good. One might conclude then that Luther is simply inconsistent, and that one cannot put together any kind of coherent ideas of reason and faith in the reformer. However, an examination of Luther's understanding of the two kingdoms demonstrates that such is not the case, and that his seemingly contradictory statements on the topic are completely consistent within the framework of two realms.

Modern scholarship has generally acknowledged that the two kingdoms is the key to a proper understanding of Luther's thought on this topic.[173] Though disagreeing on some particulars, Jerry Robbins, Steven A. Hein, and Brian Gerrish all recognize this twofold framework as necessary to grasp Luther's view. For Luther, Christians live in the midst of two kingdoms. Though this has sometimes been described as the difference between the church and the state, Luther never makes this identification. Instead, these two realms represent one's relation to God (the right-hand kingdom) and one's relation to others (the left-hand kingdom). The left-hand kingdom has reference to the state, culture, and vocation. The right-hand kingdom is connected with the church. Reason and philosophy, for Luther, are properly used in the left-hand kingdom as a means to guide the state, relationships, ethics, and other aspects of external life. In relation to God, however, reason is to be surrendered to revelation, which often speaks of truths which are opposed to bare reason. This is especially related to the chief article of justification which, according to Luther, is at odds with human rationality, which reasons that reward is based on human obedience *coram Deo*, just as it is in

---

[173] On the two kingdoms, see Biermann, *Wholly Citizens*.

the left-hand realm.

One of the problems in scholarship on this topic is that Luther's 1518 Heidelberg Disputation, and in particular, his distinction between the *theologia gloriae* and the *theologia crucis* (thesis 22), is viewed by many as central to gain an understanding of the reformer's thought on the topic. While this early work certainly contains themes which extend throughout his career, the late Luther never utilizes such a distinction. The difference between a theology of the cross and a theology of glory, which modern Luther interpreters view as a theological paradigm which is perhaps as central as the distinction between law and gospel,[174] is never given prominence in Luther's own writings. Even in the great Reformation writings of 1520, this distinction is never mentioned. The Lutheran scholastics hardly even note such a distinction, and certainly did not understand it to be somehow paradigmatic for Luther's thought. The idea was popularized by the publication of Walter von Loewenich's *Luthers Theologia Crucis* in 1929 and has since been studied by Gerhard Forde and Alister McGrath, among others. Jerry Robbins, in his essay "Luther on Reason: A Reappraisal," frames Luther's understanding of the topic through the *theologia crucis* in opposition to the *theologia gloriae*. While Robbins's conclusions generally agree with those of the present author, the prominence of the Heidelberg Disputation and lack of discussion of later writings lead Robbins to conclude that Luther "rejected all natural theology," and that he held to "contradictory propositions."[175] These ideas would put Luther at odds with the previous scholastic

---

[174] Forde, *Theologian of the Cross*.

[175] Robbins, "Luther on Reason," 203.

tradition, and the idea that contradictory propositions can coexist does, essentially, make Luther an irrationalist.

Steven Hein's approach to Luther on faith and reason offers a more balanced perspective which leads to continuity with the preceding Christian tradition.[176] One point Hein notes that is particularly significant is that even within the earthly kingdom, certain truths about God can be discovered by human reason. While the gospel, the triunity of God, and other truths cannot be arrived at through reason alone, the existence of a good God can. Hein notes a distinction that Luther makes between a *general* and a *proper* knowledge of God.[177] A general knowledge of God is discovered through reason and is evidenced through the predominance of worship in areas where the gospel has not been proclaimed. In other places, Luther can refer to this general idea of God as a "legal knowledge," because it consists in knowledge of the moral law.[178] It is in this area that Luther can praise even pagan philosophers like Aristotle, who, he states, at times had a better understanding of the law than many clergy in the church.[179] These facts demonstrate that Robbins is in error when he argues that there is no natural theology in Luther. While Luther certainly limits what can be known through natural revelation, he does not reject the concept altogether.

Where reason falls short, for Luther, is in its attempt to understand God's attitude toward sinners. If Aristotelian ethics are applied to one's place in the heavenly kingdom, one

---

[176] Hein, "Two Kingdoms."

[177] Ibid., 140.

[178] Ibid., 141.

[179] Ibid., 141.

will conclude something akin to Pelagianism. In the earthly kingdom, one receives payment in accord with one's work. Such an arrangement according to the law does not apply to one's relation to God, and a confusion of these two kingdoms is what led to Rome's moralistic approach to justification. Hein notes that there are two basic problems which Luther had with Rome's use of Aristotle: first, the righteousness of faith was replaced by one of works, and second, logic became a judge over revelation.[180] If Aristotle is used, then, outside of these problematic areas, Luther's thought is not inherently in opposition to that of the philosopher. Luther himself argued that Aristotle's logic should be retained in university curriculums.[181] The reformer's theology, then, is not irrational or anti-philosophical.

While it has been established that Luther viewed reason as a positive good within the left-hand realm, the question now arises whether there is any inherent connection between the civil and heavenly kingdoms. Some authors have proposed that Luther's division between these two realms mirrors the later noumenal-phenomenal divide in Kantian philosophy. In this way, the two serve in a completely dichotomous relationship. Robbins states that in heavenly things, unlike in the civil realm, contradiction is possible.[182] For him, the acceptance of contradictory propositions is part of Luther's *theologia crucis*. In this model of interpretation, one cannot view Luther as anything other than an irrationalist when it comes to divine truths. Such a conclusion is not necessary for

---

[180] Ibid., 143.

[181] Robbins, "Luther on Reason," 196.

[182] Ibid., 203.

a read of Luther's own writings. While Luther often derides human reason for its misunderstanding of the truths of faith, nowhere does the reformer state that heavenly realities are in actuality contradictory to one another, or to civil realities. While Luther firmly holds onto paradox, his criticisms of Aristotle and of syllogistic reasoning do not imply that divine truths are opposed to reason *as such*, but to fallen human reason.

For Luther, reason does have a role to play—even in theological discussions. While reason must not override that which is taught by revelation, it still holds a secondary function in defending theological matters. Luther's famous words at the Diet of Worms demonstrate this fact, with his insistence that his errors must be disproved by both Scripture and plain reason. Robbins notes that while Luther criticizes human reason, in faith, the sinful person's reason itself undergoes a change. This is called "regenerate reason," which is used in service of divine truth.[183] Robbins points out that reason is not absent when interpreting revelation, but is "vital for pointing out logical weaknesses in destructive reasoning."[184] Even in the mere reading and understanding of words on a page, one must utilize one's intellectual faculties. One example of this use of regenerate reason can be found in Luther's debates with Zwingli over Christ's presence in the sacrament. While the reformer founded his arguments first upon the text of Scripture, he used categories derived from his nominalist training, especially in his differentiation between Christ's

---

[183] Ibid., 200.
[184] Ibid., 196.

modes of presence.[185] Thomas Osborne notes that philosophy is used by Luther only insofar as it supports the plain meaning of the biblical text.[186] For Luther, then, scriptural truths are to be accepted on the basis of revelation rather than human logic, but this does not negate the usefulness of reason and philosophy as a secondary source of authority, even in spiritual matters.

Luther's thought on the relationship between theology and philosophy can be summarized in three points. First, in the civil sphere, reason is an absolute necessity. It has the ability to interpret natural law, and even to determine the existence of God, as well as God's desire for worship and obedience. This is a general knowledge of God which cannot bring one unto salvation. Second, the truths of the gospel are inherently opposed to fallen human reason—especially the doctrine of justification. There are, thus, many truths which cannot be grasped other than through revelation. In the matters where God speaks, in the spiritual realm, reason must submit to God's word. Third, faith leads to a new heart and a new reasoning faculty. The believer can, and should, use reason, though only in a secondary sense. Philosophy is useful only insofar as it submits itself to revealed theology.

In light of these conclusions, the relationship between Luther's thought and that of scholasticism can be defined. In particular, some conclusions can be drawn regarding the relationship between Luther and Thomas Aquinas, who sometimes is at the brunt of Luther's criticisms of the use of Aristotle. While older scholarship emphasized discontinu-

---

[185] Osborne, "Nominalist Background," 81.
[186] Ibid., 82.

ity between these two figures, ecumenical dialogues in the twentieth century brought about a renewed consideration of areas of agreement between the reformer and the angelic doctor. The author who has done the most extensive writing on the relationship between these two figures is Dennis Janz, who has published two books and several articles on the topic.[187] While Janz does not claim that these two figures had an identical theological method, he demonstrates that discontinuity has been overstated. This being the case, it is demonstrable that the Lutheran scholastic method does not differ in any substantial way with the theological method of Luther, even though their presentation might be more akin to that of Aquinas and other medieval writers in certain particulars.

The argument that there are commonalities between Luther and Aquinas is demonstrated in two ways. First, it is argued that Luther misunderstood some fundamental aspects of Thomas's thought. Second, it is contended that just as Luther is not the irrationalist he is often characterized as, Aquinas is not the pure rationalist that nineteenth-century neo-scholastics portrayed. In *Luther on Thomas Aquinas* (1989), Janz evaluates all of Luther's references to the medieval theologian and demonstrates Luther's familiarity with primary sources. In opposition to some other scholars who have argued that Luther knew Thomas only through secondary sources, Janz demonstrates that the reformer was well acquainted with Thomas's own works. Luther's familiarity with Thomas does not, however, mean that Luther correctly understood him.

---

[187] See Janz, *Medieval Thomism*, and Janz, *Luther on Aquinas*.

The Thomistic school continued to exist into the late Middle Ages, even with the rise of nominalism. Several prominent figures in Luther's own life considered themselves to be heirs of the angelic doctor, including Andreas Karlstadt and Cardinal Cajetan. As a continual critic of Luther, Cajetan's Thomism is particularly important for Luther's understanding of Aquinas. The cardinal vehemently opposed Luther's anthropology and view of grace, taking the position that morally good acts are possible without the aid of grace whatsoever.[188] This, for Luther, was at the heart of the errors of medieval scholasticism, as it promoted a neo-Pelagianism and resulted in a denial of salvation *sola gratia*. Janz demonstrates that Cajetan misunderstood Thomas's position on the issue. For Janz, Aquinas's commentaries on the Pauline epistles demonstrate commonality between his anthropology and that of Luther.[189] When Luther criticized Aquinas, especially in relation to grace, it is likely that this is due largely to Cajetan's reading of Thomas, rather than the intentions of the author himself.

This leads, then, to an examination of the theological methods of Luther and Aquinas. Opponents of Protestant scholasticism have often derided the seventeenth-century theological method as a reversion to Aquinas's system and a rejection of Luther's purer theology. The contrast between Luther and medieval scholasticism is, therefore, emphasized to a great extent. While critics of Aquinas have often accused him of imposing Greek philosophy upon the biblical text, Janz notes that contemporary Thomas scholarship has recognized that, though certainly concerned with metaphysics,

---

[188] Janz, *Medieval Thomism*, 135.

[189] Ibid., 138.

Aquinas was first and foremost a theologian rather than a philosopher.[190] One of the problems with older interpretations of Thomas is that he was often read through the lens of the Enlightenment, as an apologist and philosopher in the modern sense who attempts to rationally prove the truths of Christianity through logical syllogism. As Janz states, one cannot read Aquinas in such a context, as the entire concept of autonomous reason is an enlightenment construct.[191] Instead, when Aquinas offers his five "proofs" of the existence of God, he merely demonstrates the rationality and coherence of an acceptance of theism for the Christian. As Feser notes, Aquinas wrote his text for believers, and the *Summa* was not intended as an apologetic text.[192] In using these arguments, Aquinas does not imply that all truths of the Christian faith must, or even can, be rationally demonstrated. On these points, Luther does not fundamentally disagree, as he too argues that a general knowledge of God is rationally demonstrable. Similarly, as Luther notes that the proper knowledge of God is not discoverable through reason, Aquinas argues that the Trinity, the incarnation, and other doctrines are believed through revelation alone, rather than logical deduction.

There are, certainly, points of departure from Aquinas in Luther. Paradox is a central theme in Luther's thought, while Aquinas has a greater concern for syllogistic reasoning. This is not to say, however, that Aquinas completely rejects the concept of paradox. Janz observes that in the majority of his answers to proposed questions throughout the *Summa*,

---

[190] Janz, "Syllogism or Paradox," 3.

[191] Ibid., 12.

[192] Feser, *Aquinas*, 63.

Aquinas usually answers with "a simultaneous yes and no," which he labels a type of paradox.[193] He also notes that the centrality of the apophatic method in Aquinas's writing is opposed to rationalism. Theology ultimately leads one to mystery, and on some points, it cannot speak.[194] Janz leads to some specific passages in Aquinas's writing where mystery is emphasized, and the great theologian acknowledges paradox.[195] These passages are, primarily, in relation to the mystery of the incarnation. While Aquinas was certainly not as fond of paradox as Luther, and was certainly much more concerned to exposit a logical system, he was not opposed to leaving his theology in the context of mystery when necessary.

Luther and Thomas are two very different thinkers whose theological concerns and presentation diverge greatly from one another. However, despite such differences, they share several areas of commonality. Both praise reason, and even Aristotle, in the civil sphere, and in relation to a natural knowledge of God. Both acknowledge that the truth of the gospel is known only through revelation. Both acknowledge that there are paradoxes in the Christian faith. What this demonstrates is that when the Lutheran scholastics borrow Aristotelian terminology from Aquinas, as well as his concern for natural theology, they are not diverging from Luther's own thought. Even the reformer's concern for paradox remains in those scholastics writing in his name throughout the next century. In this way, the scholastics retain Luther's theology and concerns while simultaneously utilizing beneficial aspects

---

[193] Janz, "Syllogism or Paradox," 15.
[194] Ibid., 16.
[195] Ibid., 19–20.

of Aquinas's method.

Aristotle and the Scholastic Method after Luther

Critics of scholasticism in seventeenth-century Lutheran thought often place the blame on Luther's student Melanchthon for deviating from the theology of his older contemporary. While Luther taught a pure gospel-centric theology, Melanchthon instead began to impose rationalistic philosophical categories onto Reformation theology. The process that began with Melanchthon then continued throughout the scholastic era, as writers began to revert to a pre-Reformation theological scheme.

The thesis of a great divide between Luther and Melanchthon gained prominence through Albrecht Ritschl and Adolf von Harnack, who both favored the earlier reformer as a purer source of Christian truth.[196] This contention continued to be promoted by scholars associated with the Luther renaissance begun by Karl Holl throughout the beginning of the twentieth century.[197] Authors such as Werner Elert and William Lazareth continued this trajectory, especially as they contended that Melanchthon was influenced by Calvin on the subject of the third use of the law, which greatly differentiated him from Luther.[198] In some ways, such a divide is not new, as the debates in post-Reformation Lutheranism which led to the writing of the Formula of Concord depended upon two opposing schools of thought,

---

[196] See Lotz, *Ritschl and Luther*.

[197] Holl, *What Did Luther Understand*.

[198] Murray, *Living God*, 27.

sometimes labeled as the Philipists and the Gnesio Lutherans. Because of this, some second-generation reformers spoke ill of Melanchthon, often giving him the labels of Crypto-Calvinist and Sacramentarian.[199] There are generally two places of proposed discontinuity between the two authors: theology and method. For the present work, the second question is more essential, but the first is addressed due to its connection to the proposed differences in theological method between the two reformers.

In his article "Melanchthon versus Luther: The Contemporary Struggle," Bengt Hagglund outlines what he perceives as the two most pronounced areas of supposed disagreement between Luther and Melanchthon: free will and the Lord's Supper. There are also practical disagreements regarding church fellowship and adiaphora, but these will not be addressed here. The nature of free will is one of the most prominently discussed issues between Melanchthon and Luther, as it is often argued that the younger reformer became a synergist following Luther's death, especially in his insistence that one's free will is a factor in conversion, alongside of the Word of God and the Holy Spirit. This is opposed to Luther's thoroughgoing monergism as promoted in *The Bondage of the Will*. Hagglund argues, in opposition to this, that though Melanchthon utilized language which might be misconstrued, he never rejected the *sola gratia* principle, and is thus not rightly categorized as a synergist.[200] While Hagglund's contention has not remained unchallenged, what he does demonstrate is that such divergences may not be as

---

[199] Gritsch, History of *Lutheranism*, 76.

[200] Hagglund, "Melanchthon versus Luther," 124.

great as is often proposed.

Whatever conclusion one comes to regarding Melanchthon's later writings and his obscure statements regarding free will, what is apparent is that Melanchthon demonstrated different concerns than Luther in relation to this issue. This much is apparent in the formation of the Augsburg Confession. It was Melanchthon alone who authored articles XVIII "Of Free Will" and XIX "Of the Cause of Sin," in which possible misunderstandings of Luther's language on these topics is clarified.[201] While Luther usually rejects free will without qualification, Melanchthon is careful to nuance such a remark in article XVII by distinguishing between free will in things related to *civilem iustitiam* (civil righteousness) and actions connected with *iustitiae spiritualis* (spiritual righteousness). In civil things, one does have free will; in spiritual things, one does not. Melanchthon's later article on the cause of sin similarly is an attempt to clarify Luther's language, such as his remarks that "all things happen of necessity,"[202] so that such phrases do not imply God to be the author of sin. One might conclude that this demonstrates, already, that Luther and Melanchthon are on fundamentally opposing paths. However, if such were the case, why did Luther himself fail to recognize it? One does not find, in Luther, any indication that he disagreed with these articles. Certainly, it is true that Luther and Melanchthon approached the theological task differently. Luther used sharp polemical language, and Melanchthon used more carefully nuanced terms to describe his thoughts. It is in this sense that perhaps Melanchthon can be rightly

---

[201] Kolb, Arand, Nestingen, *Lutheran Confessions*, 102.

[202] Ibid., 103.

called the father of Lutheran scholasticism. However, Luther did not fundamentally oppose Melanchthon's use of such distinctions at all. One does not have to propose absolute continuity in every particular to recognize the similarity and even complementarity of these two reformers' theological systems.

Regarding the Lord's Supper, the differences between Melanchthon and Luther are more pronounced than with perhaps any other doctrine. While Hagglund attempts to argue that the differences are due Melanchthon's desire for ecclesiastical unity rather than actual theological diversion,[203] other scholarship has demonstrated that real theological disagreement is at the heart of this division. Scaer argues that the primary difference between these two thinkers surround not the topic of *whether* Christ is present, but of *how*.[204] For Melanchthon, Christ's presence is mediated through liturgical action, and thus the younger reformer does not emphasize the elements themselves as mediators of the body and blood of Christ. Luther, to the contrary, speaks in realist terms regarding the presence of Christ's body in the elements of bread and wine. Scaer notes this practical difference in the reformers' respective attitudes toward the act of eucharistic elevation.[205] Melanchthon rejected such a practice, while Luther initially desired to retain it. Though this is a genuine area of difference between the two figures, this divergence does not demonstrate a fundamental disagreement between them regarding theological method, and thus only

---

[203] Hagglund, "Melanchthon versus Luther," 125.

[204] Scaer, "Real Presence," 143.

[205] Ibid., 143.

demonstrates discontinuity on one particular topic. The discontinuity is not so pronounced that one could simply dismiss Melanchthon as wholly departing from Luther.

The theological method of Melanchthon is apparent in his *Loci Communes*, which was released in a number of different editions throughout his life. The first edition, released in 1521 when Melanchthon was just 24 years old, is sometimes viewed as the first systematic treatment of Protestant theology.[206] The work itself, however, is not intended to be comprehensive. While later editions include treatments of the Trinity and other essential doctrines, the initial edition set forth the distinction between law and gospel, the sacraments, and other Lutheran distinctives. The form of treatment here is not that of Aquinas or other scholastic writers who use an extensive systematic format of proposition, anticipated refutation, and then response. Instead, Melanchthon divides theology into various topics, or *loci*, and treats them through an exposition of the doctrine with an establishment of that teaching from both Scripture and the church fathers. Throughout the text, Melanchthon responds to those who disagree with his perspective. This treatment is certainly systematic, and utilizes both logic and rhetoric, though it differs from the obscure philosophical discussions which are prominent in other theological textbooks of the era.

Insights into Melanchthon's place as a scholastic are found in Lowell Green's essay "Melanchthon's Relation to Scholasticism." In Green's view, all of the characteristic elements of later Lutheran scholasticism are present in Melanchthon. In

---

[206] Green, "Relation to Scholasticism," in Trueman, *Protestant Scholasticism*, 282.

particular, he notes Melanchthon's use of classical dialectics and rhetoric.[207] Like Luther, Melanchthon was critical of philosophy, and of Aristotle in particular. However, despite his negative statements regarding the Greek philosopher, he continued to use, and teach, Aristotle's logic, rhetoric, and grammar. Green argues that Melanchthon's attitude toward philosophy can be best understood by using a twofold definition of the term "philosophy." On the one hand, philosophy is identified with the liberal arts, including both the *trivia* and *quadrivia*.[208] Owing especially to his humanism, Melanchthon defends these aspects of philosophy. However, Melanchthon derides the other definition of philosophy, which includes metaphysics, specifically as it is used by medieval theologians through their adoption of Aristotle. According to Green, Melanchthon wholeheartedly rejects both the metaphysics and ethics of Aristotle.[209] Despite several harsh statements of Melanchthon, however, such a total rejection is inconsistent with some of his own statements.

In his argument that Melanchthon rejects Aristotle's ethics and metaphysics, Green cites two of Melanchthon's early writings: *Didymi Faventini adversus Thomam Placentinum pro Martino Luthero theologo oratio* (1521), and *Scholia in epistolam Pauli ad Colossenses* (1527). It is worth noting that these are two early works, and it is apparent that when Melanchthon writes the Apology of the Augsburg Confession, he has a largely positive view of Aristotle. Green notes that in his treatment of Colossians, Melanchthon makes a differentiation between

---

[207] Ibid., 274.
[208] Ibid., 277.
[209] Ibid., 281.

spiritual life and bodily life.[210] Philosophy (and ethics in particular) is relevant to the bodily rather than spiritual life. It is in this way that Melanchthon approves of Aristotle as an ethicist while simultaneously rejecting those ethics as being a foundation of the gospel. Like Luther, Melanchthon functions on the basis of the framework of the two kingdoms when formulating his views of faith and reason. More particularly, Melanchthon speaks of the relationship between faith and ethics within the framework of the two kinds of righteousness. Charles Arand argues that the two kinds of righteousness serve as the framework for Melanchthon's approach to faith and works in the Apology.[211] In this framework, the Christian lives in two fundamental relationships: to God, and to others. In relation to God, Aristotle is to be rejected, because salvation arises solely by faith in the gospel promise. In relation to others, however, Aristotle's ethics give a general guide as to how ethical living in the world functions. This is not due to any inspiration given to Aristotle, but instead due to Aristotle's adherence to natural law, which is largely discoverable by way of philosophy.[212]

The question of metaphysics is an important one, as part of the goal of the present work is to defend the necessity of metaphysical discussion in theology. Green notes that Melanchthon argues against the notion that theology is in any way determined by philosophy. This relates especially

---

[210] Ibid., 277.

[211] Arand, "Two Kinds of Righteousness."

[212] See Biermann, *Case for Character*.

to metaphysical questions.²¹³ Philosophy, instead, is a mere handmaiden to theology, always submitting to the truths set forth in divine revelation. Melanchthon does not reject metaphysics as such, but its abuse in the late medieval era. Regarding the doctrine of God, Melanchthon is certainly willing to speak in a metaphysical manner regarding God's being. For example, he affirms the doctrine of divine simplicity—a hallmark of Aquinas's metaphysical system—in Article I of the Augsburg Confession, which refers to God as *impartibilis* (without parts).²¹⁴ Melanchthon does not reject extensive discussion of God's nature and attributes, or even proofs of his existence, as these are all included within later editions of the *Loci Communes*. The reformer's primary concern here is to ground knowledge of God not in speculation, but in the person of Christ. One does not reason unto the nature of God and then consequently determine theological conclusions. Instead, the Christian is called to look to Christ and affirm who God shows himself to be through his Son.

It is following the work of Melanchthon where the influence of Aristotle upon Lutheran thought becomes more explicit. Debates among second-generation reformers often utilized Aristotelian categories of substance and accident in discussions surrounding the nature of sin and of free will (FC SD I), as well as contentions regarding causation in the application of salvation (FC SD III). God was also often described through Aquinas's concept of being, in which there is no distinction between existence and essence within the divine nature. Aris-

---

[213] Green, "Relation to Scholasticism," in Trueman, *Protestant Scholasticism*, 381.

[214] On divine simplicity see Dolezal, *God Without Parts*.

totle's categories, particularly of causation, are used even more extensively in the period that Robert Preus labels "high orthodoxy"[215] than in the so-called "golden age" of the Formula of Concord. Perhaps the most explicit Aristotelian of the era is Johann Gerhard, who is generally considered the most significant Lutheran thinker following Martin Chemnitz. Even in Gerhard, however, there was no explicit *ordo salutis*, which is often regarded as a high point in the development of Protestant scholastic thought. The *ordo salutis* belongs to the final age, which Preus refers to as the "silver age," which includes Johannes Quenstedt, Abraham Calov, and David Hollaz as its three most significant representatives.[216] These authors make numerous distinctions on each topic which the modern reader might find tedious. They then follow every point with a proposed refutation and response. In this manner, then, the method of Aquinas and other medieval thinkers is followed rather closely. A more recent example of this method can be found in Conrad Lindberg's *Christian Dogmatics and Notes on the History of Dogma*, first published in English in 1922.[217] Throughout this volume, on nearly every topic, Lindberg cites the formal, material, sufficient, primary, and secondary causes, all using traditional Latin scholastic terms. While some might contend that these authors are merely complicating themes which need not be, the theologians themselves are attempting to be as clear and precise as possible.

There are two primary aspects of the scholastic method

---

[215] Preus, *Theology of Post-Reformation Lutheranism*, 45.

[216] Ibid., 45.

[217] Lindberg, *Christian Dogmatics*.

discussed in this chapter which are often given to criticism by those who are unsympathetic to post-Reformation Lutheranism. First is the scholastics' commitment to traditional Greek concepts of being as described by Plato and Aristotle. These commitments are outlined and explored in light of Luther's continual negative assessment of Aristotle and of Thomas Aquinas. Second is the notion of causation and its application to ideas such as the *ordo salutis*, especially as it is taught in the "silver age" of Lutheran orthodoxy. This is discussed in light of contemporary Thomistic philosophy and Humean notions of causation, which have led to significant misunderstanding of scholastic thought.

The Utilization of Essentialist Categories

While theology and metaphysics are distinctive disciplines, they share an intimate connection with one another. One's general beliefs surrounding the nature of reality have an impact upon one's view of God and created things in relation to him. For Aquinas and other medieval theologians, such a connection was obvious, as an extensive amount of space in the *Summa*, along with other medieval dogmatic texts, is devoted to such issues. In general, theology since the Reformation has relegated such metaphysical questions to a secondary position. This is not to say, however, that metaphysics was not a concern for the theologian in the immediate post-Reformation era. While Protestant scholastics made a conscious attempt to utilize more biblical theological language than in preceding centuries, metaphysical claims were far from absent. Language related to being is discussed, most often in the treatment of the doctrine of God, as well as the doctrine of man. While differences arise between various writers on these particulars, the Protestant scholastic authors were committed to an essentialist metaphysic.

The term "essentialism" is subject to a variety of interpretations, as this word has been used to describe a number of different philosophical perspectives. Thus, a working definition of the term is merited here so that further discussion of the idea can proceed. In recent discussions in analytic philosophy, essentialism is described as the philosophical conviction that every object has specific characteristics or properties which are essential to it. Without such properties, it is impossible for a thing to be what it is. There are, for example, certain characteristics of what makes a dog a dog, as opposed to a human or a chair. Without these characteristics, one could not categorize it as such. This concept relies on a distinction between accidental properties and essential properties, wherein essence is identified with the latter. This idea is found in Saul Kripke,[218] and is expanded in the so-called "new essentialism" of Brian Ellis.[219] In a more traditional essentialist schema, however, essence is not identified with essential properties as such. Rather, properties are subsequent to essence. It is precisely because a thing has a certain essence that it contains specific properties.[220] For the present purposes, essentialism is defined as the belief that there are universal real forms which things either participate in *or* contain within themselves that determine what they

---

[218] Kripke, *Naming and Necessity*.

[219] Ellis, *New Essentialism*.

[220] See the criticisms of new essentialism in Feser, *Scholastic Metaphysics*, 230–35.

are. A dog is a dog because it participates in, or contains, the universal essence of "dogness." The category of *dog* is, then, something real, rather than a mere linguistic aid to categorize particular objects which just happen to have similar features. This is why such a concept is often referred to as "realism." Further, the label "real-essentialism," borrowed from David Oderberg, is used throughout to distinguish this from other perspectives which utilize the essentialist title.[221] Yet, even the idea of a real-essentialist metaphysic is subject to a variety of interpretations, and various approaches are explored below in relation to the ideas of Lutheran scholastic authors.

Platonic Essentialism

In general, there are two strands of essentialism which are prominent in the history of both philosophy and theology: Platonic and Aristotelian. Plato's approach to essences is often categorized as idealism, due to its privileging of ideas over concrete physical reality.[222] Platonic idealism purports that reality ultimately exists within the realm of the "forms." This is an ideal world which, though real, exists apart from ordinary material reality. This realm of ideas is one in which all things participate, and through which they have their being. Going back to the previous example of a dog, then, every canine is such because it participates in the form of "dogness." The form is the perfect version of each object. Thus, the form of a dog is a perfect dog. One can participate more or less in such a form and thus become more real in accordance

---

[221] Oderberg, *Real Essentialism*.

[222] Copleston, *History of Philosophy*, I:163–206.

with the ideal. A dog with four legs is more real than one that lost two legs in an accident, because it conforms more accurately with the form. An illustration Plato often uses is that of shadows.[223] The physical particular instantiations of a form are like shadows that come from real objects, and the form is the thing itself.

The philosophy of Plato developed in a number of different directions in the centuries following him. Historians of philosophy have generally distinguished between three periods of Platonism: early Platonism, middle Platonism, and Neoplatonism.[224] For the development of Christian theology, middle Platonism and Neoplatonism are most important, as they both had a profound impact on the theology of the first centuries of the church. Middle Platonism arose in the first century B.C. and extended through the third century A.D. In this era, philosophers began combining the ideas of Plato with those of other popular philosophical systems such as Stoicism and Aristotelianism. The most important figure in this era, for discussions of the relationship between philosophy and faith, is the Jewish philosopher Philo of Alexandria.[225] Though the date of his birth remains unknown, Philo was a contemporary of Jesus, and his ideas were important for early Christian thinkers. Philo is perhaps the first thinker to consciously attempt a synthesis of Hellenistic and Hebraic forms of thought. He argued that there is continuity between Plato's philosophy and the revelation given to Moses. For Philo, such continuity is a result of the fact that the Greek philosophers had some

---

[223] Plato, *Selected Dialogues*, 279.

[224] Copleston, *History of Philosophy*, I:451–75.

[225] Ibid., I:458.

acquaintance with the writings of Moses. Several convictions of Philo are influential upon the development of Christian theology. Among these, two are especially important for the development of a Christian version of Platonic essentialism. The first is his idea of the *Logos*.[226] For Plato, there is a scale of being, as some objects are more real than others. At the top of such a scale is the realm of ideas which is connected to Plato's concept of God. Platonists argued, in light of the teaching of their founder, that some kind of intermediary (or intermediaries) was necessary to connect an individual to God as the highest form of being (alternatively described as one *beyond* being). For Plato, as described in the *Timaeus*, this was the role of the Demiurge, or master craftsman, who put the world together. In connection with this, Philo described the Logos (divine reason) as this intermediary between God and man, who connects the immaterial God to the material world.[227] For Philo, this Logos has a divine character, as he describes it in personal terms. As early Christians would, Philo connects the Logos with the Angel of the Lord who appears throughout the Old Testament. It is important to note, however, that Philo's idea of the Logos is not identical with that of later Christian theology, as the Logos is not of the same essence as God. At best, Philo's approach would be described as an Arian one, differing from the Nicene view of the relationship between God and the Logos. The second important aspect of Philo's thought for Christian Platonism is his connection between the realm of ideas and the mind

---

[226] Ibid., I:459.

[227] Allen, *Philosophy for Understanding Theology*, 72.

of God.[228] Philo, believing in the personal God of the Old Testament, argued that there is no realm of independent forms, but that these are concepts contained in the Logos, which are then manifest through physical reality. Though Philo is not usually cited by early Christian thinkers, it is undeniable that his views had a strong impact upon Christian Platonism.

Following the era of Middle Platonism, a popular school of thought known as Neoplatonism arose with Plotinus (A.D. 204–270). Though thinkers categorized as Neoplatonists differ on a number of points, they share a common belief in oneness as the ultimate reality. For Plotinus, there is a single transcendent unity called "the One" who is above all things and forms the basis of all reality.[229] This singular unity exists beyond all things, including both being and non-being. Nothing can be properly spoken of this One, as it is above all language and thought. However, Plotinus does speak of this One as good in an analogous sense. For Plotinus, the One, also called "the Good," is not a personal God. It is the source of creation, but it did not willfully make the universe. Instead, all things are emanations from the One, as an overflow of its being. Like Plato, Plotinus argues that some things are less real than others, and one's place in a scale of being is dependent upon how much one participates in the One. Singularity is, thus, the highest reality, and multiplicity is the result of a downward overflow of the One.[230] An illustration often used to describe this concept is that

---

[228] Copleston, *History of Philosophy*, I:460.

[229] Plotinus, *Six Enneads*, 353–60.

[230] Allen, *Philosophy for Understanding Theology*, 75.

of the sun and its rays. The sun naturally produces rays which are consistent with its own nature, and they diminish in brightness the farther one is from the sun itself. One especially important development in Plotinus is the religious nature of his philosophy. For Plato, knowledge of the forms was primarily a rational enterprise, and there is some debate whether Plato had any mystical notions whatsoever.[231] In Neoplatonism, philosophy is experiential, rather than simply rational. This connection between philosophy and mystical experience became foundational for Christian Platonists. According to Plotinus, one can attain union with the One in this life through ecstatic experience. Plotinus himself claims to have achieved such a union at different points in his life. This move is particularly important, because middle Platonists generally held that experience of the ultimate reality is only a product of the next life.[232] Though modified heavily, these ideas were adopted by certain figures within the Christian tradition.

Early Christian forms of essentialism are largely Platonic in nature, though in some significant ways early Christian thinkers differentiate themselves from the Greek philosophers. The connection between Greek philosophy and Christian thought is a complex one, as early writers had a variety of views regarding their interrelation. It is well known that Tertullian rejected any strong contact between the two, asking, "What has Athens to do with Jerusalem?"[233] Yet, in spite of such protests, even he utilized certain terms and

---

[231] Copleston, *History of Philosophy*, I:196.

[232] Allen, *Philosophy for Understanding Theology*, 71.

[233] Tertullian, "Against Heretics," VII. ANF 3, 246.

concepts from Greek philosophers.[234] The Alexandrian school, especially through Cyril and Origen, sought a one-to-one correlation between Greek and Christian ideas in certain areas.[235] These writers borrowed the idea from Philo that Plato had contact with the writings of Moses, and thus spoke about the God of divine revelation. Clement of Alexandria also makes a connection between the law given to the Jews as a schoolmaster leading them to Christianity with philosophy given to the Greeks. Thus, there is a quasi-revelatory status given to Greek authors.[236] The majority of Christian writers acknowledged both continuity and discontinuity between Christian thought and that of Plato, rejecting both a pure antagonism between the two as perceived by Tertullian, and a near total adoption of Greek thought forms as held by Clement.

In order to understand Christian essentialism in its Platonic form, there are two important figures who must be understood who utilized elements of Neoplatonism in their respective theological systems. First is Pseudo-Dionysius, and second is St. Augustine. The first became definitional for the development of Eastern Christian thought, and the latter for Western, both Roman Catholic and Protestant. Each of these authors uses certain categories as developed in Plotinus and other Neoplatonist authors, but both diverge from Platonism in certain important points. First, areas of divergence from Neoplatonism will be described, and second, the systems of Augustine and Pseudo-Dionysius will be explained.

Whatever differences Christian Neoplatonist authors have,

---

[234] Wolfson, *Church Fathers*, 104.

[235] Ibid., 106–9.

[236] Clement, "Exhortation," VI. ANF 2, 191.

all are agreed as to the problems of Plotinus' system. First, Plotinus' thought is opposed, at heart, to the concept of a personal and triune God. For Plotinus, the One is not to be identified with God but as an impersonal principle which is the source of all being. This One cannot enter into any personal relationship with creation. Any doctrine of the Trinity, for Plotinus, is fundamentally opposed to his emphasis upon unity as the ultimate source of being. While Christians emphasize God's unity in regard to the divine essence, as well as the doctrine of divine simplicity, multiplicity as such is not an imperfection, as God contains both unity and multiplicity within himself. Thus, the philosophical question of the relationship between the one and the many has a fundamentally different answer for Plotinus and Christianity. For Plotinus, multiplicity is simply an overflow of oneness and implies imperfection. For Christianity, both unity and multiplicity are found within God's own self. The second major area of difference between the two forms of thought is that Plotinus views creation not as a free act of the One, but as a necessary overflow of being. For Christianity, creation is a free act of God rather than a necessary one. It occurs *ex nihilo*. Finally, the concept of the incarnation is an impossibility for Plotinus, as material reality is a lesser overflow of the One, and then would not be consistent with the essence of the ultimate reality. With these important divergences in view, the adoption of Neoplatonist categories by Dionysius and Augustine will be described.

The work of Pseudo-Dionysius is definitional of the metaphysics of the Eastern church as it developed its own unique theological tradition. Pseudo-Dionysius' thought was highly influential upon Eastern thinkers such as Maximus Confessor and Gregory Palamas. Both of these writers continue to retain a strong influence upon Eastern Orthodox thought, especially through the Neopalamite school of Vladimir Lossky.[237] Thus, in order to understand the essentialism of the Eastern church in its Neoplatonic form, one must grasp the basic convictions of the Areopagite. Dionysius wrote under the name of the Areopagite converted by St. Paul, and thereby granted himself a significant amount of authority as a faithful representation of apostolic theology.[238] This fact resulted in a significant influence of his works on the patristic and early medieval church in both the East and West. It is universally acknowledged today, as it was by many in the later Middle Ages, that the author is not the biblical Dionysius, as he exhibits a clear influence from Plotinus, who did not write until 150 years after the death of the apostles. The first mentions of the work do not appear until the sixth century, and it is likely that Dionysius draws upon the writings of the Neoplatonist philosopher Proclus, who died at the end of the fifth century. Therefore, the text was likely written sometime in the late fifth and early sixth century. Its actual author remains unknown, and he is simply given the title of Pseudo-Dionysius the Areopagite.

What one finds in Dionysius is a speculative theology which is highly metaphysical. He hardly mentions the events of Christ's own life and does not demonstrate a significant concern for redemptive history. His most influential work is titled *The Divine Names*, which presents an apophatic theology, wherein God is known by way of negation. Like Plotinus, Dionysius characterizes God as the ultimate unity and source

---

[237] See Lossky, *Mystical Theology*.

[238] Copleston, *History of Philosophy*, I:91–100.

of being.²³⁹ God, as the source of being, then engages in the "bounteous act of Emanation," in which unity divides into multiplicity in the realm of created things.²⁴⁰ This is not an admission of pantheism, wherein God is identifiable with all things. Rather, Dionysius promotes a participationist ontology, wherein nothing can have being without participation in God. He, like other Neoplatonists, uses the analogy of a sun and its rays, noting that the sun sends forth rays, not through an act of the will, but as a necessary emanation of its nature. God, similarly, sends forth "the rays of Its undivided Goodness," which interpenetrates all created things.²⁴¹ In traditional Platonic fashion, for Dionysius, one can have more being the more it comes to participate in divinity. Salvation is defined as participation in God through these emanating rays. This gives the groundwork for the developed Eastern understanding of salvation as theosis.

The Dionysian metaphysic leads to a doctrine of God which differentiates itself from earlier Christian treatments through its apophatic emphasis. For the Areopogite, ultimately nothing can be properly stated of God. Like Plotinus, he argues that God is beyond all human concepts, including being itself. Even the ideas of triunity and oneness are incapable of describing God's own self.²⁴² The basic concept of goodness cannot properly be ascribed to God. Knowledge of God, then, is most properly a negative enterprise. He is to be described, not by what he is in essence, but by what he is not. The most

---

[239] Dionysius, *Divine Names*, 53.
[240] Ibid., 71.
[241] Ibid., 87.
[242] Ibid., 188.

proper understanding of God leads one to the point of lack of both "speech and thought," since both are incapable of grasping his nature.[243] The highest form of prayer, which is pure contemplation without word or thought, can lead to an ecstatic experience and ultimately unity with God. This mirrors Plotinus' conviction regarding the possibility of unity with the One. Later Eastern Orthodox writers mirror this emphasis, especially through the practice of hesychastic prayer.[244] These Neoplatonic themes result in a unique form of Plato's essentialism which is definitional for the Eastern Orthodox Church.

While Dionysius is the chief propagator of Neoplatonism in the East, the Western church is indebted primarily to Augustine in its adoption of Platonic ideas. In his early intellectual pursuits, prior to his conversion to Christianity, Augustine discovered the philosophy of Platonism, and particularly that of Plotinus.[245] He became convinced of the philosophical school and was an ardent disciple for some time. John Peter Kenney notes that the primary appeal in this ideology, for Augustine, was the concept of transcendence.[246] In his time as a Manichean, Augustine adopted the theory that God was both finite and material, yet this did not allow for any true rest for his soul, and it did not account for God and the existence of evil in the world. A discovery of monotheism in relation to a God who is above the world and is the source of all things led Augustine closer to the truths of Christianity

---

[243] Ibid., 198.

[244] Lossky, *Mystical Theology*, 209.

[245] Augustine, *Confessions*, VII.

[246] Kenney, "Mysticism of Augustine," 9.

that he would eventually accept. Though Augustine rejected several ideas related to Plato's philosophy after his conversion, he continued to praise the work of the Greek philosopher throughout his life. Even in his great work *The City of God*, Augustine states that Plato more closely approached the truths of Christianity than any other philosopher.[247] Augustine's divergence from Plotinus, as well as his utilization of Platonic philosophy in certain areas, is expressed here in order to give an account of Augustinian essentialist philosophy.

Augustine's relation to philosophy can best be understood by what H. A. Wolfson labels the "double faith theory." Throughout his writings, Augustine uses the language of faith in two different senses. In the first, Augustine refers to belief in general, which for the Christian is an acceptance of the truths given in revelation. One is called to accept what is revealed in Scripture because of the authority of the one who revealed it. In another sense, Augustine refers to faith as consent to a proposition.[248] It is in this second sense that Augustine connects faith with reason. Augustine takes from Stoicism the idea that consent is based upon reasonable probability.[249] This does not mean that Augustine is a rationalist in that he has a requirement for every idea revealed in Scripture to be logically demonstrable, as he acknowledge that some truths cannot be discovered by pure reason. While Augustine rejects the idea of any divine inspiration in Plato, he argues that in areas where Platonism or other philosophies are in agreement with revelation, they should be used, and

---

[247] Ibid., 13.

[248] Wolfson, *Church Fathers*, 129.

[249] Ibid., 134.

even praised by the Christian.[250] It would be proper to define Augustine's use of philosophy as a ministerial rather than magisterial one, as philosophical conclusions are always to be judged by Scripture.

There are certain convictions of St. Augustine that agree with those of Pseudo-Dionysius. For example, like the Areopagite, Augustine admits that God must first be known by way of negation before positive affirmation is possible.[251] The apophatic element of Augustine's thought, however, is not pronounced. He speaks often of God being known by way of the contemplation of creation, and then a consequent reasoning upward. In *De Trinitate*,[252] he mentions the concept of "goodness" which is ascribed to various things in creation. One speaks of food as good or money as good, and Augustine asserts that there must be a source for this concept of the good. On this point, he is a realist, as goodness is not a mere abstract term identified purely by human attribution, but something real which can be known and identified. From here, Augustine argues that God himself is the good from which all goodness derives. Thus, like Plotinus, Augustine utilizes the notion of God as the source of all being. Goodness, like other ideas, has its ultimate foundation in God's own self. He further contrasts derivative goodness from the source of goodness by making a distinction between "changeable good" and "unchangeable good."[253] The latter necessarily implies the former. If attributes are known in an imperfect

---

[250] Ibid., 128.

[251] Augustine, *De Trinitate*, VIII.2.4.

[252] Ibid., VIII.3.4.

[253] Ibid., VIIi.3.5.

way by earthly objects, it is implied that a perfection of those attributes exists as the source of the limited form of such attributes. Connections between Augustine's thought and Plato's regarding the forms are clear. Augustine connects abstract objects such as love, goodness, and beauty with God himself, which the human creature is an imperfect reflection of. Like Philo, he connects the forms with God, rather than some kind of separate ideal world that contains distinct forms which earthly things participate in. This leads to a participationist ontology which is different from that of Plato. Augustine's notion of participation is perhaps most evident in his theology of deification, which involves human participation in God.[254] However, despite his participationist ideas, Augustine does not speak of created objects as emanations of God as does Dionysius. His thought might, then, be most properly categorized as a moderated Neoplatonism.

Though there are a wide variety of views found in figures who adopted aspects of Platonism within the Christian tradition, there are two general trajectories in adoption of Platonic essentialism amongst Christian philosophers. In the East, Dionysius' view tends to predominate, especially as modified by Gregory Palamas. For Palamas, all of creation participates in God, and thus receives being from him. This is not a pure participation in God's essence, but in his energies, which are identified as that which emanates from God as rays do from the sun. This has eschatological significance, as like Plotinus, the Eastern church emphasizes unification with the One, identified by Christian thinkers as the triune God. This is

---

[254] Puchniak, "Augustine Revisited."

a reality in which all creation participates.²⁵⁵ These ideas were also transmitted in the West through the mystical tradition, such as in Boethius and Johann Tauler. In the Augustinian tradition of the West, Plato's idealism is transmitted through the conviction that objects have an essence which corresponds to the mind of God. This orientation is prominent in Anselm and the early scholastics, and is modified with the introduction of Aristotle's philosophy in the thirteenth century. Some of the ideas described here are used by Lutheran thinkers, especially through St. Augustine's influence upon Reformation thought. Yet Plato is not a sole influence upon the development of Lutheran scholasticism, as Aristotelian ideas are even more prominent in thinkers like Johann Gerhard and Conrad Lindberg.

Aristotelian Essentialism

The other form of essentialism which is prominent in both philosophy and theology is the Aristotelian version. Like Plato, Aristotle argues that there are real universals which unite all things of a common kind together, and that there are certain characteristics of an object which are necessary in order to make it what it is.²⁵⁶ Unlike Plato, he rejects the notion that forms exist in the ideal world of the mind, but instead promotes the idea that forms are found within objects themselves. Participation, then, is merely perceptual rather than real, as no ideal world exists. Such forms, then, are accessible through one's sense perception, and one is not

---

²⁵⁵ Staniloe, *Experience of God*, 1.

²⁵⁶ Aristotle, *Metaphysics*, 32–38.

led simply to the realm of contemplation where true reality is, as in Platonic philosophy. Aristotle therefore removes the third category of "being" which stands between God and the material world which exists as a mere image. There is, as a consequence of this, no necessity of a Logos or emanations which connect God and the world of images. A further distinction Aristotle makes is that between matter and form. This results in an approach to reality often labeled hylomorphism.[257] All things are made up of both matter and form, meaning that there is the material which makes up a thing (such as wood being the matter which a chair is made out of) and the form that matter takes (the actual form and shape which that wood is placed into so that it can function as a chair). The concept of "form," however, is not always necessarily tied to the physical shape of an object. Rather, form identifies what a thing is. For example, matter is engaged in the formation of a human person who has the identity of "human." At the moment of death, the soul is gone, and even though the body retains its shape materially, it no longer has the form of "human" in the sense that it did previously. Similarly, matter does not always have a physical connotation; Aristotle uses the example that letters are the matter of which words are made.

Along with the distinction between matter and form, another important concept for Aristotle's metaphysics is his discussion of substantial and accidental properties of objects, which he identifies as two differing components to every existing thing.[258] First, there is the substance of a thing. This

---

[257] Owens, *Elementary Christian Metaphysics*, 58.
[258] Ibid., 71–79; Feser, *Scholastic Metaphysics*, 164–71.

is what makes a thing what it is. Without certain properties, a thing's form would cease to exist. To go back to the previous example, the form "human" necessitates both soul and body. If the soul departs upon death, then the actual essence of the thing changes. Because the soul is an essential property, the lack of a soul means that what exists is no longer human, though the matter remains. Second, there are accidental properties which are subject to change, and are not necessary to make a thing what it is. A wall, for example, may be white, and that same wall may be painted brown. In this instance, both whiteness and brownness are simply accidental properties, because they can change and have no impact on whether the object they are connected with is a wall or something else. The form of "wall" remains. In relation to humanity, if an individual cuts one's hair, grows, or loses a tooth, the actual essence of the person is still the same. The person remains human despite such changes, because those changes are merely accidental rather than substantial. This schema differs from Plato's philosophy due to Plato's notion of participation. Changes in objects, for Plato, result in either more or less participation in the ideal form of that thing. In order to understand this difference, take the instance of a dog who has gotten its hair cut. Both Plato and Aristotle have an explanation for both the consistency of essence and the change which occurs in the world. For Plato, the dog retains its essence as such because it continues to participate in the ideal form of "dogness." What changes, however, is the mere shadow which reflects the real. The form itself remains constant. For Aristotle, this change is explained through the substance/accidents distinction. The cutting of hair allows the dog to remain as such, because a specific hair-length is not absolutely essential to the form of "dog." Instead, it is an accidental property. Thus, change in an object can exist while there is continuity in the subject itself through such change.

Alongside the distinctions between matter and form, as well as between substantial and accidental properties, a third essential distinction in Aristotle's thought is that between act and potency.[259] This concept is used by the philosopher as a way to explain the nature of change in the world. One of the earliest questions that arose in pre-Socratic philosophy was that of consistency of objects in view of the fact of change which occurs. One solution to the problem is to say that change is really an illusion instead of an actual movement of things from one state to another. This is Parmenides' view, representative of the Eleatic school, which purported that change must occur in an object due to the influence of something other than itself.[260] Since all that exists is "being," changes in a thing's being must come from something other than itself, which is "non-being." However, non-being is nothing, and therefore cannot actually cause any change. Therefore, change is impossible. The opposite view, held by Heraclitus, is that movement and change are the essence of reality.[261] He used the illustration of a river to demonstrate that when one steps into a river multiple times, it will fundamentally differ from what it was previously, since water is always in motion. Aristotle formulates an approach to the question of change and constancy through his distinction between act and potency.

---

[259] Owens, *Elementary Christian Metaphysics*, 31–42.

[260] Nahm, *Early Greek Philosophy*, 89.

[261] Ibid., 70.

For Aristotle, the primary problem with the Eleatic position is that it posits only two possibilities—being and non-being.[262] Were this the case, then being could not actually undergo any change, because that would imply a descent into non-being. Thus, Aristotle posits a third element into the equation: potentiality. Everything carries within itself not only the nature of its present being, but potentiality to become something else, or to be acted upon by other objects. Contemporary Thomistic philosopher Edward Feser uses the example of a rubber ball to indicate the nature of act and potency.[263] There might be specific characteristics which define what the ball is in the present, such as its color, size, and texture. These are all aspects of what the ball is in actuality. Yet, the ball also has the potential to take on other characteristics. One might paint the ball a different color or heat up the ball so that its texture changes. If these changes occur, then the potentiality to be a certain way becomes actuality. The potential for the ball to be painted blue becomes actual when the painter does it. For Aristotle, potentiality only becomes act when it is impacted by another agent. The ball could not become blue by itself, but only through the outside objects of the painter, the brush, the paint, and several other factors. Since, for Aristotle, all things are moved by another, there must necessarily be a beginning point in this chain which gives motion to all things. This beginning point must therefore not have the ability to be moved by anything other than itself (or then it could not be the source of motion). This is Aristotle's conception of God as an unmoved mover,

---

[262] Aristotle, *Metaphysics*, 21–22.

[263] Feser, *Aquinas*, 10–11.

which later becomes definitional of Thomistic thought.

While Plato was the most influential philosopher upon the early Christian church, Aristotle's influence predominated the later Middle Ages through St. Thomas Aquinas. Though certain ideas of Aristotle were transmitted to the early church through Stoic and other philosophical groups who took some influence from the Greek writer, Aristotle's own writings remained untranslated into Latin throughout the early medieval period, and were thus not widely known. Familiarity with Aristotle began through the writings of the Islamic philosopher Averroes, who wrote commentaries on the writings of both Plato and Aristotle in Arabic, which were translated into Latin during the thirteenth century.[264] Aristotelian philosophy soon became standard in Western thought through Thomas Aquinas, and his thought remains influential unto the present day. As Aquinas is Aristotle's most important interpreter, his use and modification of the philosopher is explained here in order to properly explain the metaphysical assumptions of the Lutheran scholastics in connection to Aquinas.

Though he might be popularly characterized as a pure repristinator of Aristotle, Aquinas distances himself from Aristotle in a number of important ways. Just as the church fathers borrowed concepts from Plato while rejecting his beliefs which were contrary to Christian revelation, Aquinas is quick to dismiss aspects of Aristotle's philosophy which are inconsistent with Christian theism. Chief among such differences is Aristotle's doctrine of God. While the philosopher does speak about an "unmoved mover," this being

---

[264] Leinsle, *Introduction to Scholastic Theology*, 136–38.

is not identified as a personal Creator. For Aristotle, the universe itself is eternal, and thus, though he confesses a clear distinction between God and the material world, there is no creation *ex nihilo*. The primary function of God in Aristotle's philosophy is to give motion to all things, while himself remaining unmoved by anything.[265] He does this through his nature as the final cause of all things, toward which all things move. This unmoved mover spends eternity contemplating himself, and is thus unconcerned with the world. In adopting Aristotelian thought, Aquinas combines the truths of revelation with those discoverable by reason.[266] For Thomas, natural reason is able to comprehend certain important truths about the world, including God's existence and the contingency of all things upon him. However, the dogmas of the incarnation, the Trinity, creation *ex nihilo*, and other distinctively Christian doctrines are known only by way of revelation. It is in terms of natural revelation that Aristotle is particularly praised.

For the present purposes, it is Aquinas's utilization of Aristotle's basic metaphysical assertions which are most important. The nature of causality also plays a large role in the formation of Thomas's thought, as it did in later Protestant scholasticism. However, this is dealt with in a separate section below. The three central distinctions of Aristotle's metaphysics are all adopted by Aquinas, and he also adds a fourth: the difference between essence and existence.[267] For Thomas, the essence of a thing is its identity. It is the *what* of

---

[265] Allen, *Philosophy for Understanding Theology*, 127.

[266] Nieuwenhove, *Introduction to Medieval Theology*, 175.

[267] Aquinas, *Introduction to Metaphysics*, 31–35.

an object. This is what is otherwise called the form of an object. Like Aristotle, Aquinas rejects an idealist understanding of essence, wherein universals are derived from the ideal form of an object. Yet, universals do exist, and there is then something of "humanness" which exists within each human person that unites them all as a species. Distinct from the essence of an object is a thing's existence. This is not the question of *what* a thing is, but *whether* it is. One might have an idea of the identity of a unicorn and some of the attributes which constitute unicornness. This means that this object has cognitional being.[268] Yet, the fact that such an essence can be constructed does not mean that this creature actually exists beyond the mind. It most likely does not. Therefore, there must be a distinction between the essence of an object and the existence of an object. This is an important aspect of Aquinas's doctrine of God, who is defined as one in whom essence and existence are identical.[269] In contingent objects, essence never necessitates existence, as no essence is by nature necessary. However, God's essence differs from all others in that his essence necessitates his existence.

It is in Aquinas's doctrine of God that Aristotle's metaphysical categories find their *telos*. Among the most essential aspects of God's being, for Thomas, is his simplicity. God is not composed of parts.[270] This does not mean merely that God does not have physical parts, but that he is not a composite being in *any* sense. For a being to be composite is to say that it can be broken down into some kind of reality which

---

[268] Owens, *Elementary Christian Metaphysics*.

[269] Dolezal, *God without Parts*, 62.

[270] Aquinas, *Introduction to Metaphysics*, 103.

is greater, or more basic, than itself. If God were composed of atoms, for example, then those atoms, rather than the divine nature, would be the ultimate foundation of reality. The self-existence of God, then, necessitates that he is a simple rather than a complex being. For Aquinas, this simplicity is defined in light of Aristotle's important distinctions as discussed above. In God, there can be no division between substance and accident.[271] In more traditional theological language, there can be no real distinction between God's essence and his attributes, because if such were the case, he would be a composite being. As in the example of the atoms, this would necessitate that attributes were separable from the divine essence, and thus were a more basic form of reality than God. Consequently, God would not truly be the ground of being. If love, for example, were merely an accidental attribute of God rather than his essence, then love would be something which is able to be divorced from God. The question then would be, by what standard is God loving? If love were not the essence of God himself, then some standard of love must exist outside of him and thus be prior to him, thus negating his own self-existence and self-dependence. For Aquinas, there is no standard by which God is loving, just, merciful, or good, because he himself *is* that standard. The second Aristotelian division, between act and potency, is similarly tied to divine simplicity.[272] Thomas describes God as "pure act," because there is no potentiality within God which has yet to be actualized. For Aristotle, movement from potentiality to actuality is a movement from lesser to greater, as actuality

---

[271] Dolezal, God *without Parts*, 58.

[272] Aquinas, *Introduction to Metaphysics*, 100.

is the result of an object achieving its final cause. For God's own being, there can be no final cause, because such would imply imperfection in the divine nature, or some kind of self-actualization which denies his self-sufficiency and perfection. These ideas, alongside Thomas's argument that in God, there is an identity between God's essence and his existence, form his concept of God as an absolutely simple being.

Thomas Aquinas, utilizing Aristotle, promotes a form of essentialism which affirms some of the basic assumptions of Plato and the Neoplatonist traditions, while simultaneously moving beyond the concept of an idealist view of forms. In both systems, there is an affirmation that universal essences do exist, alongside a conviction that God (or "the One" in Plotinus' case) is necessary and self-existent. On these points, Christians who follow either the Aristotelian or the Platonist tradition agree. In that sense, all are essentialists. Yet these two forms of essentialism differ in their approach to the nature of essences. While Christian Platonic thinkers view essences as ideas in the mind of God in which all things participate, the Aristotelian approach locates the essence within objects themselves, though with acknowledgement that the creation and sustenance of such essences is due to the work of God. In the following section, these two forms of essentialist philosophy are discussed in relation to the Lutheran scholastic tradition in order to establish the basic metaphysical assumptions of Lutheran orthodoxy.

Essentialism in Lutheran Scholasticism

As inheritors of the medieval theological and philosophical tradition, the Lutheran reformers and scholastics interacted with the philosophical convictions of those within the previous Christian tradition. This interaction extends from Luther through the scholastic revival of the nineteenth century. In this section, first, Luther's interaction with Platonic and Aristotelian essentialism is engaged in order to compare Luther's own philosophical convictions with those of previous authors. Following this, the seventeenth-century Lutheran scholastics are examined in order to explain their metaphysical convictions. Most particularly, Johann Gerhard is discussed as an exemplar of this tradition. This seventeenth-century approach is then compared to the scholastic revival involving nineteenth- and early twentieth-century Lutheran theologians. Finally, a proposal is offered for an essentialist metaphysic which is consistent with Luther and the following tradition.

While Luther's relationship to Aristotle has already been discussed, some observations regarding his relationship to essentialist ontology are merited. While critics of essentialism in Luther are engaged in the following chapter, some preliminary remarks must be made on the subject. While Luther does not spend an extensive amount of space writing on his views of metaphysics, and the nature of essence in particular, there is one writing which does engage the ideas inherent in both Platonic and Aristotelian essentialism: the Heidelberg Disputation. Opponents of Lutheran scholasticism often utilize the Disputation as an anti-scholastic document, especially in the theological theses. However, Luther's remarks are not merely theological, but he engages specific metaphysical ideas in his philosophical theses, and not always in a negative manner. These ideas have simply not been engaged in the majority of works on the Heidelberg Disputation, and there are a few significant reasons for this. First, the critical edition of Luther's works did not include the defense of Luther's philosophical theses until 1979. This omission simply did not allow for an in-depth treatment of the issue. Second, the English edition of *Luther's Works* still fails to contain a translation of these portions of writing. The most important part of the theses for the present work is his eighth point, in which he argues that Aristotle wrongly condemns Plato's theory of forms. Eric Parker provides a translation of the defense of the eighth proposition, which is worth quoting at length:

> *That the philosophy of Plato is better than the philosophy of Aristotle appears from this, namely, that Plato always depends upon the divine and immortal, separate and eternal, insensible and intelligible, from whence he also recommends that singulars, individuals, and sensible things be abandoned because they cannot be known on account of their instability. Aristotle, being opposed to this in every way, ridicules the separable and intelligible things and brings in sensible things and singulars and thoroughly human and natural things. But, he does this most cunningly:*
>
>   *Firstly, because he cannot deny that the individual is transient [fluxa], he invents a form and different matter, and so the thing is not knowable as matter, but as form. Therefore, he says that the form is the cause of*

> *knowing [causam sciendi], and he calls this "divine, good, desirable" and he assigns the intellect to this. And so he frustrates every mind, while he examines the same thing in two ways.*
>
> *Secondly, this "form" is a quiddity and the sum of his Metaphysics. So, he destroys all the ideas, putting in their place his own forms and quiddities conjoined to matter, ridiculing and denying [the existence of] the ideas separable from matter, as appears in many places, especially Metaphysics and [Nicomachean] Ethics. But, it is well known by way of blessed Augustine, Iamblichus and all the Platonic disputants that the ideas of Plato are separate [from matter]. And so it is well known that the philosophy of Aristotle crawls in the dregs [reptat in faecibus] of corporeal and sensible things, whereas Plato moves among things separable and spiritual.*[273]

Luther's comments on these matters prove to be quite problematic for interpretations of the Reformer which place him at odds with all traditional Greek thought-forms. He rejects Aristotle's metaphysics, not for its essentialism, but for its denial of the reality of forms existent in the mind of God. It should not be surprising that, as an Augustinian monk, Luther prefers the philosophical convictions of the bishop of Hippo over that of Thomism. The specifics of Luther's criticisms of Aristotle are dealt with below, in an attempt to formulate an essentialist approach which is both scholastic and consistent with Luther.

Following the death of Martin Luther, the leadership of the

---

[273] Parker, "Platonism of Martin Luther."

Lutheran movement eventually fell into the hands of Martin Chemnitz, sometimes affectionately labeled "the second Martin." A more philosophical thinker than Luther, Chemnitz demonstrates a strong adherence to a classic essentialist metaphysic. Through the second-generation reformer, Aristotelian metaphysical convictions are included within the Lutheran confessional documents, and were then transmitted to the seventeenth-century scholastic tradition. Chemnitz's thought is complex enough, especially in his exposition of Christ's two natures, to merit a full-length study, but for the present purposes, it only must be demonstrated that he utilized classical Greek philosophical categories in his construction of Lutheran thought. Thus, here some passages in the Formula of Concord and Chemnitz's *Two Natures in Christ* are explored to demonstrate this point, and his comments are supplemented with passages from other scholastic writers which affirm and reiterate such convictions.

Perhaps the most important metaphysical statement in the post-Reformation era for the Lutheran tradition is made in Article I of the Formula of Concord, under Chemnitz's influence, in resolution to a debate surrounding the nature of sin upon the human creature.[274] The Philipists tended to speak more optimistically about the nature of the human will after the fall than did the Gnesio-Lutherans. This led to a number of disputes between representatives of both schools of thought. At the height of this controversy, a public disputation was held as an attempt to arrive at a resolution on the subject. Victorin Strigel and Matthias Flacius met in 1560 to settle the question of the role of the human will in conversion. In

---

[274] The history is catalogued in Preus, *Contemporary Look*, 115–17.

the dispute, Strigel argued that sin was an accidental, rather than substantial, quality. As such, Strigel argued, there was goodness intact in the human person in regards to one's substance. Not having a strong understanding of Aristotelian categories, Flacius rejected the idea that sin was an accidental quality and instead retorted that it became the very essence of the human creature in the postlapsarian state. In spite of several calls to recant his statement, Flacius refused, and was eventually rejected by the other Gnesio-Lutherans for his latent Manicheanism. This debate led to a confessional statement on the subject which rejected the positions of both Strigel and Flacius.

In Article I, the authors make two basic contentions. First, the language that sin is "accidental" does not mean that it is insignificant. The corruption of sin has a radical impact upon the person, placing one under God's wrath and rendering one devoid of spiritual freedom (FC SD I:1). It is a misunderstanding of Aristotle's language to assume that just because something is not a substantial property, it is as inconsequential as painting a wall a different color. A more apt illustration might be of someone driving a car into a wall, cracking and bending it while leaving the wall itself barely intact. The second contention of the Formula is that though the impacts of sin are devastating upon the human person, they do not negate one's humanity and essential value as a creation of God (FC SD I:26). This leads to a metaphysical discussion related to the value of utilizing the Aristotelian categories of substance and accident. Were they opposed to essentialism (at least of the Aristotelian variety), the authors of the Formula had an opportunity to voice such criticisms here; yet the opposite is the case. The metaphysical system of

Aristotle, at least in some form, is adopted by the Formula.

In this discussion, the Formula notes approvingly that the church fathers often used metaphysical language, as such is sometimes necessary in academic dispute. It is argued that such language should not be used heavily in preaching for the sake of the unlearned—there is a proper place for such ideas to be expounded by theologians. A substance is defined as a "self-existent essence," and an accident, in contrast, "does not exist by itself essentially," but is separable from a substance (FC SD I:54). An essence is unchanging, while the accidental properties of a thing are subject to continual change. This division is further described as an "indisputable truth" (*immota veritas*) among all learned people (FC SD I:57). The Formula further attempts to demonstrate that Luther was not opposed to using such language, and at times did so himself (FC SD I:62). In light of the acceptance of such language, it is argued then that Flacius's position is mistaken, and that sin is an accidental property after the fall (FC SD I:61). These statements are highly significant because they do not represent the opinion of one individual theologian, but became a standard part of the Lutheran confessional documents as published in *the Book of Concord*.

The metaphysical assumptions here played a significant role in the development of the anthropology of Lutheran scholasticism. In the scholastic texts, there are two primary topics of discussion under the topic *anthropology*: the *imago Dei* and original sin. Both concepts use Aristotelian metaphysics. The early twentieth-century scholastic writer Adolf Hoenecke explains the doctrine of the divine image as expounded by Lutheran orthodox theologians. He notes that the *imago Dei* is spoken of in two distinct senses. First, there is the image *late dicta* (in a general sense), which includes man's attributes, such as freedom, intellect, and dominion.[275] Lindberg refers to it as the "formal image," which consists of mind, will, and emotion.[276] This broader sense of the image includes the entire nature of man and is thus part of the human essence. This image is not lost in the fall, because if it were, then the human essence itself would be obliterated. The other manner of speaking about the *imago Dei* is the image *stricte dicta* (in a strict sense), which is identified with spiritual righteousness.[277] Lindberg uses the title "material image."[278] The narrower sense of the image refers to an accidental quality, whereby one can lack spiritual righteousness and retain a genuinely human essence. Though Lutheran theologians differ on several points related to anthropology on topics such as the propagation of the soul, the distinction between soul and spirit, and the nature of the broad sense of the divine image, all of the Lutheran scholastics are committed to an Aristotelian essentialism which accepts that there are both essential properties of the human nature, and accidental ones which are lost in the fall.

Along with the use of such language regarding the divine image, the Lutheran scholastics also follow the Formula in expositing sin as an accidental quality. In his compendium of Lutheran scholastic thought, *The Doctrinal Theology of the Evangelical Lutheran Church*, Heinrich Schmid summarizes the position of the seventeenth-century writers on the topic of the

---

[275] Hoenecke, *Evangelical Lutheran Dogmatics*, III:320.

[276] Lindberg, *Christian Dogmatics*, 156.

[277] Hoenecke, *Evangelical Lutheran Dogmatics*, III:320.

[278] Lindberg, *Christian Dogmatics*, 156.

relationship between sin and nature.²⁷⁹ Like Chemnitz, the scholastics guard against two primary problems in relation to original sin. First is the Pelagian or Semi-Pelagian position, wherein sin does not have a fundamental impact upon man's essence at all. This is what Quenstedt refers to as "a mere *accident, lightly and externally attached.*"²⁸⁰ This is not to say that sin is not an accidental property (as Quenstedt upholds the affirmations of Article I of the Formula), but that it also has a broader impact upon human nature as such, though without eliminating the human essence. He refers to original sin as "internally and intimately inhering."²⁸¹ Though the human essence is impacted and corrupted by sin, Quenstedt is also quick to note that the essence of humanity remains even after the fall, in opposition to Flacius.²⁸² Under each of these topics, the Lutheran scholastics affirm the basic Aristotelian definition of substantial and accidental qualities, and thus demonstrate the adequacy of such categories in theological formulation.

Alongside his use of Aristotelian categories in the debate with Flacius, Chemnitz also utilizes such distinctions in his exposition of the two natures in Christ. In Luther's debate with Zwingli over the nature of the Lord's Supper, an extensive disagreement began between the two reform movements surrounding the humanity of Christ. Zwingli argued that Christ's human nature remained only at the right hand of God the Father in heaven, whereas Luther contended for Christ's

---

²⁷⁹ Schmid, *Doctrinal Theology*, 246–49.

²⁸⁰ Ibid., 247.

²⁸¹ Ibid., 247.

²⁸² Ibid., 248.

omnipresence according to both natures. At the height of this debate following Luther's death, Martin Chemnitz wrote *The Two Natures in Christ*, in which he gives a detailed scriptural and theological exposition of the theme, focusing on the question of the communication of attributes in Christ. Throughout the book, Chemnitz uses scholastic categories, and thus the entire text could be examined to demonstrate all of the particularities of his philosophical convictions. For the present purposes, however, only a small section in the beginning of the text is discussed, which carries the title, "Definition of Certain Terms."[283] This first chapter of his work is a short prolegomena of sorts, wherein Chemnitz outlines the use of various philosophical and theological terms in discussions about Christ's two natures. In this text, it is apparent that Chemnitz is an adherent of an essentialist metaphysic consistent with that of Aquinas.

This discussion begins by citing John of Damascus on terminology related to substance, in which Chemnitz argues that substance, nature, and form are used as interchangeable terms.[284] These terms relate to that which is common to individual members of the same species. There are thus essential properties which make up various genera and species. Chemnitz further states that there are individual members of each species which are described through language of subsistence, hypostasis, or person. The individual thing "subsists in itself," and it is defined by particular attributes.[285] These terms are then applied to the Trinity, wherein God is

---

[283] Chemnitz, *Two Natures*, 29–36.

[284] Ibid., 29.

[285] Ibid., 29.

described as one essence which subsists in three persons. In light of this, Chemnitz explains that the eternal begetting of the Son and procession of the Spirit include a communication of the whole divine essence from the Father.[286] Chemnitz makes further distinctions in relation to the incarnation of Christ. In the person of Christ, a self-subsistent divine nature is united to the human nature, which subsists not in itself, but in the divine nature.[287] In describing Christ, there is a difference between the "abstract" and "concrete" manner of referring to him. Terms referring to natures as natures are "abstract," because they deal with essence as such. However, when speaking of the person, he is spoken of "concretely."[288] It is important that the terms utilized in this section arise from both the church fathers and medieval scholastic thinkers. Chemnitz does not view himself as an innovator, but as an inheritor of the previous tradition, which is highly indebted to Greek philosophical concepts.

Among these scholastic terms, Chemnitz again returns to the substance-accident distinction. He divides all attributes into two categories, essential and accidental.[289] All created things have both of these categories of attributes. In God, however, there are no accidental qualities. Furthermore, there is an exact identification between God's essence and attributes, so that essential characteristics of the divine nature cannot be abstracted from substance. Chemnitz reasons that God is a perfectly simple essence, because if God were

---

[286] Ibid., 30.

[287] Ibid., 31.

[288] Ibid., 31.

[289] Ibid., 34.

composed of essence and attributes, then such attributes would improve the divine nature and thus deny God's own perfection and self-sufficiency.[290] This is a clear reaffirmation of the Thomistic position regarding divine simplicity. Chemnitz then concludes his discussion by noting that Christ has accidental attributes according to his human nature, as is characteristic of all created natures. The essential properties of Jesus' divine nature are never transferred to the human as *essential* attributes, as such would result in a complete dissolution of the human nature itself. Rather, divine attributes are communicated to the human nature by grace and are thus exercised through this nature, without an essential transformation of one into the other.[291] Throughout his exposition of terminology, it is apparent that Chemnitz self-consciously utilizes the metaphysical terminology of both patristic authors and medieval scholastic thinkers. He is followed in this regard by the later Lutheran scholastics.

The most extensive metaphysical treatment of God among the scholastics is that of Johann Gerhard. In earlier authors, there was not a lengthy treatment of God's essence and attributes, as Melanchthon and Chemnitz emphasized triunity. In his *Theological Commonplaces*, Gerhard devotes an entire volume to an exposition of God's essence and attributes, in which a Thomistic conception of deity is affirmed and defended. In order to understand Gerhard's underlying philosophical convictions surrounding essence, his thoughts on two subjects are explored: arguments for the existence of God, and divine simplicity.

---

[290] Ibid., 34.
[291] Ibid., 35.

For Gerhard, the existence of God is something which can be proven both by reason and by Scripture. Apologetics, then, is an essential part of the theological task. Gerhard outlines three reasons why such an enterprise is important: first, to refute skeptics; second, to strengthen the faith of believers; and third, to perfect one's natural knowledge of God.[292] The third point is important, as it establishes continuity between Gerhard and Aquinas. As addressed above, both Luther and Aquinas argue that certain truths about God are discoverable by reason alone, though God's triunity, the incarnation, and other truths are accessible only by means of revelation. Gerhard speaks of natural knowledge of God as consisting in his being, will, power, and operation.[293] God's unity and existence, for Gerhard, are known by way of natural reason, but God's triunity is not. Like Luther, Gerhard also distinguishes between the knowledge of the law as natural and knowledge of the gospel as supernatural. Gerhard refers to the natural law as the "legal will" of God, which leads to external obedience on behalf of the heathen.[294] Gerhard then uses "grace perfects nature" type of language, which is characteristic of Aquinas. He writes that natural knowledge of God is "imperfect and weak, [and that therefore] we must surely strengthen, perfect, and complete it from the divinely revealed Word."[295] Gerhard's Thomistic leanings are clear here, and are further demonstrated in his exposition of proofs for the existence of God.

---

[292] Gerhard, *Nature of God*, 56–57.

[293] Ibid., 57.

[294] Ibid., 57.

[295] Ibid., 58.

Gerhard gives five proofs of the existence of God which are apparent by way of nature alone. First, Gerhard follows Aquinas in arguing for the necessity of an unmoved mover.[296] Everything that is moved is moved by another, because nothing can actualize its own potency. There cannot be an infinite progression of movers, because such would necessitate that there are only secondary causes, which is an impossibility. By definition, secondary causes are subsequent to a primary cause. Thus, there must be a primary cause, whom Gerhard identifies as God. Gerhard affirms here some of Aristotle's most fundamental metaphysical claims—most particularly, the distinction between act and potency. Gerhard is so fond of Aristotle that, following Aquinas, he even gives him the affectionate title "The Philosopher"![297] His second argument is similar to the first, as he contends that efficient causation necessitates a primary cause who is not caused by another nor is self-caused. Third, Gerhard uses an argument from Anselm, which is also echoed in Augustine, wherein the degrees of goodness in the world necessitate an ultimate goodness by which all things are measured. It is in this context that Gerhard also speaks about things having "more being and less being."[298] This is significant because such a statement demonstrates that Gerhard does not rely *solely* on Aristotle's metaphysic, but he also draws from Augustinian Neoplatonism, in which being is described as participation in God, and of which there are gradations. Fourth, Gerhard returns to Aristotle and argues from final causation, that an

---

[296] Ibid., 60.

[297] Ibid., 60.

[298] Ibid., 60.

intelligent source must be instrumental in directing things toward their particular ends.[299] Finally, Gerhard argues from natural human instinct that God's existence is imprinted upon the human mind. In all of these proofs, it is clear that Gerhard argues from the perspective of classical metaphysics, drawing primarily from Aristotle, but also utilizing aspects of Neoplatonism.

Gerhard's philosophical convictions are further seen in his treatment of that topic, "What God Is," in which divine simplicity takes a central position.[300] The theologian defines God as "sheer and purest act."[301] He defines actuality by use of the Aristotelian distinctions as filtered through Thomas. Gerhard notes that God is not composed of matter and form, genus and species, substance and accidents, act and potency, or individuated substance and nature.[302] In using such distinctions, Gerhard confirms his commitment to the Aristotelian categories presented. Gerhard is thus a strong proponent of hylomorphism. He further distinguishes by active and passive potency, noting that God is devoid of passive potency. This distinction, which is prominent in Aquinas, distinguishes between the ability to have a potency which can be actuated by something outside of oneself (passive potency), and the ability to actuate the potency of something outside of oneself (active potency). God possesses the latter, but not the former. All of the basic elements of Aquinas's metaphysical system are affirmed by Gerhard, but he also utilizes aspects of

---

[299] Ibid., 61.
[300] Ibid., 92.
[301] Ibid., 93.
[302] Ibid., 93.

Neoplatonism through St. Augustine.

From Luther to Gerhard, philosophical essentialism is affirmed by Lutheran theologians, as it was throughout the scholastic tradition even into the twentieth century. Chemnitz, the Formula of Concord, Gerhard, and later scholastics primarily utilize Aristotelian categories, especially as they relate to two topics: man's relationship to sin, and God's simplicity. It is in these two areas that a distinction between substance and accident is adopted, as well as distinctions between act and potency, and between matter and form as they relate to the simplicity of God. A problem has arisen, however, in relation to Luther's own thought and that of later thinkers. Most of Luther's statements about Aristotle are rather negative, although positive affirmations about his ethics and logic can be found. Yet Luther nowhere accepts Aristotle's metaphysical schema. In fact, in Luther's most supposedly anti-philosophical phase, he completely rejects Aristotle in favor of Plato. This leads then to the often-made conclusion that a philosophical chasm separates Luther from the scholastics. Is one then left simply to choose between the Platonism of Luther and the Aristotelianism of the confessions? While such a decision might seem inevitable, there are ways in which these ideas can be synthesized. As noted, Gerhard does not avoid Platonic language, especially when derived from Augustine. Here, it is contended that a consistent Lutheran scholastic metaphysic utilizes elements of both Aristotelianism and Platonism, as Aquinas himself did. Before such a synthesis can be exposited, however, some remarks surrounding Aristotle's view of causation, which is a prominent aspect of the Protestant scholastic tradition, are merited. Following this is an exposition of the archetype-ectype distinction, which then leads to a proposal for a synthesis between Platonic and Aristotelian ideas in Lutheran thought.

Causation

One of Aristotle's most important contributions to philosophy is his concept of causation. In contemporary language, one generally uses the term "cause" in one particular sense, as an act or event which results in some further action as its consequence. This is what Aristotle describes as an "efficient cause," which is merely one aspect of causation. According to Aristotle, there are four distinct types of causes: material, formal, efficient, and final. Each of these demonstrates a different aspect of reality. In this section, these four types of causation are defined, followed by an exposition of how the reformers and scholastic theologians used such distinctions in the formation of theology.

Aristotle's four types of causation are connected with his other distinctions explained above, as all of these ideas are interwoven throughout his *Metaphysics*. The first type of cause is the *material*. This refers to that which a thing is made of, as matter, for Aristotle, refers to whatever makes up a thing. The matter of words, for example, are syllables, and the matter which makes up a chair is wood. The second type of cause is the *formal*. Because Aristotle defends hylomorphism, everything has both a material and a formal cause. Matter (with the exception of "prime matter") takes up particular structures, which are a thing's form. The formal cause of a chair is its shape, which allows for sitting. The formal cause of a word is the order and structure in which syllables are placed. The third type of cause is the one most commonly understood today, known as the *efficient*. This is related to the idea that for anything's potential to be actuated, it must be impacted by something else. As Aquinas argues, everything that is in motion is moved by another. In every object, other than the unmoved mover, a motion occurs by way of an efficient cause. Nothing is self-caused. It is important to distinguish this idea from a notion that the relationship between cause and effect is simply one of time, wherein a cause is described as temporally prior to its effect. This misunderstanding is explained further below. The last type of cause described by Aristotle is the *final cause*. This is the notion that not only is everything moved by something else, but motion is directed toward something. Actions are goal-directed. This type of goal-directedness does not relate only to humans, but it is inherent in all objects. A seed, for example, grows for the final cause that it become a tree or a plant. This goal-directedness brings forth a teleological element into all of reality, which for Aristotle is directed toward the unmoved mover.

The language of causation taken from Aristotle was part of several early debates in the Reformation, especially related to the role of the human will in conversion. The language of causation became part of theological discourse in the Reformation primarily through Philip Melanchthon, who often utilized the four causes as defined by Aristotle.[303] While Luther used such ideas on occasion, it was Melanchthon who was the more systematic thinker, and the four causes helped to give clarity to certain concepts. In his later editions of the *Loci Communes*, Melanchthon sparked a controversy by utilizing the language

---

[303] Trueman, *Protestant Scholasticism*, 280.

of causation in connection to conversion. He spoke about three causes of conversion, which included the Holy Spirit, God's Word, and the human will.[304] This led to a debate between Philipists and Gnesio-Lutherans over the efficient cause of conversion, as many feared that Melanchthon had neglected the position of his predecessor for a synergistic approach. In the Formula of Concord, this debate was settled through an article on the subject of free will. Article II speaks about the *causa efficiente* (efficient cause) of conversion, and identifies both the Holy Spirit and the Word of God as such (FC SD II.70). The Epitome similarly summarizes the formulators' position that there are two *efficientes causae* of conversion (FC Ep. II.19). Throughout the scholastic era following *the Book of Concord*, the four Aristotelian causes were applied to nearly every theological topic.

Gerhard is perhaps the first writer to use language of Aristotle's causes on more than an occasional basis within the Lutheran church. He does so to characterize various topics, but here, one in particular is presented as an example of his mode of theologizing. In the beginning of his *Theological Commonplaces*, Gerhard includes a short prolegomena section which explains the nature of theology. In this text, he explains the efficient, formal, material, and final causes of theology. The efficient cause of theology is divine revelation.[305] This concept is further divided into a *principal efficient cause* and an *instrumental efficient cause*. These two distinctions are used throughout later writers. The principal efficient cause of theology is God himself, and the instrumental cause is

---

[304] Kolb, *Lutheran Confessions*, 206.

[305] Gerhard, *Nature of Theology*, 24.

Holy Scripture, which is the instrument through which God reveals himself.[306] He explains this in another manner by distinguishing between the principle of being (God) and the principle of knowing (Scripture). The material cause of theology is those theological truths which are drawn from the revealed word. The formal cause is that specific structure that theology takes when one is writing.[307] Regarding the form, Gerhard notes that this is not essential, as theologians have differed in mode of presentation while retaining the same matter of theology. Theology's final cause, for Gerhard, is twofold. He distinguishes between its *principal end* and its *intermediate end*. The principal end of theology is the glorification of God. Like Aquinas, Gerhard views God as both the efficient and final cause of all things. The intermediate end, for Gerhard, is further divided into an *internal* immediate end and an *external* intermediate end. The internal is the inner work of the Spirit in preparing people for salvation, and the external is the reception of eternal life.[308] The foundation laid here by Gerhard is built upon by the later scholastic authors, especially in discussions about the *ordo salutis*.

In general, non-scholastic thought has rejected the concept of a systematic order of salvation as an imposition of Aristotelianism upon theology. According to these authors, there is no need to speak about cause and effect with reference to salvation. However, in the scholastics, there is benefit to such a discussion as a manner in which one grasps more fully the multifaceted nature of salvation. Contemporary

---

[306] Ibid., 24.
[307] Ibid., 28.
[308] Ibid., 29.

rejections of this idea often lead to a justification-centric approach to salvation which neglects non-forensic elements of soteriology. The adoption of Aristotle's categories here are not viewed by the scholastic authors as some pagan imposition upon the biblical text, but as a useful tool to explain what is implicitly in Scripture.[309] Within these discussions there is some disagreement surrounding certain elements of the *ordo*, but a general order adopted by the Lutheran scholastics is as follows: the call, illumination, conversion, regeneration, justification, mystical union, sanctification, and preservation. Sometimes, glorification is included as part of the order.[310] Some elements of this system are explained in order to exposit the utilization of the ideas of causation in later scholastic thought.

The first part of the *ordo salutis* is generally referred to as the call (*vocatio*). This is the invitation of God, through the means of grace, by which one is beckoned unto salvation.[311] The efficient cause of the call is twofold. The primary efficient cause is the Holy Spirit, and the instrumental cause is the divine word. Through these means, one is brought to repentance and faith. Though a material and formal cause are not generally attributed to these various elements of the order of salvation, final causality is a central element of the *ordo salutis*. In relation to the call, there is a twofold final cause. The first, proximate end is the sinner's awakening unto the need of salvation. The second, final end is conversion.[312] A second

---

[309] Weidner, *Pneumatology*, 19.

[310] Lindberg, *Christian Dogmatics*, 298.

[311] Weidner, *Pneumatology*, 31.

[312] Lindberg, *Christian Dogmatics*, 305.

example will suffice to demonstrate the use of these categories in the context of the application of salvation. Sanctification is defined by the Lutheran scholastics as a continual renovative act, wherein holiness is increased and sin expelled.[313] In describing the efficient cause, there is a threefold division. First, there is the principal efficient cause, which is identified with the triune God.[314] Second is the terminative efficient cause, which is the Holy Spirit. Third, the human person is described as an efficient cause of sanctification in a secondary sense, as moved by the Holy Spirit.[315] The final cause of sanctification is explained with the same twofold division used above in relation to the call: the proximate end and the final end. The proximate end of sanctification is the furtherance of the work of renewal, which progresses day to day. The final end is entrance into eternal life.[316] These categories are used throughout the *ordo salutis* in order to establish the relationship between the cause and effect of God's acts, as well as the final end toward which salvation moves.

Unlike many modern thinkers, the Lutheran reformers did not criticize Aristotle's concept of causation in favor of some other model. Luther used it on occasion, though it did not play a central role in his theological formulation. Melanchthon taught the fourfold definition of causation, and used it to categorize certain topics in theology. Gerhard viewed the four causes as a beneficial means by which various theological topics can be explained, and he brought them into discourse

---

[313] Weidner, *Pneumatology*, 181.

[314] Ibid., 184.

[315] Lindberg, *Christian Dogmatics*, 357.

[316] Ibid., 357.

on a variety of questions. The later Lutheran scholastics follow Gerhard, and further used language of efficient and final causes to explain the *ordo salutis*.

The final area of metaphysics to be discussed among Lutheran thinkers is analogical predication and its relation to the distinction between archetypal and ectypal theology.

The Archetype/Ectype Distinction and Analogical Predication

The division between archetypal and ectypal theology is a common one in the later seventeenth century. This concept, utilized in both Lutheran and Reformed scholastic writers, is based upon a fundamental differentiation between the knowledge that God has of himself and the derivative knowledge attained by God's creatures. Archetypal theology consists in God's own self-knowledge, which according to those who accept the doctrine of divine simplicity, is identical to God's essence, as there is no fundamental differentiation between his essence and attributes. Such a knowledge of God is an impossibility for the human creature, because to have such knowledge is to possess the divine nature. The knowledge that creatures (both human and angelic) have, therefore, is derivative and analogical. This is ectypal theology, which is a picture of—though not identical with—the archetype. This concept is important for present purposes because it establishes continuity between the Protestant scholastics and the *analogia entis* of Thomas in opposition to the univocity position as held by many contemporary theologians.[317] Here,

---

[317] See Hinlicky, *Divine Simplicity*, 152–61.

the scholastic doctrine of the archetype/ectype distinction is explained, followed by a comparison between this concept and that of the *analogia entis* of Thomas.

The earliest systematic theological works of the Protestant scholastic writers did not include extensive treatments of prolegomena, and thus many of the important distinctions for later writers were not as explicitly elucidated. The shape of theological prolegomena for the Protestant authors, both Lutheran and Reformed, was the result of Reformed theologian Franciscus Junius' work *A Treatise on True Theology*, first published in 1594. This short treatment of the subject was expanded by Lutheran authors who defend the distinction while marking areas of divergence from the Reformed approach. In his discussion, Junius first explains the nature of archetypal theology as "divine wisdom of divine matters."[318] Yet he notes that even such a definition is improper to ascribe to God, as wisdom, like God's other attributes, is only predicated of him analogously. The word "divine," as used here, demonstrates the differentiation between wisdom in God and that which is attained by the creature. For God's wisdom is one with his essence.[319] The phrase "archetypal" is defined in this context as a knowledge of God which is "uncreated . . . essential, absolute, [and] infinite."[320] This knowledge is also present simultaneously to God, as he does not experience knowledge in succession as do creatures. This knowledge, according to Junius, is incommunicable and is attributable to the divine nature alone. This fundamental aspect of God's self-

---

[318] Junius, *Treatise on True Theology*, 107.

[319] Ibid., 108.

[320] Ibid., 110.

knowledge then leads to an exposition of ectypal theology.

For Junius, ectypal theology is knowledge only in a secondary sense, which is an "offspring" of God's own self-knowledge.[321] It is the knowledge that creatures have of the Creator, and it is only received by divine communication, as a derivation of archetypal theology. Using an analogy which was popular among Neoplatonists, Junius relates God's self-revelation to the sun and its light. Just as the sun shines forth light from its own essence to the moon, so does God reveal his light to his creation. It is through such light that the mind is enlightened, and thus humans are able to gain an understanding of God.[322] This knowledge, in contrast to archetypal theology, is communicable. Junius further connects this revelation of God to the Aristotelian causes. God is the efficient cause of ectypal theology as revelator, and he is also its final cause, as knowledge of the Creator leads one back to him. Due to human limitations, ectypal theology is not simple, but complex. The creature learns by way of succession, and through analogy. These ideas expressed in Junius were brought into the Lutheran scholastic tradition, and continued to remain a consistent element of prolegomena through the beginning of the twentieth century.

At the height of the supposed silver age of scholasticism stands Johannes Quenstedt, who spent a significant amount of space in his *Theologia Didacto-Polemica, Sive, Systema Theologicum* on issues of prolegomena, largely taking his topics from Junius. Among these is Quenstedt's treatment of the archetype/ectype distinction in Christian theology. Quenstedt

---

[321] Ibid., 113.

[322] Ibid., 115.

first distinguishes between a true theology, which is that of the Christ, from the false theology of pagan religions.[323] Significantly, he includes certain elements of scholastic theology in the medieval period as false theology insofar as these elements override truths of revelation by way of logical syllogism. True theology is further divided into two distinctive spheres: prototypical (archetypal) and ectypal. Like Junius, Quenstedt defines God's self-knowledge as immediate, perfect, and indivisible. It is inseparable from his own essence.[324] Thus, Quenstedt contends that to know God in an archetypal sense is to *be* God.[325] He further contends, like his Reformed predecessor, that divine knowledge is identified with God's pure actuality.[326] Despite these important areas of agreement, there is one aspect of the designation of archetypal theology which differs between Lutheran and Reformed thinkers. While Junius contends that archetypal theology is incommunicable, Quenstedt argues that such knowledge is communicated to the human soul of Christ through the incarnation. In opposition to Calvinist authors, he contends that texts such as Colossians 2:3 attribute perfect knowledge to the God-man without solely noting the divine nature.[327] Such a difference arises from continued disagreements between the two traditions regarding the relationship between Christ's two natures. Yet, in spite of such a difference, the basic elements of Junius' treatment of this issue remain in Lutheran thought, including

---

[323] Quenstedt, *Nature and Character*, 18.

[324] Ibid., 23.

[325] Ibid., 25.

[326] Ibid., 24.

[327] Ibid., 27.

their discussions of ectypal theology.

In his explanation of ectypal theology, Quenstedt uses Neoplatonic terms to describe the relationship between God's self-knowledge and that of creatures. Ectypal theology is an "outflowing and effulgence, a kind of emanation" of the archetype.[328] As Plotinus describes being as rays which extend from the sun as an overflow of the One, so does Quenstedt explain God's knowledge as communicated to creatures. This communicated theology is a reflection of the archetype, and is thus derivative and incomplete knowledge, though it is true and proper knowledge. The scholastic theologian also connects ectypal theology to the human nature of Christ, as this is his natural orientation as a true human person.[329] As it is for creatures, this is a learned theology. Quenstedt makes a further distinction among types of ectypal theology between paradisiacal theology and pilgrim theology.[330] In the prelapsarian state, Adam and Eve had a perfect inherent knowledge of divinity as an aspect of the *imago Dei*. This innate knowledge is labeled "concreate" theology, as it is a product of man as created.[331] Along with this concreate knowledge, Adam and Eve also received "revealed theology," which is that taught through external means.[332] After the fall, concreate theology is corrupted, and nature is able to reveal only some aspects of God's character and law. Pilgrim theology, in the state of redemption, is primarily expressed by way of

---

[328] Ibid., 24.

[329] Ibid., 29.

[330] Ibid., 35.

[331] Ibid., 36.

[332] Ibid., 36.

revealed (also called supernatural) theology as explained in Holy Scripture.[333] The study of theology is further explained, as it is in Junius, as having a specific efficient and final cause. Its efficient cause is God, who alone initiates knowledge of himself, and its final cause is twofold: the glory of God, and the salvation of humanity.[334] These ideas expressed in Quenstedt demonstrate continuity but also expansion of the archetype-ectype distinction from Junius.

The two authors examined above represent only a small portion of writers who include treatments of the archetype-/ectype distinction. Nearly all of the other authors in the Protestant scholastic tradition, however, explain these ideas in the same fashion as these two thinkers. These representative figures demonstrate some important aspects of the Protestant scholastic method, especially regarding the nature of one's knowledge of divinity. Only God's knowledge of himself is complete and comprehensive. As creatures, humans cannot have perfect knowledge of the divine essence, but only a derivative understanding. Explanations of the character of God are not univocal, though they do constitute real knowledge. This is demonstrated through the analogy between a sun and its rays, which lighten the moon. In a similar manner, knowledge of God is directly given from its source, and this light illuminates one other than himself. These convictions lead to an understanding of God which is nearly synonymous with the *analogia entis* of Thomas.

One of the most discussed aspects of Thomas's thought, especially since the publication of *Analogia Entis* by Erich

---

[333] Ibid., 39.

[334] Ibid., 59.

Przywara in 1932, is Thomas's concept of the analogy of being between God and creatures. Though the precise phrase is not used, this concept can be understood through a study of Part 1, Question XII of the *Summa*, on the topic, "How God Is Known by Us."[335] Throughout this section, Aquinas discusses the nature of the beatific vision, wherein creatures are able to see God's essence. After defending such a possibility, Aquinas then asks about the nature of man's comprehension of God in such a state. He asks the question, "whether those who see the essence of God see all in God."[336] Those who answer in the affirmative might state that since God sees all things, it is of God's essence to see all things. Therefore, if a creature is to see God's essence, that creature too will see all things. Aquinas responds to this objection by pointing out that the human intellect is incapable of grasping the entirety of the divine nature. Instead, God is wholly known only to himself. He notes that God is infinite, and human knowledge is, in its essence, finite.[337] It is therefore beyond the scope of creaturely existence for one to attain to such infinite knowledge. Aquinas distinguishes between knowledge of a truth and comprehension, the latter of which he defines as perfect knowledge.[338] As an example, Aquinas speaks about a triangle.[339] One might know through mathematics that the three angles of a triangle are equal to two right angles. This can be proven, and thus, one is able to comprehend this

---

[335] Aquinas, *Introduction to St. Thomas*, 70.
[336] Ibid., 85.
[337] Ibid., 84–85.
[338] Ibid., 83.
[339] Ibid., 84.

truth. Another may never have thought through the reasoning which results in such a conclusion, but merely accepts it as a probable truth based upon the authority of others. In this second instance, one does not have complete comprehension of the concept of triangularity, but one is still acquainted with the truths of the idea. One can still *recognize* a triangle and have some grasp of what such a shape is. This demonstrates the kind of knowledge which humanity is capable of in regard to God. Unlike the possibility of comprehending the triangle, the infinite essence of God is beyond the understanding of the intellect. Thus, one's knowledge of God is real, but not comprehensive.

The ideas presented here anticipate the later discussions surrounding archetypal and ectypal theology. Aquinas, like Junius and Quenstedt, argues that God's knowledge of himself is not communicable to creatures. His knowledge of himself is perfect, incomprehensible, and instantaneous. The knowledge of God is identical with his essence, and thus cannot become the property of creatures. The distinction made between comprehension and knowledge also mirrors these later ideas, as comprehension belongs to God alone (archetypal theology), and partial but real knowledge is attributed to humans. This serves as an important backdrop for Aquinas's idea of the analogy of being.

In the following section of the *Summa*, Aquinas discusses the names ascribed to God, and in doing so, he defends the concept of analogy as a proper way in which to understand God. Thomas asks whether God can be named at all, due to the Neoplatonic emphasis on the unknowability of God, and he answers that God is able to be named, since words are signs, or a similitude of things. Due to the function of words, then, one uses names of God as a *sign* of his essence, while no name can express the true *nature* of the divine essence.[340] He rejects a pure apophatic mode of understanding, wherein words about God are used to describe only what he is not, and instead argues that positive terms can properly be spoken of the divine essence, though they do not perfectly represent him. Such is possible because a human understanding of God's essence is derived through its image in creatures. Creatures reflect God's own nature and character, and thus when an attribute such as "goodness" is predicated of some object in creation, it is a reflection of something which exists in God as its source.[341] Such an idea then leads to the question of exactly how the same attributes can be applied to both God and creatures. There are three solutions to this problem raised by Aquinas. The first is that all language of God is metaphorical, including ideas of goodness and other attributes, in the same way one might call God a rock. While Thomas affirms that metaphors are a genuine way in which God describes himself, attributes such as goodness, love, and life are attributed to God in a proper sense, rather than a metaphorical one.[342] He does not, then, allow for descriptions of God as purely equivocal, as this would disallow for any true knowledge of God whatsoever.[343] The second contention some make regarding knowledge of God is that of univocity, wherein attributes of creatures are applied to God in the same sense, though perhaps in a greater degree. Thomas rejects this concept, as attributes such as goodness

---

[340] Ibid., 98.

[341] Ibid., 101.

[342] Ibid., 102–3.

[343] Ibid., 107.

and wisdom fundamentally differ between God and creatures. If a person is loving, this is an attribute distinct from one's essence. For a human to have love, wisdom, and goodness is for the person to be complex as a combination of essence and various attributes. Due to God's simplicity, such cannot be said of the divine nature, in which there is no division between essence and property.

In response to these two views, Aquinas proposes a third: the analogical. In this approach, there is an analogy between God and his creation so that he can be understood in a real sense without collapsing the Creator-creature distinction. Goodness, for example, can be spoken of in relation to God and a man. This does not mean that goodness is the same between both, because if it were, then man would be good in essence (rather than simply having the property of goodness) and thereby would be God himself. It also does not *only* mean that God is the source of goodness in man, because God could produce something which did not reflect his own being, and thus such a label would be essentially meaningless. Further, this does not imply that God is good only in the sense that he is not bad. Instead, that which man has as a *property* is what God is *essentially*.[344] There is a distinction between "being good" and goodness itself. God is to be known, then, not through his bare essence, but through his operations in the world wherein his attributes are demonstrated.[345] The intellect is unable to grasp God as a purely simple being, and he is thus known by diverse attributes which are displayed in creation.[346] Though

---

[344] Ibid., 111.

[345] Ibid., 116.

[346] Ibid., 125.

composition in God is not real *essentially*, this is the only manner in which the human mind is able to grasp his nature. For Thomas, then, God is known through the analogy of being. Ideas of goodness, love, and truth are derived from one's experience in the world, and they are imperfect reflections of God's nature. Since the human intellect is limited, God can only be known through his operations in the world, and explained by way of a real but analogous manner of speaking about him.

The *analogia entis* is affirmed in the archetype-ectype distinction, and is explicitly taught in other Lutheran sources. Because creatures are unable to have archetypal knowledge (what Thomas labels "comprehension"), they cannot thereby perfectly describe God's essence. Instead, they are only able to use language which is reflective of the knowledge God has of himself. Early twentieth-century Lutheran dogmatician Francis Pieper discusses these ideas in the first volume of his *Christian Dogmatics*. In his exposition of the divine attributes, Pieper begins by affirming the doctrine of divine simplicity with the contention that there is an absolute identity between God's essence and attributes.[347] He contends, however, that knowledge of this unified perfect essence is an impossibility for the creature, and thus God condescends to human limitations, and describes himself through a number of different attributes and so "divides Himself," not essentially, but in accord with human speech. Like Aquinas, Pieper then discusses how it is that this incomprehensible God can be spoken of in relation to his creation. Pieper denies that such can be done univocally, as this would negate the distinction

---

[347] Pieper, *Christian Dogmatics*, I:428.

between creature and Creator. Properties are not attributed to God and creation merely equivocally either, as this would make speech about God meaningless. Instead, Pieper defends the notion of analogy, that God and creatures share similar attributes, though not in precisely the same "manner or degree."[348] Pieper defends the Augustinian notion that one can reason through the imperfect attributes which belong to creatures to the perfection which is in God.[349] Pieper serves as merely one example, but throughout the scholastic Lutheran tradition, these concepts surrounding knowledge of God are affirmed.

The archetype/ectype distinction and the *analogia entis* are essential aspects of the scholastic theological method. These distinctions demonstrate the underlying concepts regarding speech about God, which is at the heart of the discipline of theology. It is recognized by the scholastics that there exists a quidditative difference between creatures and the Creator, and that defines and limits what is to be properly said of God. Comprehensive knowledge belongs solely to God himself, and ectypal theology is a reflection and derivation of God's self-knowledge. In utilizing such distinctions, the Protestant scholastics build upon the foundations of Thomas Aquinas along with a use of Neoplatonic language surrounding the emanation of God's self-knowledge to his creatures. Continuity is therefore established between these writers and earlier Christian and philosophical thought.

---

[348] Ibid., I:431.

[349] Ibid., I:431.

Toward an Aristotelian-Platonic Synthesis

Now that the foundational concepts of faith and reason, essence, causation, and the analogy of being have been explained throughout Lutheran sources, a synthesis is here constructed of these various ideas into a consistent metaphysical system which is scholastic in orientation. As is apparent from the primary sources, Luther and later thinkers did not draw purely on one philosophy in order to construct their thought. Instead, they borrowed from earlier Christian sources, and fluctuated between Aristotelian and Neoplatonic ideas. Drawing from the German mystical thinkers, Luther is generally more Neoplatonic in his orientation, whereas thinkers like Gerhard draw primarily on Aristotle. Here, a synthesis is provided of ideas from both Plato and Aristotle, which gives a consistent account and summary of the metaphysics previously explained.

It is an unavoidable conclusion that there are philosophical differences between Plato and Aristotle. Aristotle often speaks negatively about the idealism of his teacher, as he rejects all notions of participation in favor of the conclusion that essences are found only within things themselves. However, Christian thinkers have never seen themselves as purely beholden to the ideals of any one particular pagan philosopher, especially as some of the most prominent ideas in both contradict divine revelation. Christian Aristotelians do not adopt the conclusion that matter is eternal, and neither do Christian Platonists insist that all knowledge is simply recollection from a preexistent soul (with Origen being the possible exception). There are, then, elements of both systems which are consistent with biblical teaching and can be utilized in theological formulation. In this section, the ideas of Plato and Aristotle are discussed, and then a proposal is offered which borrows from both thinkers, as did the scholastics. Two ideas are addressed extensively here: participation and being. An examination of these related concepts demonstrates that aspects of Neoplatonism can be adopted to further define aspects of reality of which Aristotle's metaphysic is inadequate.

Platonism: An Evaluation

Elements of Plato's thought have been adopted by Christian thinkers since the time of Justin Martyr. Even so, the Christian tradition has also recognized inadequacies in the thought of the Greek author. The discussion here proceeds first with some of the beneficial aspects of Plato's metaphysic, especially as adapted by Luther and later writers. Second, the inadequacies of Plato's system are described. Following this evaluation of Platonism is a similar discussion of Aristotelianism.

The aspect of Platonic thought which is perhaps most clearly retained within Lutheran writing is the notion of participation. For Luther, as well as for the scholastics, all of creation participates in God. Sammeli Juntunen observes the importance of this theme in the reformer's writings.[350] While such an idea is not expressed explicitly in most places (with the exception of the Heidelberg Disputation), it stands behind some of Luther's most prominent themes. One aspect of Luther's thought related to this that has been studied in recent decades is his concept of creation as *larvae Dei* (masks of God). For Luther, God is intimately involved in every

---

[350] Braaten, *Union with Christ*, 150–51.

aspect of earthly life, and works within his creatures as if he were a man wearing a mask. Such an idea necessitates more than the notion that God is abstracted from physical reality, but that in some mysterious way, the created world participates in divinity. The Finnish Luther interpreters also connect this to Luther's notion of deification, wherein the human creature is defined by participation in Christ, which transforms the human subject.[351] Such Neoplatonic elements of Luther's thought are likely a product of the influence of Johannes Tauler and the *Theologia Germanica* upon Luther's theology. In particular, these writers speak about self-emptying, which leads to union with God.[352] This type of language is echoed in Luther's notions of the empty hand of faith the believer has *coram Deo*, which results in the granting of Christ to the sinner. In his introduction to the *Theologica Germanica*, Bengt Hagglund makes the case that Luther utilizes the mysticism of Tauler in his explanation of the human experience of God, particularly in his notion of the hidden God.[353] Hagglund uses a distinction taken from Nathan Soderblom between "personality-mysticism" and "infinity-mysticism" to further explain Luther's thought in connection with mystical ideas. A personality-mysticism is defined by connection with a personal God in an I-Thou (to use Buber's language) encounter. The concept of infinity-mysticism relates to the idea of the immersion of the self in an "impersonal Beyond."[354] Such a distinction demonstrates

---

[351] Ibid., 152.

[352] See Clark, *Great German Mystics*, 36–54.

[353] Hagglund, *Theologia Germanica*, 16.

[354] Ibid., 20.

Luther's connection with the Neoplatonic ideas of mysticism and participation, while simultaneously distinguishing him from the type of mysticism which one encounters in Plotinus, as Luther is christologically and biblically oriented.

These thoughts are not those of Luther alone, but extend throughout the scholastic tradition. Described here are two particular places wherein such notions of participation in God are used. First is the discussion of mystical union, which is a consistent aspect of the *ordo salutis* as expressed in the later dogmaticians. Second, devotional literature consistently draws upon such language, especially that of Johann Gerhard. Treatments of the mystical union in the Lutheran dogmaticians generally follow justification and precede sanctification. The indwelling of God is a result of justification and the cause of the work of renewal by the Holy Spirit. In such discussions, union is divided by two distinct elements. First is the union of God with all creation, and second is the special union of the triune God with the regenerated person. Hoenecke summarizes the conclusions on this topic by the later seventeenth-century authors in the third volume of his *Evangelical Lutheran Dogmatics*. The general union is defended upon the basis of passages like Acts 17:28, which connect God's being to all of humanity. Hoenecke rejects any notion that such a general union is purely one of will, or of reliance of the creation upon God's providence. He refers to this as a "union of the substance of God" with that of creatures.[355] This goes beyond a mere *relational* connection between God and the world to one which is substantial, and thus ontological. There is a real sense, then, in which creation participates in

---

[355] Hoenecke, *Lutheran Dogmatics*, III:390.

God. Such is consistent with Luther's emphasis on God's immanence within the world expressed through the concept of the masks of God.

Along with his exposition of this general sense of union, Hoenecke explains the nature of the particular union that God has with the regenerate. This, again, is described as a "substantial presence," which is distinguished from purely relational or volitional understandings of one's union with God.[356] Such an idea is certainly metaphysical, as Hoenecke speaks of a permeation of God's substance within the human essence.[357] This is also described as the "participation of the believers in the life of God."[358] This theme is connected with St. Peter's language that one is made a partaker of the divine nature (2 Pet 1:4). Calov describes the mystical union as an eternal marriage between the believer and Christ, wherein one lives in the "divine life," which culminates in union with God in heaven.[359] These ideas indicate commonality with Neoplatonism in that they adhere to a concept of participation in God, both in a general sense with regard to creation, and in a particular gracious sense related to the regenerate.

The Lutheran author who is perhaps most commonly associated with Neoplatonism is Johann Arndt, who is often cited as the forefather of Pietism. Unlike Chemnitz and other early scholastics, Arndt was concerned with practical theology more than dogmatic formulation. He published numerous prayers and devotional texts, along with several reprints of older

---

[356] Ibid., III:386.

[357] Ibid., III:386.

[358] Ibid., III:392.

[359] Schmid, *Doctrinal Theology*, 483.

mystical works such as the *Theologia Germanica* and Thomas à Kempis's *The Imitation of Christ*.[360] In his most popular book, *True Christianity*, Arndt describes union with God as the initial purpose of creation, as well as the end toward which all things strive. In Arndt, a system of thought which is Neoplatonic in orientation is clear, especially as such a system is more commonly that of Christian experience in mystical sources, rather than the utilization of Aristotle's categories in dogmatic formulas. Arndt even allows for the possibility of ecstatic union with God during prayer, which connects him firmly with the German mystical thinkers and Plotinus.[361] While debates which occurred during the rise of Pietism between the followers of Spener and of the Lutheran orthodox caused the scholastics to differentiate themselves from Arndt, in his time, he retained a strong influence upon Lutheran theology. Peter Erb notes that the entire *ordo salutis* expressed in later writers has its roots in Arndt's thought.[362] Perhaps Arndt's most important influence, however, is in the writing of his most prolific student, Johann Gerhard.

Though known largely as a dogmatician, Johann Gerhard had a strong conviction that the task of theology was never to be divorced from a life of devotion and piety. While he tended to neglect some of the excesses which appeared in Arndt's writings, Gerhard continued to emphasize the importance of union with God as explained by his predecessor. It is notable that while Gerhard uses precise Aristotelian terminology in his dogmatic texts, his devotional material has

---

[360] Arndt, *True Christianity*, 6–7.
[361] Ibid., 9.
[362] Ibid., 8.

a Platonic orientation, particularly as he utilizes concepts from St. Augustine. In the introduction to his *Sacred Meditations*, Gerhard cites Thomas à Kempis, Augustine, and Tauler as influences on his writing.[363] A few selections from this text demonstrate the use of these concepts in Gerhard.

In the beginning of this work, Gerhard writes about the nature of repentance, and in doing so, he uses concepts which are common to Platonic thinkers. Gerhard defines God as the "infinite and incomprehensible Good."[364] Sin, in contrast to God, is an infinite evil insofar as it opposes him. Repentance consists in moving toward and participating in the good, rather than evil. Gerhard then speaks of the necessity of self-renunciation, which then leads to the filling of oneself with divine love through Christ.[365] Some of the language here is taken directly from Tauler, as Gerhard expresses these notions of participation. In another section, Gerhard explains that the beauty of God is expressed through creation. The soul has an appetite which can be satisfied only by God, and created objects serve as mediating factors. One is to reflect upon the beauty of physical creation so that the soul can then extend beyond such things to the infinite and unseen God.[366] Gerhard speaks about love of creatures as a love which "dies within us," so that love of God might be perfected.[367] This, for Gerhard, is part of theosis. He argues that love has an inherent uniting power, whereby the soul and the

---

[363] Gerhard, *Sacred Meditations*, 17.

[364] Ibid., 29.

[365] Ibid., 30.

[366] Ibid., 47.

[367] Ibid., 49.

thing loved "become one."³⁶⁸ Through love of sin, one transforms through such affections, but through love of God, one will "become divine."³⁶⁹ Gerhard cites Athanasius' famous summary of deification, that God became man in order that man might become god.³⁷⁰ These ideas of participation reflect a Platonic metaphysical orientation on these points within Lutheran thinkers.

The place in which Platonic language is used most frequently in all of these authors is in relation to participation in God. Lutheran scholastics were not primarily philosophers, but theologians. Consequently, it was their desire to explain biblical teaching rather than argue for the validity of one particular metaphysical system. It was primarily for exegetical reasons, particularly dealing with texts such as Acts 17:28 and 2 Peter 1:4, that such a notion of participation is explained. None of the writers are realists in the strongest sense, though, as no separate ideal world of forms is affirmed as it is in Plato. However, there may be some indication that Luther does adopt some form of idealism in the philosophical section of the Heidelberg Disputation, when he points to the instability of individual particulars, in favor of the transcendent and eternal.³⁷¹ This need not be understood as some kind of total adoption of such a strong realism on behalf of Lutheran thought. The primary criticism Luther gives to Aristotle is that he studies essences within the things-in-themselves, and consequently, he points the philosopher to sensible things, rather

---

[368] Ibid., 48.

[369] Ibid., 48.

[370] Ibid., 64.

[371] Parker, "Platonism of Martin Luther."

than spiritual reality. The concern of Luther is addressed in Gerhard's utilization of Augustine. That Gerhard adopts Aristotle's basic convictions about essence is clear in his *Theological Commonplaces*. However, despite speaking of essences within things-in-themselves, he also argues that creation leads to contemplation of God, who supersedes sensible reality. This is particularly true insofar as the beauty and goodness inherent within creation reflect their source in God. Though these ideas commonly associated with Platonic essentialism are affirmed, there are problems with Platonism which are to be rejected as inconsistent with Lutheran scholasticism.

Treatments of the philosophical problems in Plato's metaphysic are manifold and will not be addressed here. There are, however, some theological concerns with the Platonic theory which are explored in brief. The primary issue addressed here is that of the sacramental nature of Luther's theology. Platonism identifies reality not with the sensible things of earth, but with that which is represented by them. While Luther himself might affirm such an idea at times, a question arises in relation to the consistency of such a position and the emphasis which Luther gives on earthly particulars as means by which grace is given. Luther's theology is a very physical one, as he rejected previous forms of piety which were based upon either moral action or mystical experience. While the reformer certainly did not deny the importance of ethical formation of the Christian experience, his foundational themes of justification and assurance are dependent not upon either, but upon the concrete promise of God given to man through word and sacrament. In his article "Why Luther Is Not Quite Protestant," Philip Carey argues that Luther's theology of justification arose through his strong understanding of the sacraments.[372] For Luther, the sacraments are concrete promises of God given to the individual. In baptism, God's promise is delivered to the one receiving the sacrament through the triune name and the element of water. In holy communion, God's promise is given through Christ's presence by means of the elements of bread and wine. Luther's theology of absolution carries a similar tie between God's promise and the external word. If this is the case, then reality is indeed found in the things-in-themselves, and the sacraments are not mere signs which point to a reality elsewhere.

The relationship between Luther's theology of the sacraments and language of signification has been explored by Herman Sasse. Sasse argues that the Augustinian language of the sacraments as signs is inconsistent with Lutheran theology and leads to a Reformed approach to baptism and the Lord's Supper.[373] His approach to the bishop of Hippo is quite negative, as Sasse contends that Augustine was impacted by pagan philosophy, which impacts his sacramental thought. This led to a distinction between the sign in the sacrament, and the thing which is signified by that sign (*res*).[374] This definition was followed by the Western church throughout the medieval period until the time of Luther. This, according to Sasse, is a vestige of Neoplatonism. In essence, his argument is as follows. For Platonism, reality is not to be found in physical particulars, but instead in eternal, unchanging ideas. Augustine utilized such a distinction in his doctrine of the sacraments. The reality in the sacrament is that which is

---

[372] Carey, "Why Luther."

[373] Sasse, *We Confess the Sacraments*, 12.

[374] Ibid., 16.

signified (*res*), rather than the sign itself. Instead, like Plato's idea of particulars, the sign points beyond itself to something higher. This then leads to Calvin's idea of the Lord's Supper, wherein the bread in the sacrament remains what it is, serving a mere representative purpose for the individual who partakes of Christ by faith. This is fundamentally opposed to Luther's realist view of the Eucharist.

The thesis that Augustine was merely Platonizing in his use of signification language is questionable, as he does not divorce the sign and signified in the manner that later Calvinist thinkers would. Sasse also too quickly dismisses Thomas's language of efficacious signification as inadequate.[375] The Augsburg Confession and later Lutheran thinkers use the sign-signified language of Augustine without adopting the conclusions of other Protestant groups who assign a mere symbolic function to the elements. Despite these problems with his thesis, however, Sasse correctly demonstrates that Luther simply does not fit into a purely Platonic mode of thought. For Luther, the sacraments and the word are performative. The believer need not look beyond them to something represented in an ideal realm, whether in heaven or in the mind of God. Instead, the promises are concrete and physical. It is in this way that, while elements of Platonism are used by Luther and Gerhard, a strong idealism is an inadequate metaphysical basis for Christian thought.

Just as figures such as St. Augustine had done in the early church, the reformers and Lutheran scholastics utilized Platonic ideas when consistent with biblical teaching, and rejected his ideas when incommensurate with theological

---

[375] Ibid., 16.

truths. Through the influence of St. Augustine and Johann Tauler, Luther preferred the Platonist approach to reality over the Aristotelian, especially for Plato's emphasis on rising above physical objects to unchanging spiritual reality. Luther also spoke often about participation in Christ, and wrote of God's immanence within creation in such a manner that creation participates within God. Johann Gerhard similarly uses Platonic ideas throughout his writings, and especially in his devotional literature. He does such primarily to emphasize participation in God through a form of theosis, as well as the idea that particular physical objects are a reflection of the unchanging God who is the source of beauty and goodness in the world. As is the case for Luther, Gerhard's two primary influences here are Augustine and Tauler. Notions of participation are further taught in Lutheran scholastics in their exposition of union with God, both in the general union and in the mystical union.

Despite such areas wherein Plato is drawn upon, the dualism inherent in Platonic philosophy is rejected by Lutheran thinkers, especially in their sacramental theology, wherein spiritual reality is given concretely through material particulars. The elements of Platonism used by these thinkers is not the apophatic mysticism of Pseudo-Dionysius, but the moderated and more biblically oriented ideas of St. Augustine. Along with these elements of Platonism, Aristotle's metaphysics are also an essential foundation for the scholastic method.

Aristotelianism: An Evaluation

Just as there are both helpful and inadequate aspects of Platonic philosophy in its relation to Christian theology, so are there with Aristotle. While some of the problems in Plato's philosophy were addressed by his student, there are several areas of his thought which are rejected by Lutheran thinkers. Here, both the benefits and problems with Aristotelian philosophy are addressed, so that the metaphysical system which underlies Lutheran scholastic thought may be understood. First, the beneficial aspects of Aristotelian philosophy are explored, followed by a discussion of problems in Aristotle's system. This leads to a discussion of divine ideas and participation in Thomas's thought, which synthesizes elements of both Plato and Aristotle.

In this treatment so far, the positive elements of Aristotle's system have been apparent. While Luther and Melanchthon rejected the overuse of the Greek philosopher, his categories had a profound impact upon the development of Lutheran theology. The four causes were adopted almost immediately by Melanchthon as an organizational tool to explain theological matters. Luther continued to promote Aristotle's rhetoric and logic, despite disagreements on other issues. The language of causation is also a beneficial means whereby the different aspects of salvation are to be explained without either confusion or the need to exposit a system of temporal succession between elements of the *ordo salutis*. Non-Aristotelian ideas of causation simply do not allow for such nuanced discussion, as is argued in the following chapter. These fundamental ideas of causation also serve as a background for arguments for the existence of God, which Gerhard defends while utilizing Aquinas. Along with his concepts of causation, Lutheran thinkers also recognize the usefulness of his other metaphysical categories. The distinction between substance and accidental properties, for example, allows for an explanation of certain biblical truths such as the fact that sin impacts the human creature, while one's identity as human remains constant. Modern approaches to this issue which use other philosophical categories tend to conflate man's essence with sin. Finally, the Lutheran scholastics recognized that Aristotle's distinctions between act and potency, form and matter, essence and existence, and substance and accident help to give a thorough account of God's self-dependence as exposited through the doctrine of divine simplicity. Through these categories, God's self-sufficiency and constancy can be affirmed while also explaining his activity in a world of change. A final benefit of Aristotle's system is that his connection between essence and concrete particular objects is more consistent with a strong sacramental theology than is Plato's dualistic thinking.

These benefits do not imply a complete adoption of an Aristotelian metaphysical system by the Lutheran scholastics. There are several areas of his thought which are inconsistent with biblical revelation and are thus to be rejected. Luther's most central problem with Aristotle is his system of ethics, which, while useful in the civil sphere, does not apply in the realm of justification, wherein God's work alone saves sinners, apart from ethical action. The logic of Aristotle is also problematic when applied to spiritual truths, which often transcend the limits of human logic. While syllogistic reasoning is applicable in the left-hand kingdom, the Lutheran tradition has always adopted a strong view of mystery with regard to heavenly truths. This leads to certain theological affirmations which appear inconsistent, though it is affirmed that a higher unity of such ideas does exist in God. Human wisdom is acknowledged to have significant limitations. Another problematic area of Aristotle's thought is in his concept of the divine mind. For the philosopher, God's thoughts are singular. He contemplates only himself, without any regard for the external world whatsoever. Christian Neoplatonism argues for a rather different approach, as the divine ideas are connected with Plato's idea of forms, thus affirming the connection between God's thoughts and the created world. The problem is further clear in that because Aristotle does not use any language of participation, there is no room for the strong idea of immanence expressed either in Luther's concept of the *larvae Dei* or the doctrine of a substantial union which God has with creation. These problems are addressed through an examination of Thomas Aquinas's approach to divine ideas as taught in the *Summa*. The concepts of divine ideas as exemplar causes, and motion as a means of participation, provide a balanced system of the philosophies of both Plato and Aristotle in a consistent Christian philosophy.

Thomas addresses the divine ideas in question fifteen of the first part of the *Summa* as part of his discussion surrounding God's knowledge. In the first article, Thomas asks whether there are divine ideas. He answers in the affirmative, contending that ideas are "forms of things, existing apart from the things themselves" (II, Q.15, Art.1). Such a form, he argues, can be spoken of in one of two ways in relation to the object: either as an exemplar of the object, or as a principle of knowledge of the object. He explains the former. In order to give a more adequate comprehension of Thomas's thought here, his illustration of the relationship between God and the builder of a house is useful. An architect, prior to creating a building, has a concept of what such a building will look like. Thus, a form of the object exists in his mind, though it does not yet exist in a physical state. Similarly, divine ideas serve such a function, as the idea of an object is logically prior to its physical existence. In article two, Aquinas then addresses the question of whether there are multiple divine ideas, as one might argue that the doctrine of divine simplicity necessitates singularity in the divine mind. Thomas argues that plurality in the created world necessitates a plurality of divine ideas. Just as a builder has a concept not only of the intended building but also of its parts, so must God have ideas relating to the various parts of the created order. Aquinas demonstrates that this is not inconsistent with God's simplicity unless one posits that such ideas are the result of a plurality of ideas outside of himself (II, Q.15, Art.2). All created things share a likeness to God, and thus participate in his essence. God's complete knowledge of his own essence, therefore, means that he also has comprehension of the various ways in which creatures participate in this essence. Therefore, archetypal theology necessitates knowledge of all created things. The third point made by Thomas regarding divine ideas is that there are divine ideas of everything known by God (II, Q.15, Art.3). Aquinas defends this notion through citations of both Augustine and Plato. He defines these ideas as twofold. First, they are described as exemplars, which is the "the principle of the making of things" (II, Q.15, Art.3). Second, these ideas are described as a likeness to created things, wherein God knows even those things which never come to pass. This is further described as a speculative knowledge. This idea, which is labeled "exemplarism" by Gregory Doolan,[376] connects God's thoughts to the created world in a manner that Aristotle did not, and thus provides a more adequate concept of divine knowledge.

The second important notion in Aquinas's thought which differentiates him from Aristotle is that of participation, which has been a prominent subject of discussion within the past half century of Thomistic thought. This idea was first recognized by the French philosophers Cornelio Fabro and L. B. Geiger, who argued for the importance of this theme in Thomas. Joseph Koterski summarizes Aquinas' approach to this issue in his essay "The Doctrine of Participation in Thomistic Metaphysics," which is consistent with Gerhard's use of Aristotelian metaphysics alongside a strong teaching of participation in divinity. Koterski differentiates between Plato's strong realism, wherein participation is connected to the world of forms, and that of Thomas. In connection with this, Koterski gives a definition of participation which is consistent with Aquinas, writing that participation means "to receive only part of what belongs to another fully, and so merely to share in it without exhausting it."[377] Koterski defines three distinct kinds of participation in Thomas's thought. First, a genus participates in its species as a matter of categorization. Second, substances participate in their accidental qualities. A red wall does not exhaust the nature of redness, for example, but simply partakes of it as a manner of composition. The third idea of participation is that which is most prominent in Thomas: that of causation. An effect

---

[376] Doolan, *Divine Exemplarism*.

[377] Kotersky, "Participation," 189.

participates in its cause.

Aristotle, though his system is based upon the language of causation which Thomas uses, does not speak about participation in this context. Koterski argues that the differentiating factor between these two thinkers is Thomas's strong doctrine of creation, which is absent in Aristotle.[378] It is in his articles on the procession of creatures and the emanation of all things that Thomas utilizes such language most extensively (Q.44–Q.45). Aquinas contends that being most properly belongs to God as subsistent being. Subsistent being is necessarily singular, and thus created things cannot possess being essentially. Therefore, Thomas reasons, all things other than God are "beings by participation" (II, Q.44, Art.1). For Koterski, this is differentiated from Platonism due to Aquinas' speaking of participation through the language of efficient rather than formal causality. There is, therefore, no need for objects to participate in transcendental forms, but instead, they participate in a "communication of being."[379] In God, essence and existence are identical, but creatures are composite; there is no identity between essence and existence. Therefore, existence is necessarily received from outside of oneself through the agency of God. Consequently, everything that is *participates* in existence, while only God is *identifiable* with existence. Koterski speaks of the act of creation as "an influx of being," which extends from God to creatures. This notion of participation corrects the problems inherent in Aristotle's approach to the relationship between God and the world.

---

[378] Ibid., 194.

[379] Ibid., 192.

These concepts which appear in Thomas's thought of both the divine ideas as exemplar causes, and creation as participation in being, allow for an essentialist theory which uses prominent Aristotelian distinctions while still retaining valuable elements of Platonism. The notion of exemplarism contends that there are indeed a multitude of divine ideas, and that such ideas are causative, in some sense, of created things. This can be affirmed without a belief in the separate existence of forms in the Platonic sense. Aquinas's writing on participated being is useful in comprehending Gerhard's use both of Aristotelian metaphysics and a strong teaching of participation in God. The Thomistic version of participation allows for a strong teaching regarding God's immanence in creation without subscribing to the pantheistic tendencies of Neoplatonism.

Conclusion

In this chapter, the methodological foundations of Lutheran scholasticism have been defined and explained. Here, the conclusions reached above in this discussion are summarized in preparation for the following chapter, in which the scholastic method is defended from criticisms offered by Radical Lutheran writers. The conclusions drawn from the research in the present chapter are discussed in relation to three topics: faith and reason, essentialism, and the *analogia entis*.

While some modern caricatures of Lutheran thought imply that the Reformation tradition is inherently anti-rational, and opposed to philosophy as such, it has been demonstrated that such an evaluation is inconsistent with Luther and the following Lutheran tradition. It is certainly true that the reformer had a strong conviction about the necessity of mystery in Christian proclamation, and that he places philosophy within significant limits. However, despite such contentions, reason is not inherently opposed to revelation. Martin Luther defended the validity of reason, especially within the context of the two kingdoms. The kingdom of the left is guided by reason, while the right-hand realm is dependent upon special revelation. In the kingdom of grace, reason still remains useful as regenerate reason, which can be used to defend the truths of the gospel. Logical argumentation is used as a secondary tool of critique in opposition to false theological propositions.

Following Luther, the later tradition continues to defend both the usefulness of reason and its significant limits. This is done through a distinction between a ministerial and magisterial use of reason. In its ministerial use, reason is always submitted to the truths of revelation, even when logical syllogism seems to overthrow revealed truths. This is not because revelation is contradictory to logic as such (as God himself is inherently logical), but due to the limitations of the human subject. An example of such limits is found in the contention that God's saving will is universal, while salvation is a monergistic act which some reject. This idea, sometimes known as the *crux theologorum*, has no logical solution, but the theologian consents to the truth of both propositions because of their clarity in revelation. A magisterial use of reason is when logic is placed above Scripture, and revealed truths are forced into a logical system foreign to the text. It has often been the contention, for example, that the Reformed approach to double predestination is the result of this misuse of logic, as is Thomas's philosophically oriented approach to transubstantiation. Misuses of logic do not imply that reason is opposed to theology, but merely that it must be used in its proper sphere.

These conclusions surrounding the relationship between faith and reason lead to the question of metaphysics. It has been argued here that an essentialist approach to reality is necessitated by Luther and Lutheran orthodoxy. Luther himself did not have a strong affinity for metaphysical discussion, as he contended that these debates in scholastic thought overshadowed scriptural exposition. Yet this does not mean that Luther himself did not have metaphysical presuppositions that he, too, utilized throughout his career. Despite some contentions that Luther was devoted to the nominalist ideas of his teachers, he was influenced largely by Neoplatonic thinkers, such as Johann Tauler and the anonymous author of the *Theologia Germanica*. In Luther's harshest criticisms of Aristotle, which appear in the Heidelberg Disputation, he affirms the philosophy of Plato, rather than arguing for a rejection of classical Greek thought in general. As Finnish interpreters have observed, Luther also has a doctrine of participation, which is expressed in his ideas about created objects as masks of God, as well as through his emphasis on union with Christ as a participatory reality in faith. Despite his harsh criticisms of Aristotle and his affirmation of Platonism, there are also ideas that appear in his writing which are inconsistent with Platonic dualism. In particular, Luther's theology is a strongly sacramental one, wherein reality is to be found in the earthly elements, rather than in an ideal realm. Thus, whether he recognized it or not, some of Luther's thought is consistent with Aristotelian ideas.

In the post-Luther era of the Reformation, metaphysical discussions were more prominent. Melanchthon uses Aristotle's conceptions of causation as organizational tools for his doctrine. He affirms the doctrine of divine simplicity in Article I of the Augsburg Confession, which has certain metaphysical convictions as its prerequisites. Beyond Melanchthon, debates between Philipists and Gnesio-Lutherans were, at times, philosophically oriented. In the debates which arose surrounding the impact of original sin, some of the foundational elements of Aristotle's philosophy were affirmed by the Formula of Concord, which distinguished between a substance and its accidental properties. The scholastic tradition continued to use such distinctions, from Chemnitz through the early twentieth century. The seventeenth-century scholastics distinguished between a substance and its accidental properties especially in their discussions of original righteousness and sin in relation to the human person. None of these authors questioned the usefulness of Aristotelian language in connection with these ideas.

The doctrine of divine simplicity was similarly defended by the Lutheran orthodox. Though affirmed by Melanchthon and Chemnitz, it is Gerhard who gives its first detailed exposition in his *Theological Commonplaces*. For Gerhard, this is definitional of the Christian God, and he often cites Aquinas on the subject. Inherent in his discussion are the Aristotelian distinctions between substance and accident, and matter and form, along with Thomas's distinction of essence and existence, which are all identical in God. The doctrine of divine simplicity is affirmed and defended in a similar manner by later writers, including the early twentieth-century theologian Francis Pieper, who identifies God's attributes with his essence. These concepts necessitate an affirmation of significant elements of Aristotle's philosophical system.

Causation also plays a prominent role in the exposition of theology in the post-Reformation era. Melanchthon's use of Aristotle's fourfold concept of causation continues into the following writers, who then use the concepts of both efficient and final causation to define a variety of concepts. Gerhard exposits several of Aquinas' arguments for the existence of God, and in doing so affirms some of Aristotle's most significant insights. In arguing for the necessity of an unmoved mover, Gerhard affirms the distinction between act and potency along with the belief that God is pure actuality, who is capable only of actuating the potency of things outside of himself. The later scholastics, such as David Hollaz, Johannes Quenstedt, and Abraham Calov, exposit a precise *ordo salutis* in which the application of salvation to the individual is explained through a series of causal events. These acts are defined in respect to both their efficient causes as well as to final causes. These convictions constitute a strong Aristotelianism in Lutheran orthodoxy.

The use of Aristotelian concepts does not necessitate a complete adoption of his philosophical convictions. Several of his beliefs stand in contradistinction to Christian theism, and are thus rejected. As biblical theologians, rather than philosophers, the Lutheran scholastics are willing to affirm elements of other philosophical systems as they enable the proclamation of Christian truth. Thus, the Platonic notion of participation is used by the scholastics on certain points. In particular, the scholastics speak about both a general union and a mystical union with God, which both affirm a kind of participation of the creature in the essence of God. This is affirmed while simultaneously contending for a strong creature-Creator distinction. It was demonstrated that these Platonic notions can be affirmed within Thomas's system, which uses the concepts of exemplarism and participation in his philosophy. While Aquinas' philosophy need not be adopted in its entirety, these elements of his system demonstrate how Aristotelian metaphysics and aspects of Neoplatonism cohere with one another in a Christian essentialist system.

Connections with Aquinas and Lutheran orthodoxy do not end with essentialism, but these theologians speak in a similar manner regarding speech about God. Reformed theologian Franciscus Junius distinguishes between archetypal theology (God's self-knowledge) and ectypal theology (derived knowledge). This concept was used by Gerhard and expanded by Quenstedt, who uses it as a foundational idea to understand the limits and function of theology. It is argued that only God has comprehensive knowledge of himself, and that the creature is limited in theological understanding. This relates to Aquinas' concept of the *analogia entis*, where it is argued that God cannot be spoken of univocally in relation to the creature. Instead, God is known by way of analogy. This forms the basis of ectypal theology, wherein true knowledge of God exists, but is far from comprehensive. Francis Pieper explains the relationship between these two types of theology by noting that while God is simple in his essence, he divides himself in human speech into a number of attributes, because such is the only possible manner in which creatures have an understanding of who he is.

These foundational elements of the Lutheran scholastic method have been demonstrated from the primary sources. An essentialist metaphysic and other elements of Thomism are used by Lutheran orthodox thinkers in the scholastic tradition, yet they are not beholden to pre-Reformation philosophy on every particular. In the following chapter, this theological method is compared with that of Radical Lutheranism. The unique methodology of Radical Lutheran authors is discussed and criticized in view of the considerations expressed in this chapter. Throughout, criticisms of scholastic thought are engaged and refuted.

4

A Defense of the Scholastic Method

Introduction

The extensive theological and methodological convictions which underlie the scholastic method have been explored, and it has been demonstrated that the Lutheran scholastics utilized a form of essentialist philosophy which borrowed elements from both Aristotelianism and Neoplatonism. They were all realists who affirmed that things have distinct essences which pervade all objects of each species. Similarly, they contended for a concept of causation which is consistent with that of Aristotle and Aquinas, which was used in the development of the *ordo salutis* as well as their definition of God's simplicity. Though these concepts were used extensively by seventeenth-century authors, as well as some early twentieth-century writers like Conrad Lindberg and Adolph Hoenecke, they have been challenged from a variety of fronts in contemporary scholarship from both Lutherans and those outside of the church of the Augsburg Confession. In particular, these ideas have been criticized by those associated with the Radical Lutheran method.

In this chapter, the scholastic method outlined previously is defended from challenges which have been offered by modern writers. These writers include those who are not confessional in the strict sense, such as Oswald Bayer, Gerhard Forde, and Steven Paulson, as well as theologians who have used certain insights offered by Radical Lutheranism while themselves remaining committed to the confessional documents, such as Robert Kolb and William S. Schumacher. The treatment here deals with several topics which have been at the heart of some criticisms of scholastic thought. First, the methodological and philosophical foundations of Radical Lutheranism are engaged. These ideas are twofold: existential and linguistic. As contended previously, many modern Luther interpreters hold to a linguistic-existential approach to reality rather than the real-essentialist proposal offered here. Connections are offered here between existential philosophy and Radical Lutheranism, as well as between twentieth-century linguistic philosophy and these writers. As these concepts are engaged, it is demonstrated that they are inadequate to serve as a general metaphysic in opposition to classical models. Alongside an examination of these philosophical schools, some particular topics are addressed which demonstrate such flaws in methodology. These include the *ordo salutis*, classical theism, and theological anthropology. It is argued that in each of these areas, modern methods are inadequate in explaining necessary theological truths which are more properly explicated through older metaphysical categories.

Existentialism

I have contended elsewhere that the theology of Gerhard Forde constitutes a form of existentialism.[380] Such a statement merits further explanation, as the phrase "existentialism" itself is quite elastic in its use, and there is no existential manifesto to which its followers subscribe. Also, many of those who are commonly categorized as existentialists either preceded the use of such a term (Kierkegaard, Nietzsche, Dostoyevsky)[381] or rejected any association with it (Heidegger).[382] Apart from Rudolph Bultmann, there were not many theologians who associated with existential thought directly and claimed the title. It is not the claim here that Gerhard Forde or Steven Paulson self-consciously echoes the ideas of Sartre or Camus,[383] but that several of their basic ways of thinking about life and reality are consistent with the thought of writers who are commonly categorized as existentialists. There are three necessary elements to the discussion which are addressed below. First is explained some background in the philosophical shift from the seventeenth century (the era of scholasticism) to the twentieth (when the Radical Lutheran movement began). This is a cursory overview, as an in-depth exposition of the movement away from classical essentialist metaphysics is beyond the scope of the current project. Second, a working definition of existentialism is composed, with

---

[380] Cooper, *Lex Aeterna*, 40.

[381] See Beardsley, *European Philosophers*, 802, and Friedman, *Worlds of Existentialism*, 18–21.

[382] Olson, *Introduction to Existentialism*, 134.

[383] Friedman, *Worlds of Existentialism*, 87–93.

which it is possible to explain in exactly what way the Radical Lutheran authors affirm such an idea. Finally, these concepts are engaged and critiqued.

The Philosophical Shift

Trends in theological thought tend to correspond to those of philosophy. The method of theologians in proceeding with their task is often determined by philosophical convictions, whether recognized or not. Thus, as the basic structures of classical philosophy began to deteriorate within the modern world following the Reformation, the church was forced to reconsider its own beliefs and modes of theological presentation. In the seventeenth century, in which the Lutheran scholastics wrote, thought forms of the ancient world were still taken for granted, as categories of Plato, Aristotle, and classical Christian theism were widely known and defended. Here, these philosophical shifts are explained, so that criticisms of scholastic thought can be properly defended in light of changing presuppositions that lead to existentialism.

The birth of modern philosophy is generally ascribed to René Descartes, who challenged the philosophical arguments of the past. His *Meditations on First Philosophy* was first published in 1641 and would have a profound impact upon Western thought.[384] In this text, Descartes attempts to discover an irrefutable starting point for human knowledge. He reasoned that the validity of one's experience of the external world could not be verified, as it is possible that one is manipulated by an evil genie or some other entity. Instead, he argued that

---

[384] Allen, *Philosophy for Understanding Theology*, 171.

certainty begins with the self. Descartes developed his now-famous phrase "*cogito, ergo sum*" (I think, therefore I am) as the starting point of all knowledge.[385] From this, Descartes then presented an ontological argument for God's existence, which then led to a conviction about God's reliability and the trustworthy nature of sense perception. This shift in philosophy, and a search for certainty, led thinkers away from classical and medieval problems addressed in previous philosophy, to new systems. While Aristotle and Plato placed metaphysics in a central position, modern philosophers emphasized epistemological questions. Descartes's position became the foundation for a new rationalism, further developed by Baruch Spinoza and Gottfried Leibniz.[386] Spinoza rejected Aristotelian metaphysics for a naturalistic monism, wherein all substance is identified with God, who is not a personal being in the Christian sense.[387] Leibniz proposed the concept that all things were made up of monads, which are small, simple, eternal objects. His ideas echo those of the ancient Greek atomists who argued for the atom as the basic structure of all existence.[388] These developments led to other philosophical movements such as empiricism, German idealism, and existentialism.

The second major philosophical shift, which had a profound impact on theology, was the rise of empiricism and Newtonian physics. For empiricists, knowledge was gained through experience and observation. Older theories of innate knowledge

---

[385] Descartes, *Key Philosophical Writings*, 123.

[386] Allen, *Philosophy for Understanding Theology*, 171.

[387] Beardsley, *European Philosophers*, 138.

[388] On Atomism, see Nahm, *Early Greek Philosophy*, 148–207.

through the soul's preexistence (Plato) or through the illumination of God (Augustine) were rejected for a view which was centered in the developing scientific method. This approach was popularized during the Enlightenment in the late seventeenth through eighteenth centuries through philosophers such as John Locke, George Berkley, and David Hume.[389] Locke argued that the mind is a *tabula rasa* (blank slate) at birth and that information is gained purely through experience.[390] Though experience results in reasonable probability with regard to the external world, Locke rejected Aristotle's claim that abstract essences can be discovered by way of reason and observation.[391] Berkley followed Locke's empiricism while offering several modifications. Unlike Locke and other previous philosophers, Berkley rejected the notion of abstract ideas, arguing instead that only particulars exist, which are then used to categorize other particulars of like qualities. Berkley defines all reality through perception. Sensible objects, which are perceived, are not material, but merely a collection of ideas. For Berkley, God is described as the eternal perceiver who thus assures the existence of all things.[392] These two thinkers led to a significant shift in the questions raised and answered by both philosophy and theology.

The most important empiricist for changes in eighteenth- and nineteenth-century Christian theology is David Hume. Known during his life as a skeptic, Hume questioned some of the basic assumptions of philosophy which were inherited

---

[389] Allen, *Philosophy for Understanding Theology*, 181.

[390] For a helpful overview and critique of Locke's thought, see Feser, *Locke*.

[391] Allen, *Philosophy for Understanding Theology*, 182.

[392] Ibid., 186.

through Aristotle. For Hume, knowledge is categorized by impressions gained through sense-experience, which are then translated into ideas. There are no abstract essences of objects which can be discovered, but merely a series of individual perceptions which the mind categorizes as composite objects. In his *Treatise on Human Nature*, Hume argues that even the self has no distinct continuous identity, but that one is instead simply a collection of perceptions.[393] Along with his rejection of essences, Hume criticizes Aristotle's ideas of causation. For the empiricist philosopher, there are no inherent powers within objects that are actualized by other objects. Instead, there are simply events which one perceives, and often one particular perception follows another. When one observes that A happens, and that B follows each time, one makes a connection between these two acts as a cause and effect.[394] There is, however, no inherent connection which one can be assured of between A and B. It is simply the application of one's experience, which can generally be assumed to have reliability. Hume's ideas of causation challenged assumptions about the world which were consistent through the Middle Ages into the era of the Reformation. These criticisms would have a profound impact upon ideas such as the *ordo salutis*, apologetics, and the doctrine of God. Humean notions of causation are often assumed in criticisms of scholastic thought, and thus will be addressed below in relation to a number of subjects in which Radical Lutheran authors contend for the inadequacy of Aristotelian ideas.

The influence of all of the philosophers explained so far is

---

[393] Ibid., 190.

[394] Livingston, *Modern Christian Thought*, 52.

overshadowed by one figure whose impact can be compared only to that of Plato and Aristotle: Immanuel Kant. Kant's impact on theology is enormous, as he shifted the entire intellectual conversation in the West through his writings. Rather than siding with either the rationalists or the empiricists, Kant combined the two ideas into a synthesis which would become the basis for the development of liberal theology through Albrecht Ritschl. While initially attracted to David Hume's empiricism, Kant describes a "Copernican revolution" in his thought, wherein he discovered the idea of the synthetic a priori.[395] In his book *Critique of Pure Reason*, Kant argues that there is knowledge which is derived from experience (a posteriori) and that which is independent of experience (a priori). It is important to note than Kant does not speak of sequential temporality here, as if a priori experience is first, and a posteriori is second. Kant contended that while Hume's arguments about causation were valid as far as observation is concerned, there must be some firmer grounding for knowledge than sense experience. Thus, Kant argued that one could, with certainty, arrive at certain propositions a priori.[396] There are, for Kant, two types of ideas which are arrived at a priori: analytic and synthetic. An analytic judgment is one in which affirmations are made about the predicate of a statement which is identified by the subject. It adds no additional knowledge to the subject at all. An example of such a proposition might be, "A bachelor is an unmarried man." This is true, of necessity, because being an unmarried man is part of the definition of "bachelor." On

---

[395] Gardner, *Kant*, 37.

[396] Ibid., 51.

the other hand, Kant argued, there are synthetic propositions, wherein some kind of knowledge is actually added in one's understanding of the subject. Diogenes Allen gives an example of this type of statement, writing, "All bodies have weight."[397] This statement is true, even though the concept of weight is not necessitated in the definition of the term "body." These synthetic a priori propositions are true universally, rather than in some particular instances. To say that "bodies weigh over 100 pounds" would be true only with regard to some bodies, and such a conclusion could only be drawn through experience, as various bodies were weighed and thus demonstrated to equal such a value. However, the connection between bodies and weight is not dependent upon experience, because such a concept is true *universally*. One need not examine every body on the planet in order for such a universal statement to be made. This leads to certainty of knowledge which is not available in Hume's empiricism, while Kant still retains elements of his skeptical outlook.

The methodology developed by Kant is sometimes known as the transcendental method.[398] Kant seeks to find the conditions through which sense-experience is understood by the human subject. He proposes space and time, for example, as preconditions for knowledge, through which the external world is understood. Since geometric statements are defined as synthetic a priori judgments, space is a transcendental category, because without it, geometry would not be possible. The certainty of mathematical formulas, as part of a priori knowledge, is opposed to the complete uncertainty of meta-

---

[397] Allen, *Philosophy for Understanding Theology*, 205.
[398] Gardner, *Kant*, 65.

physical propositions.[399] Kant argued that observations of the external world are only understood through the manner of one's own perception. This is the "phenomenal realm," wherein one has certainty of one's own perception of the world. This does not mean, however, that the actual external world can be properly understood apart from the human subject. There is, then, no affirmation of the "thing-in-itself," which is identified as the "noumenal realm." Such a conviction constitutes a radical break with Greek thought, wherein the purpose of philosophy is to discover the underlying nature of reality. For Kant, this is impossible, and philosophy does not deal with such questions, including religious metaphysical claims. These ideas impacted theology in the nineteenth century.

The theological implications of Kant's system were enormous. Kant himself outlined his approach to religion in his book *Religion within the Limits of Reason Alone* (1793), wherein he defended a moralistic approach to Christianity. All the classical arguments for the existence of God Kant regarded as inadequate.[400] He rejected the ontological argument for its insistence that existence itself is a predicate, and arguments from design as statements about the noumenal realm which, for Kant, are impossible to verify.[401] This is not to say, however, that Kant regarded the existence of God as an impossibility, or religion as an unnecessary idea. He sought, rather, to place religion within the realm of faith rather than reason. The function of theism is primarily in

---

[399] Ibid., 75.

[400] Beardsley, *European Philosophers*, 456.

[401] Livingston, *Christian Thought*, 66.

the realm of morality. Like his convictions regarding the synthetic a priori, Kant was convinced that the key to moral judgments was not in experience, but in universal moral imperatives discoverable through reason a priori. It is in this context that Kant develops his categorical imperative. God's existence, for Kant, was necessary for this universal moral imperative to have any value. James Livingston speaks about a "Copernican revolution" in theology, wherein Kant argues from morality to theism, rather than deducing moral laws from religion.[402] This was not a bare theism, however, as Kant argued for the superiority of Christianity. In his exposition of Christianity, Kant rejects some of the traditional Protestant ideas about original sin and justification, and reformulates such concepts around his ethical theory. Sin, for Kant, is selfishness, and one must, in freedom, turn from this orientation to an ethical one. It is human free decision which determines one's religious and moral character.[403] The ideas about religion which Kant defended had an influence on nearly every theologian following him. Whether one agreed or disagreed with his conclusions, every serious theologian had to contend with Kant's system.

These various ideological movements associated with the Enlightenment led to the dissolution of scholasticism as a prominent theological method. As the eighteenth century progressed, few remained committed to the method which had been standard since the later sixteenth century. Robert Preus identifies the ending of the scholastic era with David Hollaz

---

[402] Ibid., 69.
[403] Ibid., 72.

in 1713.[404] While a contingent of later thinkers remained scholastic in orientation, such as Valentin Ernst Loescher, many retreated to either Pietism or rationalism. The Pietist movement, begun with the publication of Philip Jacob Spener's *Pia Desideria* in 1675, promoted a Christianity which was centered upon religious experience and moral imperatives, rather than strict dogmatic theological categories which defined the era of Lutheran orthodoxy.[405] Initially, the two movements were not set in opposition to one another. Spener did not reject the theology of Lutheran scholasticism, and his work was promoted by scholastics such as Abraham Calov. Johann Gerhard is sometimes considered a precursor to Pietism, although he remains among the most influential Lutheran scholastic writers.[406] However, after the beginning of the eighteenth century, the two ideologies gradually divorced from one another, as Pietism became more firmly rooted in millennial expectations and the loss of the sacramental piety inherent in scholasticism. Though differing in their respective convictions, Pietists and rationalists shared a common critique of the systems of seventeenth-century Lutheranism, and a distrust of prevailing religious structures. The exact relationship between the two movements remains an area of scholarly debate,[407] but many view Pietism as an influence on the Enlightenment in Germany.

It is significant that Immanuel Kant was raised as a Pietist before his Copernican revolution in philosophy. From Pietism,

---

[404] Preus, *Theology of Post-Reformation Lutheranism*, 65.

[405] Gritsch, *History of Lutheranism*, 141.

[406] Shantz, *Introduction to German Pietism*, 38–39.

[407] Ernest, .

Kant derived an understanding of the practical nature of religion, and particularly its relationship to morality.[408] This shaped German theology for the next century. By the end of the eighteenth century, Kant's ideas had pervaded Western Europe, and theologians attempted to apply these philosophical developments to Christian doctrine. In response to rationalism, a movement known as Romanticism began to flourish as people began to search for meaning beyond bare scientific facts emphasized in Newtonian science. Rather than emphasizing rational argumentation, Christians stressed the nature of personal religious experience, as the rational arguments for Christianity adopted in the past were no longer seen as viable.[409] The most prominent Romantic theologian was Friedrich Schleiermacher who, like Kant, was raised in Pietism.[410] In view of the criticisms of older scholastic theology, Schleiermacher rejected the idea that religion was concerned with metaphysical claims. Unlike Kant, however, he also denied that the place for religion is in one's moral life. Schleiermacher instead argued that the location of religion for the individual was in feelings. This is consistent with the earlier Pietist emphasis on religious experiences of conversion. By "feeling," it should be noted that Schleiermacher does not refer to particular moments of ecstatic experience, or in one's subjective emotional state. Instead, he refers to the consciousness of the self in relation to God. Religion itself is defined by Schleiermacher as a "feeling of absolute

---

[408] Livingston, *Modern Christian Thought*, 63.

[409] Ibid., 80.

[410] Barth, *Protestant Theology*, 411.

dependence."⁴¹¹ This Romantic approach to theology led to the most significant Liberal theologian after Schleiermacher, who would apply some of these concepts to the theology of Martin Luther—Albrecht Ritschl.

Like Kant and Schleiermacher, Ritschl was also raised in conservative Pietism but departed in significant ways from this perspective. Commensurate with these authors as well, he rejected classical descriptions of metaphysics as unnecessary for theology.⁴¹² Ritschl argues that there is a fundamental differentiation, in theology, between nature and Spirit which is an impossibility for metaphysical systems to grasp.⁴¹³ There is no "common foundation of all being" which is to be discovered, as such would negate this differentiation.⁴¹⁴ Arguments for the existence of God fail, as one cannot metaphysically grasp a spiritual entity. The ideas of divinity as taught by philosophy, including the *actus purus* conception of Thomism, are dependent upon a false conception of reality which regards all things through the notions of cause and effect, and a belief in teleology.⁴¹⁵ God is to be understood, not in terms of absoluteness, but in personalist terminology. He is defined as the "loving will" who creates Christian community.⁴¹⁶ Ritschl utilized the philosophy of Kant, especially as modified by Herman Lotze. Things are not known as they are in themselves, but only in relation to their impact upon the

---

⁴¹¹ Livingston, *Modern Christian Thought*, 98–99.

⁴¹² Barth, *Protestant Theology*, 640.

⁴¹³ Ritschl, *Three Essays*, 154.

⁴¹⁴ Ibid., 154.

⁴¹⁵ Ibid., 158.

⁴¹⁶ Ibid., 164.

human subject. Religious truths are thus important only insofar as they impact the human person. This is not a pure subjectivity, as Ritschl does not deny that the things-in-themselves do in fact exist. However, such metaphysical claims are simply irrelevant to religion.

Classical metaphysical Christian claims are rejected as unimportant for faith in Ritschl's thought. There is no need for a metaphysical description of the Trinity, or of the preexistence of Christ.[417] Ritschl differentiated between scientific judgments and value judgments. The former deal with those of factuality versus falsehood. This is the nature of the scientific method. Value judgments are different, as they relate to the impact and use of ideas in relation to the human person. While he did not negate the importance of scientific judgments, Ritschl placed religion within the category of value judgments. The Ecumenical Creeds, for Ritschl, are too concerned with the former type of judgments, in attempting to establish the nature of God through the recitation of disinterested facts. The doctrine of Christ's divinity, for example, is not a metaphysical contention about his preexistent person, but instead is the notion that Christ is the one through whom God is revealed.[418] The importance of doctrine, for Ritschl, is largely in moral action.[419] Ritchl formulated this idea through Luther's doctrine of justification. For Ritschl, the scholastic approach to justification which identifies this act with the imputation of righteousness is to be discarded. This is not to say, however, that Ritschl attempts to completely divorce

---

[417] Ibid., 151.

[418] Livingston, *Modern Christian Thought*, 253.

[419] Barth, *Protestant Theology*, 643.

justification from earlier definitions. In his interpretation of Ritschl, David W. Lotz argues that justification is "the free resolve on God's part to pardon sin without regard for the sinner's own moral rectitude."[420] This act is paired with God's coterminous act of reconciliation, wherein one enters into the Christian community and engages in free moral action. The Christian community is identified as the kingdom of God, which is a cornerstone of Ritschl's thought. The kingdom of God is a moral community which engages in actions of love in the world. The end goal of justification then, for Ritschl, is moral action.[421] Though the particulars of Ritschl's Luther interpretation were not widely adopted outside the Ritschlian school, several of his ideas, and especially his anti-metaphysical stance, were adopted by Lutheran thinkers.

The ideas presented here are representative of the development of philosophy and theology between the seventeenth and late nineteenth centuries, in which classical scholastic modes of thought became less prominent. Such a groundwork is necessary in order to evaluate criticisms of scholasticism offered by twentieth- and twenty-first-century theologians, as these authors do not write in a vacuum, but in the midst of a theological movement away from metaphysics which has its roots in early modern philosophy. Descartes signals the reformulation of philosophy, beginning with different premises than classic essentialism. This resulted in various schools of thought, such as rationalism and empiricism. While these movements differed from one another in several points, both affirmed that a new philosophical starting point was

---

[420] Lotz, *Ritschl and Luther*, 37.

[421] Livingston, *Modern Christian Thought*, 256.

necessary and that older metaphysical systems are inadequate. Kant combined the insights of these two schools with his Copernican revolution surrounding the synthetic a priori, which then became a point of departure for both philosophers and theologians in the nineteenth century. Kant's critique of classical metaphysics is adopted by Schleiermacher, who places religion within the realm of feeling. Ritschl provides a more consistently Kantian system through his approach to the kingdom of God, which combines Luther's thought and that of neo-Kantian philosopher Herman Lotze. It is within this context that existentialism arose in the twentieth century and challenged some of the preconceptions of modern philosophy while simultaneously continuing in modernism's rejection of Greek metaphysics. Radical Lutheran theologians do the same in rejecting Ritschl's moralism while retaining his essential rejection of metaphysical categories in his interpretation of Luther.

Defining Existentialism

These developments in Western philosophy led to the school of thought commonly known as existentialism. Like other philosophical schools, existentialism was not a consistent group of philosophers who conscientiously attempted to arrive at similar conclusions, but a number of disparate figures who emphasized similar themes.[422] Both Kierkegaard and Nietzsche are regarded as foundational thinkers for existentialism, but they are quite different in their approaches. Kierkegaard was a Christian and Nietzsche an adamant atheist.

---

[422] Olson, *Introduction to Existentialism*, viii.

The following generation of existential philosophers show a similar breadth of thought. Sartre, like Nietzsche, promoted a form of atheistic existentialism, whereas Marcel was a Roman Catholic. Heidegger, who is among the most influential thinkers identified with existentialism, believed that Sartre's and Camus's philosophies were too individualistic.[423] Reality, for Heidegger, was always being-in-relation. Before the discussion proceeds, some definition of existentialism which unites these figures under a single banner is merited.

Various definitions have been proposed to unify the existentialist movement. John Hayward notes the difficulty in systematizing these thinkers, but proposes a definition which includes a privileging of existence over essence, along with an emphasis on personal experience over against unchangeable universals.[424] Such a definition has the benefit of describing a single core tenet of the movement, but remains quite broad. A second proposal comes from Maurice Friedman. In his compendium of existentialist writings, Friedman argues that there is no single existentialism, but rather several existentia*lisms*.[425] Despite these differences, however, Friedman proposes that there is a "temper" which is present in all these thinkers that includes a reaction against "the static, the abstract, the purely rational, the merely irrational, in favor of the dynamic and concrete, personal involvement . . . the distinction between 'authentic' and 'inauthentic' existence, and the actual situation of the existential subject

---

[423] Barrett and Aiken, *Twentieth Century*, 206–18.

[424] Hayward, *Existentialism and Religious Liberalism*, 17.

[425] Friedman, *Worlds of Existentialism*, 3.

as the starting point."⁴²⁶ This definition is more expansive than that of Hayward, yet it remains vague. Both of the explanations proposed here accurately categorize existential thinking but are still rather broad and undefined.

A third definition appears in the writings of Thomas Flynn which is more comprehensive. In his introduction to existential philosophy, Flynn, rather than proposing a singular definition of existentialism, outlines five major themes which underlie the thought of existential writers.⁴²⁷ Since characterizations of the movement are so broad, no single definition can adequately give an explanation of the movement. Thus, Flynn's characteristics are a more sufficient means to explain existential philosophy than the other attempts. They serve as a grid by which thinkers can be judged as to whether they technically fit the definition of existentialism. It is these five characteristics which are followed here. It is to be noted, however, that the Radical Lutheran authors do not adopt the *entirety* of these five concepts, and they make several modifications to what might be considered a traditional existential outlook. These concepts are as follows: the idea that existence precedes essence; the idea that time is of the essence; humanism; freedom and responsibility; and the centrality of ethical considerations. Each of these themes is discussed here at different points, and Radical Lutheran writers are critiqued in relation to such ideas. It is the first two that are most prominent, while the notion of freedom and responsibility is significantly altered by the Radical Lutheran writers in view of Luther's conviction on the bondage of the

---

[426] Ibid., 3–4.

[427] Flynn, *Existentialism*, 1.

will.

In light of Flynn's definition, existentialist philosophy is discussed here in relation to four essential aspects of Radical Lutheran thought. First is Martin Heidegger's ontology. His critique of metaphysics is followed by an explanation of Forde's and Bayer's criticism of a classical essentialist approach to theology, which echoes the concerns of existential philosophers. Second is the transition from inauthentic existence to authenticity in existential writers, often characterized by the phrase "existence precedes essence."[428] This is linked to Gerhard Forde's personalized-eschatology mediated by Rudolph Bultmann, who combined Pauline eschatology and Heideggerian existentialism. Third, this leads to a discussion about the nature of the human person in the existential system as opposed to the real-essentialist. The final concept examined is the reconceptualization of truth as event rather than intellectual acceptance of propositional statements.

Ontology

The present project is concerned largely with the topic of metaphysics, as the opposing models of being which are used in Radical Lutheranism and scholasticism are central to their respective theological methods. As such, it is necessary to examine some of the criticisms of essentialist thought which are apparent in both existential philosophy and Radical Lutheran writers. While, again, Forde and Bayer do not self-consciously echo Heidegger in this regard, there are several areas of commonality between their criticisms. Forde in particular

---

[428] Allen, *Philosophy for Understanding Theology*, 248.

uses language which is Heideggerian in orientation. It is likely that such ideas are imbibed not through Heidegger, but by way of Rudolph Bultmann, whose thought had an extensive influence upon twentieth-century Lutheran thought. Bayer uses many of the same criticisms, though he views existential analysis as inadequate in comparison to the field of linguistics.

Martin Heidegger's approach was highly influential upon the development of twentieth-century theology. Figures such as Martin Buber and Rudolph Bultmann were impacted by the German philosopher, and they used some of Heidegger's concepts to formulate their theological systems. As discussed in his magnum opus *Being and Time*, Martin Heidegger's primary concern is that of Being.[429] Heidegger distinguishes between *Being* and *beings*. The former (which is usually capitalized in English translations) is that which is most significant for Heidegger's thinking, as he seeks to redefine the entire concept of Being from the rest of the inherited Western philosophical tradition.[430] For Heidegger, this concept has been misunderstood because the latter idea of *beings* has unfortunately been the predominant philosophical concern since Plato. Philosophers think about particular objects whose essences are then abstracted. This results in a concept of being which is so abstract that it barely has any meaning at all. William Barrett refers to Heidegger's critique here as "the destruction of the whole history of

---

[429] Heidegger's *Being and Time* is notoriously difficult to navigate, so I highly recommend using Mark A. Wrathall's *Cambridge Companion to Heidegger's Being and Time* alongside the original text.

[430] Barrett, *Irrational Man*, 208.

Western ontology."[431] Rather than finding some kind of essence behind individual existents, as was the practice of the Greeks, Heidegger attempts to get behind the concept of Being itself. Unlike the pure abstraction Heidegger accuses earlier Western thinkers of, Being is a concern for everyday human persons, and it stands behind what every person knows about the world. The simple fact that the word "is" can be used in discussion and understood means that this concept is already grasped by the average individual.[432] This description of Being leads to some further distinctions which are necessary for understanding Heidegger's thought.

One of these distinctions is that between two types of inquiry in which metaphysicians can be engaged: *ontical* and *ontological*.[433] The first refers to the study and explanation of facts about particular things, which Heidegger argues is the primary way in which metaphysics has been used in the history of philosophy. The ontological inquiry, however, is concerned with meaning and intelligibility. By opting for the priority of the latter type of metaphysical discussion, Heidegger shifts the emphasis from Greek thought, which examines essences and substances, to the question of meaning. The second distinction made by the German philosopher is that of *regional ontology* and *fundamental ontology*.[434] Regional ontology concerns itself with particular areas of study, whereas fundamental ontology addresses the transcendental conditions by which Being is expressed in these regions. This

---

[431] Ibid., 211.

[432] Ibid., 213.

[433] Macquarrie, *Existentialist Theology*, 30.

[434] Barrett, *Irrational Man*, 216.

is done, according to Heidegger, by an *existential* examination of Being. This Being ultimately relates only to humanity, which he labels "Dasein," or "being-there."[435] Though many individual beings *are*, only humans truly have existence in the philosophical sense. This existential study of Dasein is then the root of all further study, and only when this concept is understood can regional ontological discussion take place properly. What is especially significant here is that contrary to the metaphysics of other Western thought, which examines the essence of specific objects, Heidegger's philosophy locates the entire subject of ontology within the human person. This must be understood in order to properly explain his priority of existence over essence.

For Heidegger, Being is always understood as being-in-relation.[436] There is no essence in the abstract, as one exists in the world with relation to other objects, and in the midst of time. Due to this fact, objects outside of oneself are understood through one's experience with them insofar as they come into contact with Dasein. Since being is always in-relation, external objects are never described through essential and accidental attributes, as in Aristotelian thought, nor through the realm of forms, as in Platonism. In this manner, Heidegger draws on Edmund Husserl's phenomenology, though the exact relation between these two philosophers remains a topic of debate.[437] For Husserl, one is not to be concerned with things-in-themselves as existent objects outside of perception, but instead with an explanation and description of

---

[435] Allen, *Philosophy for Understanding Theology*, 251.

[436] Friedman, *Worlds of Existentialism*, 180.

[437] Barrett, *Irrational Man*, 134.

experience.[438] Though Heidegger did not agree with all of the particulars of the older philosopher, he argued that knowledge of objects arises through experience instead of contemplation. Michael J. Quirk notes that this results in a "use-oriented" way of looking at the world, which avoids both the realist and anti-realist positions debated in modern philosophy.[439] The philosophical mode of inquiry is shifted from what exists outside of the mind to how objects are encountered within one's context and experience. This manner of perceiving objects in relation to Dasein is reflected in the existential theologians of the twentieth century.

The use-orientedness of Heidegger's ontology is echoed by Radical Lutheran authors, who similarly reject ancient philosophical discussion of things in relation to their essence, especially as adopted by the scholastic theologians. In my book *Lex Aeterna*, I argued that Gerhard Forde defines reality, not by *being*, but by *doing*.[440] Here, the ideas developed there are summarized so that they can be understood in connection to these developments in philosophy. The place in which Forde's metaphysical convictions are perhaps most clear is his description of God's law. For Lutheran orthodoxy, the law is defined as the eternal will of God, which has particular content tied to it, expressed in the Ten Commandments. The law is not merely one part of redemptive history, nor is it identified with any singular one of its functions. It has a strong metaphysical grounding, as the law reflects the eternal nature of God. In this classical definition, then, the law is described as a thing-

---

[438] On Husserl's phenomenology, see David Woodruff Smith, *Husserl*.

[439] Quirk, "Martin Heidegger," 5.

[440] Cooper, *Lex Aeterna*, 108.

in-itself which can be understood by the human subject apart from one's experience with it. Such a notion is dependent upon essentialist convictions in opposition to the ideas outlined by Forde.

In his doctoral dissertation, *The Law-Gospel Debate*, Forde discusses the classical approach to the law, referring to it as the "static-ontological" view.[441] He distinguishes this from a "historically oriented" view such as that of Johannes von Hofmann, wherein the law is described as one aspect of redemptive history which has been superseded.[442] Forde argues for the superiority of the historical approach over that of earlier authors, as scholastic thought is "abstract," as a pure collection of "propositions."[443] It is clear here that what Forde argues against is any approach to the law or the gospel in which these are identified with specific content. He rejects an essentialist view in which the essence of the law and the gospel can be identified with propositional truths apart from their impact upon the individual. This rejection of propositional truth (which leads to a discussion of Heidegger's conception of truth and falsehood, discussed below) also extends to Forde's approach to revelation, which similarly is described as an event rather than a collection of truth statements.[444] The atonement, similarly, cannot be identified purely as an objective fact in history whose application only comes later.[445] For Forde, this would imply that faith is a kind of intellectual

---

[441] Forde, *Law-Gospel*, 6.

[442] Ibid., 6.

[443] Ibid., 7.

[444] Ibid., 7.

[445] Ibid., 8–9.

assent to such propositional truths, rather than the dynamic act expressed in Scripture.

At the heart of Forde's thought surrounding law and gospel is his rejection of a distinction between the essence and function of the law. For the scholastics, the essence of the law has priority, as it is eternal and precedes man's fall into sin. The function of the law, which is threefold, flows from its essential nature. In a particularly illuminating passage, Forde states that "In the face of the concrete existential situation, the question about a distinction between essence and office is beside the point."[446] In his view, it is utterly irrelevant whether the law has an essence which differs from its accusatory function, because Forde divorces the study of theology from the thing-in-itself. Instead, what is theologically significant is only that which impacts the individual. That is why Forde blatantly says that the law's essence is accusation. He also states that the difference between the law and the gospel is not in terms of their content or metaphysical nature, but of how one hears the word of God.[447] Forde acknowledges that Luther does, in the Antinomian Disputations, argue that the decalogue is eternal. However, he contends that this phrase is used only in relation to the law's accusatory function, rather than the scholastic idea of the *lex aeterna*. Even in this accusatory function, however, the law will cease, as it exists only so long as sin does. Forde then concedes that the law is eternal only in the sense that its fulfillment lasts forever, but not the law itself. In his view, the law is

---

[446] Ibid., 181.
[447] Ibid., 181.

defined "in its existential sense as that which accuses."[448] It is clear that Forde opposes a classical essentialist scheme, as he purports that to construct an essence-office distinction, as does Lutheran scholasticism, is to view law from God's perspective in the realm of abstraction. This places one "above the law" rather than below it.[449] Yet it is not merely in terms of the law that Forde rejects traditional essentialist categories. He does this systematically throughout his book *Theology Is for Proclamation*.

Theology Is for Proclamation is the closest thing to a systematic treatment of Christian theology written by Gerhard Forde. The entire project of this book is to move theology away from abstraction to concrete action. In terms discussed here, it is a rejection of essentialism and an adoption of an existential approach to reality. Forde begins this treatment with a distinction between God-preached and God-not-preached.[450] In his view, the purpose of theology is to move from God-not-preached to the proclamation of the gospel through what he labels "primary discourse."[451] This idea of primary discourse is defined and critiqued below in the examination of linguistic philosophy. In order to understand Forde's basic methodological concerns, it is necessary to expound upon what he means by God-not-preached. At heart, God-not-preached, for Forde, is any metaphysical description of God as he is in himself. Forde refers to this God as "sheer timeless abstractions," such as in

---

[448] Ibid., 184.

[449] Ibid., 185.

[450] Forde, *Theology Is for Proclamation*, 14.

[451] Ibid., 2.

traditional discussions surrounding the divine attributes.[452] He further refers to classical Christian theology in a similar manner as "a collection of abstractions."[453] This supposed abstract approach to Christian theology includes the apologetic arguments for God's existence,[454] as well as any general statements surrounding the nature of God.[455] Forde refers to both apologetics and theodicy as vain exercises, irrelevant to man's concrete existential situation being under the wrath of God.[456] Forde raises the question of what the theologian is to do with this unpreached God, and he answers that he is simply to be ignored in favor of the God of proclamation.[457] In other words, classical descriptions of God's essence and attributes are simply not the concern of the theologian whatsoever. Such a conclusion signifies a radical shift in Christian theology, and demonstrates a rejection of essentialist thought.

In one part of his treatment, Forde does explicitly deal with traditional philosophy, referring to it as "substantialist."[458] He addresses these classic metaphysical ideas throughout his discussion of Christology and his proposed reconstrual of christological dogma through his linguistic-existential approach to theology. While Forde acknowledges that the basic ancient confession that Christ is both true God and true man is correct, he purports that the church was mistaken

---

[452] Ibid., 15.
[453] Ibid., 17.
[454] Ibid., 22.
[455] Ibid., 24.
[456] Ibid., 26.
[457] Ibid., 27.
[458] Ibid., 89.

in placing this concept within substantial terminology. He argues that the use of language about natures in the abstract leads to an incarnational Christology in which redemption is dependent upon a synthesis of two distinctive essences. This removes redemption from the actual story of Christ's life, death, and resurrection, and instead makes it a metaphysical reality.[459] Forde identifies two distinctive streams of christological thought in the early church, which are both identified with Platonism: the Antiochean and the Alexandrian. The Antiochenes speak about the being of Christ's two natures, while Alexandrians emphasize the idea of becoming.[460] Both of these ideas, according to Forde, are wrong, as neither fosters proclamation. While Forde cautiously allows for the retaining of substance language to a point, he contends that the primary category of exposition related to Christ's person is that of act.[461] Christ is understood primarily as the one who "does the act of God to us."[462] In his act of redemption, Forde notes that one dies to abstraction, placing traditional systematic theology in the realm of the old world, which is conquered by Christ. Like Heidegger and the other existential philosophers, Forde has a strong notion that we are "historical beings," tied to our existence in a temporal realm, and to the physical realities of life.[463] Contemplation of divine attributes is simply not the business of the reborn Christian. All of these ideas demonstrate common themes which unite Forde and

---

[459] Ibid., 91.
[460] Ibid., 94.
[461] Ibid., 101.
[462] Ibid., 105.
[463] Ibid., 103.

Heidegger.

Unlike Heidegger, Forde is not a professional philosopher, and thus does not engage in an extensive discussion about the nature of being. However, he does have clear methodological concerns which guide his understanding of the divine law, and at several points, they coincide with those of existentialism. This is clear especially in *Theology Is for Proclamation*, wherein essentialist approaches to Christian thought are criticized. As a treatment of theological method, this project must explain such concerns. The first point of similarity between Forde and Heidegger is their rejection of classic essentialism. Heidegger argues that the Platonic and Aristotelian ideas of being were inadequate due to their privileging beings over Being. This results, according to Heidegger, in an exposition of reality by way of abstraction. Man is divorced from his time-bound circumstances and existential concerns. Forde follows this line of thought in his rejection of scholasticism. The law, the gospel, the atonement, and other concepts are dismissed by Forde as abstract in numerous places, and thus Lutheran scholasticism is inconsistent with a theology which privileges the event of preaching. A discussion of the law which defines it by specific content is abstract, as are Chalcedonian Christology, apologetics, theodicy, and expositions of the divine attributes. Similarly, like Heidegger, Forde emphasizes the fact that man exists in-time, and is not in a position to explore the nature of timeless reality as in Platonism. A second point of similarity between the two thinkers is that while Forde does not use the terms "ontical" and "ontological," such a division is inherent within his writing. For Forde, things are not to be understood as they are in themselves (what Heidegger calls ontical inquiry), but in relation to their meaning for the one hearing the proclamation (ontological inquiry). This rejection of the thing-in-itself is especially apparent in Forde's argument that God's essence and attributes are merely part of the unpreached God, who is irrelevant to the theologian. An example of Forde's rejection of the thing-in-itself as relevant to theology is his contention that law and gospel are not distinguished by content, but are defined by their impact on the human subject. Third, Forde's understanding of reality, like Heidegger's, is use-oriented. It would be accurate to label Forde's view as phenomenological, since theology's primary function is to describe and foster the historical experience of law-gospel proclamation, rather than to be a study of ideas in themselves. As in Kant, everything is known as phenomenon, as it is experienced by the subject, and noumenal ideas are rejected.

Such convictions are not limited to Forde, however, but are also apparent in the writings of Oswald Bayer. Bayer discusses classical metaphysics in *Theology the Lutheran Way*, wherein he criticizes the over-utilization of Greek concepts in Christian thought. Bayer distinguishes between the metaphysical and mythological aspects of theology, arguing that Christian thought is most properly found between these ideas. Mythology, for Bayer, is the manner of theologizing which is apparent in Homer and the ancient stories of a polytheistic reality, with gods interacting with humans.[464] Metaphysics, he argues, is the examination of God as a theoretical and rational enterprise. This is the method of Plato and Aristotle. Bayer argues that Plato retained some mythical elements, but placed theology primarily within the realm of metaphysics. There are two

---

[464] Bayer, *Theology the Lutheran Way*, 3.

general principles which guide Plato's metaphysic of God, according to Bayer, which would impact Christian thought. First, because God is good, he cannot be the cause of evil.[465] Second, God is unchangeable and exists outside of time.[466] For Plato, there is a correlation between changeability and imperfection, and thus God is devoid of both. Bayer is even more critical of Aristotle, who promotes these same ideas, but eliminates any mythological conceptions whatsoever in theology. For Aristotle, theology is "entirely metaphysics."[467] Bayer completely rejects this Greek mode of thinking, arguing that God is not the unchangeable, static being posited by Aristotle. Instead, Bayer contends that the cross impacts the very being of God. Greek thought purports that God cannot suffer, as such would imply change in his perfect essence; Bayer argues that Christian thought "destroys" any notion of divine impassibility through its teaching on the atonement.[468] Bayer places these arguments within the context of Luther's theology of the cross.

According to Bayer, Luther's theological method constitutes a radical shift from the previous scholastic tradition. Rather than thinking in Greek categories, Luther discusses God from the perspective of relation (this is discussed in the *relational ontology* section below). Bayer argues that Luther's theology opposes itself both to justifying-doing and justifying-thinking.[469] The former category is one which

---

[465] Ibid., 4.
[466] Ibid., 5.
[467] Ibid., 7.
[468] Ibid., 9.
[469] Ibid., 26.

is recognized in historic Reformation thought. One cannot earn justification by works, and therefore righteousness is achieved through human passivity *coram Deo*. Bayer broadens Luther's critique to be one also of metaphysics. He defines this idea of justifying-thinking as "the attempt to mediate and reconcile all things."[470] For Bayer, such is an impossibility. The metaphysician seeks to examine particular objects with a goal of discovering universal essences behind these particulars. For Bayer, this attempt is "blind to reality."[471] One should not use rational argumentation to affirm that God is identical with truth, goodness, and beauty, which are then purported as metaphysical principles by which the world is to be understood. Such metaphysics, according to Bayer, is idolatrous. One cannot, for Bayer, even have an understanding of the divine attributes apart from the cross.[472] All of these ideas, for Bayer, are aspects of the theology of glory which Luther criticizes in the Heidelberg Disputation. Bayer argues that Aquinas's approach to Christian thought is based upon timeless principles, as God exists outside of time and thus his being is not historically dependent. Instead, Bayer writers that God is temporal. Theology is not a science wherein one gathers timeless principles about divinity, but is instead a "study of history and experience."[473] This, again, is very much in line with the existentialist critique of essentialist metaphysics. Humans are historical beings, and philosophy (or theology, in Bayer's case) is a description of both personal

---

[470] Ibid., 26.

[471] Ibid., 26.

[472] Ibid., 26.

[473] Ibid., 29.

history and experience, rather than the abstraction of timeless truths about the world.

Though they differ in their particular criticisms, there is a unified theme in both Forde's and Bayer's thought which criticizes the use of Greek essentialist metaphysics in favor of a method which shares similarities to existential philosophy. Both Forde and Bayer are particularly critical of the scholastic treatments of the divine nature. For Forde, the discussions engaged by proponents of classical theism are to be regarded as God-not-preached, since they are not directly concerned with the proclamation of the gospel to the sinner. Bayer is not quite so bold as to deny the necessity of such treatments altogether, but he argues that the classical discussions of them are indebted to Greek philosophy in opposition to Luther's more biblically-oriented historicism. Both Forde and Bayer shift the emphasis from that which is eternal to that which is concerned with both history and experience. For Forde, it is only that which is relevant to the subject that is discussed theologically. Bayer makes a similar shift by divorcing theology and metaphysics.

A Critique of Radical Lutheran Ontology

The ontological approach of the Radical Lutheran writers is vastly different than the earlier metaphysical convictions of the scholastic theologians, who argued for a real-essentialist ontology. It is the contention of this work that the scholastic perspective remains a more adequate methodological system than Radical Lutheranism. Here, a critique is offered on two points in relation to the ontological approach of Forde and Bayer. First is the scriptural text and the foundations of essentialism for Christian thought. Second, classical theism is defended in light of the contention of Radical Lutheran authors that such concepts are inherently Greek rather than Christian.

It must be granted that Scripture is not a metaphysical text. It was not given with the distinct intention of finding various essential attributes of the eternal order for the purpose of human speculation. Bayer is not wrong, for example, in his criticisms of Aristotle wherein theology is limited to the field of metaphysics. The Aristotelian God, as a being who spends eternity in self-contemplation, is clearly distinguishable from that of the triune God of biblical revelation, who expresses himself through self-giving to an unworthy creation. On this point, both the medieval and Protestant scholastics would agree as to the inadequacy of philosophy in establishing articles of faith. Also, Bayer is correct in his bottom-to-top approach to Christian theism, wherein God is known in the purest sense not by philosophizing about the concept of a highest good, but through the lowly baby Jesus lying in a manger.[474] Here, Luther's approach is clearly distinguished from that of even the medieval scholastics, whose theological starting point is often with the being of God. The Lutheran view has always been more redemptive-historical in orientation, rather than purely metaphysical. However, while Bayer is correct on these points, what he proposes is a false dichotomy: either one adopts an ahistorical Aristotelian conception of divinity, *or* one concedes that God is not immutable; God is known either through reason *or* through his self-revelation in Christ. On both of these points, Lutheran scholasticism offers a *via media*.

---

[474] Ibid., 191.

As discussed in the previous chapter, nearly all Christian thinkers who are philosophically oriented have distinguished themselves from the false conceptions of divinity taught by the Greeks.[475] A belief in the Trinity and the incarnation radically alters the philosophies of both Plato and Aristotle. Yet none of these Christian theologians then posed an absolute dichotomy between a metaphysical approach to God and a Christian one, as it was acknowledged that certain aspects of God discovered by Aristotle and Plato are also given in biblical revelation. The New Testament itself began this process of acknowledging both the value and limits of rational thought. In Romans 1, St. Paul acknowledges that creation itself testifies to God's existence and attributes, which are "clearly seen," leaving no excuse for unbelievers to reject him (Rom 1:20). There is no dichotomy here in Paul that God is known either by contemplation of creation *or* through the incarnation of Christ. While Bayer refers to discussion of God's attributes apart from the incarnation as idolatry, Paul appears to do quite the opposite. It is the rejection of such devotion to the divine attributes that is labeled idolatry. Paul does the same in his speech at Athens, wherein he acknowledges that truth about God is to be found in pagan philosophers. Paul cites the poet Aratus as speaking truth about God when he states that "in him we live and move and have our being" (Acts 17:28). Paul does not oppose rational deduction about God from creation, to the point that he praises various truths found in non-Christian philosophers and poets. What Bayer's position appears to lead to here is an opposition to natural theology, which is a distinctively biblical category. Forde's stance is even more

---

[475] Barnard, *Justin Martyr*, 27–38.

harsh, as he rejects the field of apologetics altogether. Such a position is hard to synthesize with Paul's own words.

What should be acknowledged in this discussion is the distinction Luther makes between the *general* knowledge of God and *proper* knowledge of God cited in the previous chapter. In terms of general knowledge, one can indeed deduce various truths about God's nature and attributes through the use of reason. Such reason is also utilized to discover moral truths of God's law which are built into creation. It is in this context that it is not wrong at all to deduce God's essence through a contemplation of truth, goodness, and beauty, which are reflections of the divine nature, and the source of these attributes in the world. Bayer argues, in contrast, that such a perspective on divinity is "shattered by painful disillusionment" for the theologian of the cross.[476] Yet this assertion establishes a strong break with the entire Christian tradition, which has always identified God as the source of these various attributes of the world, which are a reflection of the divine nature. Had Luther rejected this concept, surely his critique of such a strong Augustinian notion would have been mentioned somewhere. Instead, it is better to recognize that Luther's theology of the cross is in reference to *the gospel* in particular, rather than any knowledge of God whatsoever. While general knowledge of God can use human reason to discern various truths about God and the world, it does not lead to salvation. The gospel is only received through proper knowledge of God, which is revealed solely through the incarnation and death of Christ. For the theologian, then, general knowledge of God can be

---

[476] Ibid., 26.

gained through reason, but proper knowledge only by the humiliation of Christ. There is no reason to view these two ideas as mutually exclusive realities. This balance of ideas preserves Bayer's concern to centralize knowledge of God in the person of Christ, while also recognizing the validity of natural revelation.

Bayer's thesis largely depends upon his reading of the Heidelberg Disputation, which in his view, rejects classical Greek thought. Any notions of an attempt to find a unifying metaphysic is, for Bayer, a theology of glory. Metaphysics is described as "justifying thinking," which is just as problematic as works-righteousness in his view. Forde echoes this idea through his writings as well, wherein the idea of the theology of glory is quite broad, denying all earlier philosophical approaches to theism. However, as discussed in the previous chapter, this reading of the disputation is simply wrong. A read only of the various theses which discuss Aristotle might lead to this conclusion, but in his philosophical theses, Luther does not reject all metaphysical certainty as "justifying thinking" or as a "theology of glory." Instead, Luther argues against Aristotelianism not because of its adherence to metaphysical realism, but because such a realism is not strong *enough*.[477] One of the aspects of both Plato and Aristotle of which Bayer is the most critical is the assumption that things which are unchanging are to be privileged over those which undergo change. For Bayer, this assumption leads to the unbiblical notion of an unmoved mover.[478] Yet Luther's critique of Aristotle demonstrates the completely opposite assumption.

---

[477] Parker, "Platonism of Martin Luther."

[478] Bayer, *Theology the Lutheran Way*, 9.

He prefers Plato's philosophy because it does not "crawl in the dregs" of matter like Aristotelianism, and because Plato prefers singular, unchanging, and insensible things.[479] In his treatment of the supposed justifying thinking that Luther argues against, Bayer purports that such false thinking is "driven by the compulsion to demonstrate that every individual particular thing is based on something general."[480] Yet that is precisely what Luther argues in these theses is a *proper* thing to do. As an early writing of Luther, the Heidelberg Disputation does not demonstrate that Luther always remained a committed Platonist. However, what it does prove is that Luther's Heidelberg Disputation cannot be honestly used in opposition to classical philosophy.

There are also thoroughly biblical grounds to affirm essentialism. It is not a pure rational deduction from contemplation, but is the system which is most consistent with special revelation. The existence of distinct essences stands behind the entire creation account of Genesis 1. The author writes of the creation act as an orderly one, wherein God first makes distinctive realms of sky, water, and earth, and then fills those realms with creatures. Everything is said to be made "according to its kind" (Gen 1:21). A nominalist conception of reality has difficulty in making sense of such language, which clearly implies that there are distinctive essences which make up each created thing. A bird is a bird not simply because humans categorized particular creatures in such a way; they existed as a species before humanity was created. While Genesis 1 is not an extensive philosophical

---

[479] Parker, "Platonism of Martin Luther."

[480] Bayer, *Theology the Lutheran Way*, 190.

treatise, it is hard to ignore the fact that there are clear metaphysical realities exposited in the creation narrative. This fact is especially important for the unity of the human race throughout Scripture. The incarnation would be meaningless were there not a universal essence of humanness which Jesus took part in. Were there only particular individual things and no universals, Jesus had no need to come in flesh at all, as there would then be nothing to tie that human nature to others.

Such an essentialist approach to reality is denied by a vast number of contemporary Lutheran sources, even when the authors are examining earlier Lutheranism. Paulson, for example, speaks about a problem that Lutheran theology has "always had" with metaphysics and ontology, giving the impression that such a critique has been universal in Lutheran thought.[481] As has been significantly demonstrated, such is simply not the case, even in Luther. The actual content of this critique Paulson gives of metaphysics from a Lutheran approach is also heavily problematic in light of the actual source material as explained in the previous chapter. While implicating metaphysics as a field of inquiry, Paulson criticizes primarily a Platonic notion of essences, arguing that its primary problem is the search to find God apart from physical created reality through acts of thought. He refers to this as "abstraction from created life."[482] Using the narrative of Adam and Eve, Paulson speaks about the intimate presence of God through created things. He writes about a peach which an individual might eat, and argues that God is present within the peach itself, not in some abstract category

---

[481] Paulson, *Lutheran Theology*, 72–73.

[482] Ibid., 72.

of "peachiness."[483] He then argues that sin, for Adam and Eve, consisted in their rejection of God-in-things, replaced by their attempt to gain a metaphysical understanding of God by finding him apart from created objects.[484] He further gives a definition of sin itself in light of this as "seeking to have God without a preacher, and so to have God *immediately*, apart from created things."[485] The problems in Paulson's treatment of metaphysics are numerous.

The first flaw with Paulson's argument is that he simply does not accurately represent classical metaphysics. His entire notion of essence being that which exists apart from individual particular objects implicates only Platonism, but his assumption is that his critique denies any sort of Greek metaphysic. If Paulson's concern is simply that there is no essence apart from particulars, then he should have no problems with Aristotelianism. He fails to make any strong distinction between various forms of essentialism at all. Also, at least in the Neoplatonic tradition adopted by Christian theologians, God is by no means divorced from material reality. In some ways, it is the Neoplatonic tradition which is *more* literal in its connection between God and the world. For the Neoplatonist, all created things are participatory, in that they exist as an overflow of God's own being. In Eastern theology, every created object participates in God's energies. If this is the case, then God is not completely divorced from creation, as Paulson's criticism implies. While an extreme form of apophatic theology, such as that found in Pseudo-Dionysius,

---

[483] Ibid., 73.
[484] Ibid., 74.
[485] Ibid., 74.

might be accurately criticized with Paulson's arguments here, such is not the case with the entirety of the Neoplatonic tradition.

Another concern is that Paulson's contention that one is never to reason beyond created things to God's nature is a novelty within the Lutheran tradition. As explained above, Luther argues in the Heidelberg Disputation that creation does indeed point one beyond sensible things to the ideal. Paulson's exposition of Luther fails to include any mention or interaction with this concept, which would seem to overthrow his entire argument. Perhaps Luther disregarded all of his Neoplatonic influence at some point in his career and developed an opposing metaphysic. However, until such is demonstrated from Luther's own writings, an assertion cannot be made honestly. Johann Gerhard similarly speaks, as cited in the previous chapter, about the participatory nature of reality. All things participate in aspects of God's being, such as his goodness, love, and mercy. When these attributes are found in the created world, the result is contemplation of God, who is the source of such attributes. Neither Luther nor Gerhard saw these convictions as somehow in opposition to their sacramental theology or immanentist approach to God's interaction in the world, as Paulson contends.

The third flaw in Paulson's argument is that his contentions are completely absent from the scriptural text. The story of the fall has had numerous interpreters throughout the centuries, and exegetes have disagreed on the exact nature of the sin of Adam. Perhaps it was pride in his desire to be like God, or self-love, or an attempt to please his own appetites over obedience to divine commands.[486] Despite such disagreements on the nature of this sin, no one other than Paulson (as far as this author is aware) has argued that this sin involved an attempt to do metaphysics apart from created things. There is simply nothing in the text whatsoever that could lead to such a conclusion, which appears to be pure speculation. Similarly, Paulson's definition of sin as searching for God apart from created things has no biblical support whatsoever. As most systematicians recognize, sin is primarily a violation of divine commands.[487] If Paulson's approach has validity, such must be demonstrated from the text. While Lutheran thinkers have often criticized enthusiasm and other attempts to find revelation apart from word and sacrament, they do not arrive at the conclusions that Paulson does here.

Another example of the anti-metaphysical bias of modern Lutheran scholars is found in the text *The Lutheran Confessions: History and Theology of the Book of Concord,* by Charles Arand, Robert Kolb, and James Nestingen. The book is valuable and quite comprehensive in its historical treatment of the Lutheran Confessions. However, there are two sections of this text which are symptomatic of the problems inherent within the Radical Lutheran method. The first is the treatment of the Flacian controversy addressed in Article I of the Formula of Concord, and the second is Article III, which explains the nature of saving righteousness. The first article is about a dispute between Victorin Strigel and Matthias Flacius over the nature of original sin. Strigel contended that sin was an accidental property of the human nature, and Flacius replied that

---

[486] Schmid, *Doctrinal Theology,* 237.
[487] Ibid., 231.

it was instead of the *essence* of fallen humanity. Arand, Kolb, and Nestingen contend that the flaw in Strigel's presentation was in his use of Aristotelian categories, which are described as a "dead-end street."[488] Flacius's flaw, also, was not in his identification with sin and essence, but in following Strigel into the "swamp of joining biblical concepts and Aristotelian categories," which is an "alien paradigm."[489] Further, use of Aristotelian categories of substance and accident necessarily result in "contradiction" with Scripture.[490] Following their criticisms of both Strigel and Flacius, the authors discuss the response of the Formula, stating that language of substance and accidents operate on a metaphysical framework which is opposed to biblical anthropology.[491] The issue with this critique is that it ignores the actual solution of the Formula of Concord.

While the authors of the aforementioned book purport that the flaw in Strigel's approach was his use of Aristotle, the authors of the Formula have a very different view on the discussion. The use of such distinctions is never questioned by the document, nor is there any contention that substantial language has an unbiblical metaphysical basis. Quite the opposite is the case. The article states that the existence of both substances and accidental properties is an "indisputable axiom in theology" (FC SD I.55). It is further explained as an "indisputable truth" which "no intelligent man has ever has any doubts" about (FC SD I.56). This is a vigorous affirmation

---

[488] Arand, *Lutheran Confessions*, 206.

[489] Ibid., 206.

[490] Ibid., 206.

[491] Ibid., 210.

of this aspect of Aristotelian metaphysics. The solution the Formula offers is that sin is, indeed, an accidental property rather than a substantial one, as Strigel had argued. However, it is clarified that this accidental property is thorough in its impact upon the human creature, so that free will in spiritual things is no longer intact in the unregenerate person. The contrast between the Formula and its modern interpreters is striking on this point.

The second place where this text addresses metaphysical issues in relation to the Formula of Concord is in Article III, which interacts with Andreas Osiander's view of God's righteousness. This controversy surrounded the nature of justifying faith and its relation to Christ's indwelling in the human person. It is apparent that, as with the previous issue, Arand, Kolb, and Nestingen address this view in a very different manner than does the Formula of Concord. The authors of the former text note that the problem in Osiander's theology was his adoption of a Neoplatonic metaphysic, which differentiates his thought from a Hebraic manner of thinking.[492] It is argued that his view of Luther's theology was guided through his (seemingly errant) presuppositions, of which divine simplicity is identified.[493] The difference between Luther and Osiander is that the former thinker developed a manner of reasoning based on relation and "creative speaking," while the latter was bound by "categories of substance."[494] Justification, for Arand, Kolb, and Nestingen, is described solely with the categories of relation, while Osiander viewed reality as "eter-

---

[492] Arand, *Lutheran Confessions*, 218.

[493] Ibid., 219.

[494] Ibid., 219.

nal ontological substances."⁴⁹⁵ This resulted in Osiander's metaphysical approach to justification, which resulted from a union of the divine and human substance through indwelling, while Luther retained a strictly forensic approach. The problem with this treatment is that while these authors contend that the primary differentiation between Osiander and the Formula of Concord is one of metaphysics, the Formula's authors themselves do not make such a connection.

It is clear that the authors of the Formula are not opposed to writing within the categories of substance, contrary to what Arand, Kolb, and Nestingen imply. This is obvious in that Article I explicitly affirms the essentialist division between substance and accident in Aristotelian philosophy. Further, the authors here speak negatively about Osiander's supposed "scholastic" view of God's essence as simple.⁴⁹⁶ However, these writers all affirm Article I of the Augsburg Confession, which includes divine simplicity in its definition of God. In their refutation of Osiander, the authors of the Formula outline their criticism of his approach to justification as twofold. First, they contend that there is a distinction between justification and the indwelling of God. The Formula contends that justification means, "to declare righteous and free from sins," whereas Osiander associated it with making one intrinsically righteous (FC SD III.17). The problem was not with Osiander's definition of divine indwelling as such, but in his conflation of such an act with justification (FC SD III.28). This leads to a misunderstanding of the relationship between justification and sanctification, which, in turn, can lead to

---

⁴⁹⁵ Ibid., 225.

⁴⁹⁶ Ibid., 218.

burdened consciences (FC SD III.30). The second criticism of Osiander is that he identified redemption solely with the divine nature of Christ, without the human (FC SD III.60). In contrast, the authors of the Formula argued that salvation arises from the work of Christ according to both natures. The Formula's authors never criticize Platonism or argue for a linguistic or relational approach to reality.

What is demonstrated in the treatment of these two sections of the Formula of Concord by Arand, Kolb, and Nestingen is that there are fundamental differences between their approach and that of the authors of the Formula. In both articles addressed by the authors of the twenty-first-century work, extensive criticisms are given of Greek metaphysics. The underlying problem with Strigel's anthropology is identified as his use of the categories of substance and accident. The Formula stands in stark contrast to this, as the use of Aristotelian metaphysics is not only accepted, but praised as an indisputable truth. Arand, Kolb, and Nestingen identify the problem with Osiander's approach to justification, similarly, as his adoption of Greek metaphysical constructs. The Formula does not address these issues at all. The document demonstrates no disagreement with Osiander's metaphysical system, but instead with his construction of the *ordo salutis*, in which the mystical union and sanctification precede justification. The anti-metaphysical bias of some contemporary Lutheran thought has impacted how historical sources are read. This is true, also, of some treatments of the doctrine of God, which similarly oppose classical ontology.

As discussed in the previous chapter, the scholastic thinkers affirm that God is the source of all being in the world, and that as this divine source, he is simple, immutable, and impassible.

This understanding is foundational to the development of the scholastics' respective theological systems. These basic assumptions are challenged by Forde and Bayer, who argue that classical theism is not a biblical concept, but an imposition of metaphysics. In contrast to the scholastics, Bayer argues that biblical theology is in "grave conflict with Greek metaphysics and ontology."[497] To substantiate this thesis, Bayer cites a single biblical text from Hosea 11:7–11, which speaks about God relenting from his anger toward Ephraim and Israel. Bayer understands such texts in a univocal sense, rather than simply by way of anthropomorphism. This text and others demonstrate a genuine change within God himself. Bayer makes several somewhat shocking statements in this regard, stating that God "is not identical with himself; he is not consistent with himself,"[498] and that "God is not consistent but contradicts himself."[499] Bayer views God's unity not as a present ontological reality, but as an eschatological goal.[500] He is unified in the ends for which he is working, toward the unification of all things. This results in a great differentiation between his own view and that of Gerhard (discussed earlier), who describes God's essence largely through an exposition of the doctrine of divine simplicity.

The literature on these subjects is extremely vast, and all of

---

[497] Bayer, *Theology the Lutheran Way*, 188.

[498] Ibid., 188.

[499] Ibid., 104.

[500] Similar ideas are found in several theologians in the twentieth and twenty-first centuries who change the basic meaning of classical divine attributes. See, for example, Jenson, *Systematic Theology*, and Hinlicky, *Crisis of Metaphysics*. More extreme approaches can be found in the process theologians impacted by Alfred North Whitehead.

the particulars are not discussed here. As Bayer's statements regarding metaphysical unity in God are brief, a response need not be that extensive. Here, some problems which arise in that approach are demonstrated briefly. The text which Bayer cites is one of many which speak about change within the divine mind. Often, in Scripture, God is said to relent in his decisions. The division here is not between those who take such texts seriously and those who do not, as Bayer's simplistic explanation might imply. As discussed in the previous chapter, Gerhard, following Aquinas, believed that God is to be understood analogously. Scripture attributes aspects to divinity which are common not to the divine, but to the human nature. This is done due to the limitations of the human mind, because of the fact that a created thing is not able to have a proper grasp of an infinite simple divine nature.[501] This is related to the distinction between archetypal and ectypal theology. Creatures are only capable of derivative knowledge of God, and such derivative knowledge utilizes figures of speech and anthropomorphism. Such a reality is recognized by all commentators, unless one is willing to concede that God the Father has a physical body (Is 59:1) and wings (Ps 91:4). Such a response might seem simplistic, but it demonstrates the fact that a simple citation about an aspect of God does not in itself demonstrate how such a text is to be interpreted. There are several biblical reasons to affirm the basic tenets of classical theism, such as God's unity, immutability, simplicity, and impassibility.

Debates surrounding classical attributes of God cannot be decided by mere proof texting, as some model for God's being

---

[501] Feser, *Five Arguments*, 136.

must be considered in order for the texts themselves to be synthesized. One example of such a difficulty is 1 Samuel 15, wherein God speaks about the fact that he regrets having made Saul king over Israel (1 Sam 15:35). However, within that same chapter, Samuel declares of God that "He is not a man, that He should relent" (1 Sam 15:29). If one believes in consistency within the biblical text, some synthesis of these two concepts *must* be attempted.[502] Other texts which affirm classic attributes are Malachi 3:6, in which God states, "I do not change," and James 1:17, which affirms that "there is no variation or shadow of turning" within God. Such ideas are hard to synthesize with Bayer's contention that God is inconsistent with himself. In a recent book, Jordan Barrett has argued that the scriptural divine names, such as Yahweh, demonstrate classical theistic attributes such as divine simplicity.[503] Another text which is particularly illuminating in this regard is Acts 14:15. While ministering in Lystra, Paul and Barnabas are taken to be gods due to their miracle-working. In their attempt to distance themselves from divinity, Paul and Barnabas say, "We also are men with like passions as you" (KJV). While many modern translations render the text, "the same nature" (NKJV), the actual term used is *homoiopatheis*, which translates literally in the King James rendering. This is significant, because Paul and Barnabas distinguish themselves from God specifically by noting that they have human passions, or emotions. This necessarily

---

[502] See Weinandy, *Does God Change*, for an extensive work on the subject.

[503] Barrett, *Divine Simplicity*, 2017. The literature on simplicity appears to be growing in recent years, with a number of dissertations currently being written that deal with the subject.

makes a strong ontological distinction between the Creator and creatures in relation to passions, thus denoting God's impassibility.[504] These and other texts demonstrate that Bayer's case cannot be made simply by dismissing classical metaphysical notions of the divine attributes as purely Greek, rather than biblical. The scholastic tradition has a strong biblical grounding in its view of God.

The arguments against classical metaphysics given by Forde, Paulson, Bayer, Arand, Kolb, and Nestingen are without solid grounding. They are often dependent upon misunderstandings of essentialism, as is clear especially in Paulson's treatment, wherein he fails to even differentiate Aristotelian and Platonic philosophies. The arguments also fail to account for the biblical data, in which it is assumed that each created thing has a distinctive identity which unites it to other objects of that species. None of these authors attempt to deal with this issue, and Paulson reads into the Genesis narrative his anti-metaphysical bias, which is nowhere apparent in the text at all. It has also been demonstrated that these Radical Lutheran convictions are often applied to the study of historical Lutheran documents, which is not consistent with the teaching of those texts. The Heidelberg Disputation, for example, is often treated in opposition to classical metaphysics, but Platonism is actually affirmed in the philosophical theses in the text. The clearest example of this divergence is Article I of the Formula of Concord, in which the document defends the use of Aristotelian metaphysics, while the interpreters do precisely

---

[504] See Baines's argument for this in *Confessing the Impassible God*, 193–97. This subject has been debated within the last few years in the Association of Reformed Baptist Churches in America.

the opposite. These divergences are further explored through the existential prioritizing of existence over essence.

Existence Precedes Essence

The most fundamental aspect of existential thought is the contention that *existence precedes essence*. This phrase, initially proposed by Sartre, has become a common principle used to define the movement.[505] This is significant for the present project, as a division is apparent between a metaphysic which prioritizes essence and one which prioritizes existence. The prioritization of essence is a presupposition of the scholastic method, whereas it is not in Radical Lutheran sources. It is important to note that in this context, existence has a more specific definition than simply the fact that a thing *is*. Etienne Gilson, for example, has proposed a kind of existentialism in Aquinas, wherein existence has primacy over essence.[506] However, existential thinkers are not using the term *existence* in its Thomistic manner, and thus Gilson should not be considered an existentialist in the sense of the term used here. For the existentialist, existence, instead, is related to one's decisions in the world. The self is not some type of abstract entity whose nature determines action. Instead, one is self-creative. For classical philosophy, there is a distinctive human essence, which is shared between each individual. For the existentialists, this is false, as each person defines his own being through free action. Each of these

---

[505] Barret, *Irrational Man*, 102.

[506] Gilson, *Being and Some Philosophers*. Another more contemporary take on Gilson's existential Thomism is found in Norris Clark's *One and Many*.

thinkers speaks of some kind of a movement from captivity to freedom, in which one's essence is actualized. The nature of such a transition is described in different ways depending upon the philosopher. For Kierkegaard, one must make a leap of faith which is opposed to rational deduction, which leads to a life of freedom.[507] For Heidegger, one makes the transition from inauthentic to authentic existence by recognizing the oppressive systems into which one is thrown and then choosing to live through free individual decision.[508] In whatever ways philosophers categorize the nature of this leap into existence, all agree that there is some kind of existential act which determines essence, rather than the reverse which is proposed by essentialism.

Because of his influence on Rudolph Bultmann, Heidegger's approach to authenticity is perhaps most significant for theology, though Sartre, Camus, and Kierkegaard all posit similar conceptions of such a transition.[509] Heidegger speaks about humans as having been "thrown" into existence. No one chooses to be born, or to be a part of any specific culture or time. The reality of this situation is described as one's "facticity." One's thrownness results in a number of expectations which are placed upon each individual, which, again, are never self-chosen. The actions that one takes are not self-determined, but guided by others, whom Heidegger refers to as "They."[510] This "They" places expectations upon everyone so that decisions are not truly free. One is bound

---

[507] Bretall, *Kierkegaard Anthology*, xxi.

[508] Olson, *Introduction*, 134.

[509] Barrett, *Irrational Man*, 213.

[510] Olson, *Introduction to Existentialism*, 136.

by others, without even recognizing such to be the case. Self-identity is essentially non-existent, as one is simply lost in the masses. This leads to a state of "alienation" from one's own self. This kind of mindless existence under the power of the "They" is *inauthentic* existence. This lack of freedom leads one to despair and anxiety, along with the recognition that death is an inevitability. In order to control such anxiety, one pushes off the thoughts of death, living as if existence is eternal, and continues to find one's identity in factors such as work or culture, avoiding any true understanding of identity. Heidegger proposes a solution to this dilemma through his conception of authenticity.

For Heidegger, humans come to several moments of decision in their lives, and such moments lead to free actions which are self-determinative.[511] A man who was raised in a family of doctors where it is the expectation of all of his family members that he will do the same might come to the realization that he is only on this path due to circumstances outside of himself. He was never truly free in making such a decision. At the point of this recognition, the man is at a moment of crisis. He can simply ignore his discovery, and fall back into the comfortable world of the "They," accepting the norms pressed upon him by family members and thus continue in the occupation laid out before him. This remains a position of inauthenticity. However, he has the ability at that moment to take hold of his own identity, recognizing that he has the ability to make free personal decisions. At this crucial moment, he might then make the decision to disregard the external expectations placed upon him, and then do something different. Perhaps

---

[511] Friedman, *Worlds of Existentialism*, 134.

he rejects his family occupation to pursue art. Yet, even at this point, he can fall back into inauthenticity. He might attend an art school and simply adopt whatever painting techniques are taught by instructors, then living again purely for the "They" of the art world, pursuing whatever norms are placed upon those within it. Life is continually made up of such moments of decision.

John Macquarrie has demonstrated that the basic structures of Heidegger's thought on these points are found in Rudolph Bultmann, and especially in his interpretation of St. Paul. One of the areas of commonality between Heidegger and Bultmann is in their respective interpretations of the world. For the philosopher, the world is a kind of imprisonment, as one's destiny is bound by his own circumstances and culture.[512] This notion is tied to St. Paul's conception of the term *kosmos*, which is not simply a locative phrase, but instead refers to the oppressive forces outside of oneself. For Bultmann, demonic powers are simply a mythological way of explaining such a situation. Macquarrie argues that Paul has a concept of facticity, like Bultmann, wherein one's being-in-the-world limits the possibilities of each individual. This results in a situation of depersonalization, wherein personal identity is absorbed by the masses of society. For the Christian, however, one is freed from the oppressive factors of the *kosmos*, yet one still remains within it. This being-in-the-world expressed by both St. Paul and St. John is one's facticity, and the freedom in Christ over the tyranny of the world is one's possibility.[513] The situation of fallenness, for Bultmann, is not defined by a legal

---

[512] Macquarrie, *Existentialist Theology*, 86.

[513] Ibid., 98.

guilt over sin, but instead, sin refers to a concrete situation in which man is alienated both from God and from one's fellow creatures. Macquarrie refers to sin as an "ontological conception," which is definitional for one's experience in the world.[514] In this existential mode of understanding, Bultmann rejects theological explication through language of substance, seeing, for example, the spirit-and-body dualism in St. Paul not as essential qualities of a human essence, but as two simultaneous existential realities. The spirit is possibility, but the body facticity. This existential examination of fallenness is used by the Radical Lutheran authors.

For Radical Lutheran thinkers, including Forde, Paulson, and Bayer, the primary manner in which inauthentic existence is described is through language of law. In Gerhard Forde's *Where God Meets Man*, he argues strongly against what he describes as the "ladder scheme" which is definitional of scholastic theology.[515] In this conception, the law is defined by a specific set of moral commandments given by God to his creation. This law is eternal in nature as a reflection of God's moral character. The gospel, then, is defined by the law, as a legal exchange. Jesus actively obeys the law on behalf of sinners, and then dies to pay the penalty owed to God by those who have broken it. Forde rejects this scheme for its understanding both of the law and of the gospel. He rejects the notion that the law is something "static and unchangeable,"[516] but he instead defines it as a "voice" which

---

[514] Ibid., 109.

[515] Forde, *Where God Meets Man*, 15.

[516] Ibid., 111.

confronts man throughout life, silenced only in death.[517] In a telling statement, he argues that "the law is not only a specific set of demands as such, but rather in terms of what it does to you."[518] Law is removed from the realm of the metaphysical into the existential. Forde gives a helpful illustration of the difference between these two approaches by speaking of the law as a ladder and a circle. In the scholastic view, the law is like a ladder which one must climb in order to reach God. Sin has removed the possibility from humans of climbing that ladder. Jesus, therefore, comes as a substitute in order to climb the ladder in the place of humanity. Even the gospel, then, includes the concept of the law as a ladder to God. Forde rejects this conception, and instead argues that the law is like a circle which surrounds each individual, and one is unable to escape. Using Sartre's language, Forde declares that the law proclaims: "NO EXIT."[519] Forde, like Bultmann, changes the definition of sin from earlier thinkers; it is not as a violation of divine precepts, but an existential situation in which man finds himself.

This existential approach to the law is followed by other authors. Paulson rejects what he labels the "legal scheme," which is identical with the ladder theology explained by Forde. One important aspect of Paulson's treatment is his explanation of the relationship between the law and God's wrath. Like Forde, Paulson rejects any attempt to define the law as an eternal moral standard. Instead, he defines the law by its association with the wrath of God, arguing that "the

---

[517] Ibid., 15.

[518] Ibid., 15.

[519] Ibid., 36.

law is an expression of God's wrath."[520] It is not simply that God's law has an essence apart from wrath which incurs the anger of God only after sin, but that such wrath is definitional of its nature. Paulson argues that there is no proportionality between the extent of one's sin and the wrath which then corresponds to it.[521] The gospel, then, is radically different from the law, as Christ comes outside of the law itself.[522] What Paulson's portrayal ultimately leads to is a God whose wrath is arbitrary. In scholasticism, it is affirmed that God is perfectly just, and the need to fulfill such justice is behind the substitutionary atonement. In Paulson's scheme, God can hardly be declared just, as his wrath is poured out without any regard to the actual sins which exist in those it affects. He argues that the law is not "blind lady justice," which executes punishment justly upon those who are guilty,[523] and thus it accuses Jesus of sin along with everyone else. Such an approach is incompatible with any contention that God himself is just, as God simply has wrath toward everyone according to the law without any regard whatsoever for their actual sins. The reason Paulson can speak in such a way is because sin is associated with man's existential situation, rather than with a violation of divine commands. Law, wrath, and sin are all descriptive existential terms which define the human situation apart from the gospel. The legal definitions of such concepts is rejected, and there are profound theological implications of this formulation.

---

[520] Paulson, *Lutheran Theology*, 67.

[521] Ibid., 79.

[522] Ibid., 81.

[523] Ibid., 104.

Oswald Bayer also speaks of man's situation under the law in existential terms. He defines this in some detail in his work *Living by Faith: Justification and Sanctification*. For Bayer, the central question of all human existence is that of justification. All people are in need of acknowledgment and affirmation. He categorizes both "being" and "non-being" by way of such acts by others.[524] Use of such a concept of being is Heideggerian in orientation, rather than essentialist. Like Heidegger, Bayer raises the question of why one is existent rather than nonexistent, and he argues that this basic human question seeks an answer through justification by way of others.[525] For Bayer, such a dilemma is always societally conditioned. The human person is never to be isolated, but can be understood only by way of one's relatedness to others. Here, again, a connection with Heidegger is clear, wherein people live not for themselves but for approval in the eyes of others (the "They"). This is the struggle which the doctrine of justification answers. This kind of inauthentic existence, wherein people seek to find acknowledgment through the approval of others, is universal, and authentic existence is that which is achieved through God's act of justification.

Human attempts to solve this need to be mutually recognized are twofold: moral and metaphysical. For Bayer, salvation by law is "justifying doing."[526] Recognition and meaning are sought in moral acts, wherein people prove their right to exist by way of ethical effort. In doing so, one finds meaning in the self, and is unable to truly escape this battle for

---

[524] Bayer, *Living by Faith*, 1.

[525] Ibid., 3.

[526] Bayer, *Theology the Lutheran Way*, 21.

justification. This is connected with the traditional Lutheran understanding of man existing under God's law. The law offers only a justification by doing, but such is an impossibility. The second form of seeking recognition is the study of metaphysics. Bayer sees classic essentialist philosophy as an attempt to achieve justification by way of thinking. Metaphysics seeks to overcome the divisions and difficulties in the world by positing a unified ontological principle.[527] In each of these modes of self-justification, one remains entrenched in guilt. Apart from faith, we "experience the world as the wrath of God."[528] While it would not be accurate to simply say that Bayer's view of God's wrath is one of pure subjectivity, his emphasis on law and wrath tends to be that of an experience of the world, rather than the objective violation of divine law. Throughout Bayer's work, man's situation under the law and the subsequent doctrine of justification are framed existentially.

Forde, Paulson, and Bayer all explain a type of inauthentic existence which has common characteristics with existential philosophy. None of these writers describes the law as the eternal and objective will of God which corresponds to his own nature, as is the contention of Lutheran scholasticism. Sin is not a violation of divine precepts which need to be satisfied in order to appease God's just will. For Forde, life under the law is one of being entrapped by the experience of God's wrath and unable to escape. Paulson follows Forde on this point, arguing that there is no proportionality between God's wrath and human sin. Bayer uses further conceptions of justification

---

[527] Ibid., 22.

[528] Ibid., 30.

not merely as a theological term to describe the imputation of Christ's righteousness, but as a search for meaning. This search for meaning leads one to a place of non-being, where one is dependent upon the acknowledgement of others, often through moral striving. These approaches to divine law are all decidedly existential in orientation. The solution to such a dilemma is also existential in nature, and it promotes a priority of existence over essence as in the classic existential formula. The difference between the Radical Lutheran authors and existential philosophers (and it is certainly no *minor* difference) is that one is released from the inauthenticity of existence not by a free act of human decision, but through the work of God.

For Heidegger, Dasein can make a transition from inauthentic to authentic existence. This is done through a moment of free decision in which one determines not to allow outside forces to define the self by the expectations of the "They." Macquarrie argues that the Christian life, from Bultmann's perspective, might "fairly be called the authentic existence of man."[529] As fallenness results in the loss of one's true being through entrapment in sin and death, the Creator brings man back into being. This is the function of Paul's language of *pneuma* (spirit), which is not an ontological contention regarding the essence of humanity, but instead identifies a way of being in which one is "oriented to God."[530] Here, Bultmann utilizes the concepts in Heidegger but radically changes them into a Christian form. For Heidegger, one turns toward pure nothingness while facing and accepting the reality of death.

---

[529] Macquarrie, *Existentialist Theology*, 137.

[530] Ibid., 138.

The turn in Bultmann is toward God and the promises of life. Such a turn is not Pelagian in orientation, as one might infer from the existential notion of radical freedom. Instead, this conversion occurs by grace. This grace is not a substance or mere status, but an *event* through which Christ meets the hearer in the kerygma and opens up the possibility of true existence.[531] For Bultmann, the saving work of Christ is not so much the past work of redemption, but the event of the present in which the proclamation of Christ gives authentic being by grace.

This conception of grace as event is formulated in Bultmann's unique eschatological approach. The German theologian sets his ideas forth in a series of lectures published under the title *The Presence of Eternity*, in which he formulates a Christian approach to history in relation to other philosophers and historians. Bultmann contends that man is a historical being, related to the past but not bound by it. One is always before an open future, full of possibility.[532] Faith, for the Christian, involves opening oneself up to these new possibilities in Christ. The act of salvation, for Bultmann, is eschatological, as one remains both a time-bound being but is also removed from the world by grace.[533] It is the paradoxical nature of this existence which Bultmann refers to as Luther's *simul iustus et peccator* principle.[534] History, for Bultmann, is always to be described as present history as it relates to the human subject, as one cannot stand objectively as a spectator viewing reality

---

[531] Ibid., 156.

[532] Bultmann, *Eternity*, 141.

[533] Ibid., 152.

[534] Ibid., 154.

outside of personal experience. Instead, history is to be found in a personalized eschatology, wherein Christ opens up the individual for a new free life, not bound by law.[535] Several of these basic conceptions of an eschatological approach to personal history are used by Gerhard Forde.

I have categorized Forde's approach to the law and gospel as a "personalized eschatological" one.[536] While Lutheran scholastics identify both law and gospel as objective historical realities, Forde places them in the category of event. The law is identified with the experience of wrath, and the gospel with that of salvation. In doing this, Forde utilizes an eschatology which is similar to that of Bultmann, emphasizing the dual nature of the individual as one who simultaneously exists in this age (law) and the age to come (gospel). The place in which this idea is explained in the most depth is his text *Justification by Faith: A Matter of Death and Life*.

In this text, Forde argues against the scholastic understanding of the Lutheran doctrine of justification. He speaks about two metaphors which have been used in the exposition of the teaching: the moral or legal, and the death-life.[537] While Forde does not eschew legal terms altogether, he opts for the priority of death-life speech. Forde argues that soon after the Reformation, such terminology was lost and replaced with pure legal language. Forde's opposition to strong legal language arises from his approach to the gospel, which does not include either the satisfaction of justice in the atonement, or an imputation of Christ's fulfillment of the law's require-

---

[535] Ibid., 155.

[536] Cooper, *Lex Aeterna*, 86.

[537] Forde, *Justification by Faith*, 3.

ments to the believer.[538] Since justification does not consist in the imputation of the active and passive obedience of Christ, its essence is not in anything legal, but instead in the act of death and resurrection. For Forde, justification "*is death and resurrection.*"[539] Justification is an event, and in that event the old self dies and the new is raised. This leads to a radical understanding of regeneration, wherein the subject himself ceases to exist. Forde is critical of the legal metaphor in which "the subject is a continuously existing one."[540] He further argues that to "preserve the continuity of the subject" is to kill God himself.[541] These ideas in Forde's treatment demonstrate some important similarities between his thought and that of Heidegger, and also demonstrate some of the profound theological problems with such an approach.

Forde's contention that the death-life metaphor is important in talking about the application of salvation is a rather uncontroversial one. Certainly, the doctrine of regeneration has historically been spoken of in such a manner. However, the way in which he places both the law and the gospel in such a scheme, and particularly justification, demonstrates something beyond the older orthodox contention. Forde is operating from a personalized-eschatological framework which echoes that of Bultmann. Salvation is understood from the perspective of the experience of the subject, rather than through an objective forensic decree based upon Christ's satisfaction of the divine law. This results in an approach

---

[538] Cooper, *Lex Aeterna*, 91.
[539] Forde, *Justification by Faith*, 4.
[540] Ibid., 17.
[541] Ibid., 62.

to law which is existential (defined by its acts upon the subject rather than an inherent essence) and a similarly existential idea of the gospel, which is also identified with its impact in the event of proclamation. Throughout *The Law-Gospel Debate*, Forde criticizes legal approaches as negating the eschatological nature of the gospel. It would be accurate to say that justification, for Forde, results in a kind of authentic existence. The transition to such an authentic eschatological existence does differ from that of Bultmann in an important detail. For Bultmann, though authentic existence is achieved by grace, one must act freely in faith in order for this authentic existence to be received. For Forde, any freedom of the human subject under law is completely negated. This transition, for Forde, is God's act of election—the human is merely bound.[542] This idea of Forde's results in a more Lutheran form of existential teaching than is apparent in Bultmann.

These connections to existentialism may still seem tenuous unless the fundamental dogma of such a movement—namely, that existence precedes essence—can be demonstrated to be found in Forde's writings. The place in which such a prioritization is clear is in Forde's rejection of the continuity of the human subject in the transition from death to life. In an essentialist approach, which is found in the Book of Concord, there is a consistency of a personal human essence which persists throughout life, including a transition into the regenerate state. Forde's denial of any traditional notion of essence is here apparent. The human subject is determined not by any created substance, but instead by an existential act. Certainly, Forde differs with Heidegger and other existential

---

[542] Ibid., 67.

thinkers on the question of exactly who is *doing* that act, but the fundamental conviction remains the same. The theological problems with such a claim are innumerable, and demonstrate the importance of retaining substance language in theological discourse. In Forde's view, since there is no continuity of the subject before and after justification, redemption is simply nonexistent. There is no fundamental "I" who is ever redeemed, but instead an ego which is destroyed and a newly created, differing subject which now exists. This leads to other questions, such as whether this discontinuity relates only to an initial conversion or to the daily actions of repentance. Is the conscious subject consistently changing? Furthermore, this denial of the continuous "I" is at heart a denial of the existence of the soul altogether. Christian philosophers contend for the continuous "I" which is distinct from physical processes as the nature of the soul, which is important in contemporary debates about physicalism and the spiritual nature of the human person.[543] On this point, Forde appears to have agreement with the eliminativists, who argue that consciousness is a mere illusion.[544] In Forde's view, there apparently can be no continuity of a subjective consciousness. Though he himself never draws such conclusions, they seem to be an inevitability in his approach.

Paulson follows Forde on these points. Along with his teacher, Paulson emphasizes the eschatological nature of the gospel, particularly through his elaboration on Luther's *simul*

---

[543] Some great works on this subject are Moreland, *Body and Soul*; Feser, *Philosophy of Mind*; Augros, *Immortal in You*; and Hart, *Experience of God*.

[544] See Churchland, *Neurophilosophy*.

iustus et peccator principle.⁵⁴⁵ The Christian lives simultaneously in both the old aeon (under the law) and the new (under the gospel). This, for Paulson, is definitive in Paul's exposition of the law in Romans 7. Throughout his argument on this topic, Paulson criticizes von Hofmann, Pannenberg, and others who place the law into the context of God's own justification in the process of history.⁵⁴⁶ Rather than in world history, for Paulson, the solution is found in personal history. Paulson notes that Bultmann is the first within liberal theology to understand that in faith, something truly new is brought into being.⁵⁴⁷ However, Bultmann fails to grasp the nature of the *simul* and wrongly imports the notion of a free decision into the concept of conversion.⁵⁴⁸ Paulson's view results in the concept that there are two "yous," which are defined by the law and the Spirit.⁵⁴⁹ Since he rejects the traditional definition of a human as defined by a created essence, the person is defined relationally, either by the law or by Christ. If such is the case, Paulson, like Forde, cannot defend the notion that a single continually existing conscious subject persists from spiritual death to spiritual life. This is why he consistently speaks of regeneration as creation *ex nihilo*, as the new self is discontinuous with the old.⁵⁵⁰ Because of his rejection of the classic Aristotelian substance-accident distinction, Paulson rejects Article I of the Formula in its argument that

---

[545] Paulson, *Lutheran Theology*, 188.
[546] Ibid., 189–91.
[547] Ibid., 191.
[548] Ibid., 192.
[549] Ibid., 196.
[550] Ibid., 157.

sin is an accidental quality, writing, "The sins were not just possessions of mine, but they were *me*."[551] Though Paulson is not as blunt as Forde in stating explicitly that the old human subject ceases to exist in faith, such appears to be the logical conclusion of his approach. If the "I" is identified with sin, then the redeemed and sinless person at the resurrection must be a different "I" altogether. There is thus an "existence precedes essence" ontology in Paulson, wherein the essence of the human person is defined by God's existential act, which occurs in preaching. This act recreates the entire person as a wholly new subject.

Along with Forde and Paulson, Bayer uses some of the same themes in his approach to justification. However, he adds some unique elements related to the place of linguistics in reality; these issues are dealt with in a separate section below. As Bayer describes man's situation of fallenness as a continual attempt to seek affirmation and justification from others, so does his approach to authentic existence before God also use such concepts. In faith, the need to "prove our right to exist" through both justifying thinking and justifying acting is destroyed.[552] In Christ, such a need to achieve affirmation through societal pressures is alleviated. This faith is described as an experience in which such needs are put to death, as one receives the ability to live outside of the self in another.[553] This leads to a new way of living in which one is open to the world, with an acceptance of personal finitude, and is able to live for

---

[551] Ibid., 159.

[552] Bayer, *Theology the Lutheran Way*, 21.

[553] Ibid., 25.

the good of others.[554] In the old sinful way of living, creation is experienced as divine wrath,[555] but it is now experienced as the voice of God addressing his creatures.[556] Bayer's approach here combines several themes inherent in Heidegger's concept of authentic existence. Like the philosopher, Bayer argues that one is free to live outside of the expectations of the world in search of affirmation. He also, with Heidegger, argues that part of such an existence is an acceptance of finitude and death. For Bayer, however, such acceptance only happens through the justifying act of God, rather than through any free decision to live authentically.

As these figures are examined in light of the fundamental existential conviction that "existence precedes essence," it is apparent that important elements of this idea are adopted by the Radical Lutheran authors. In all of them, there is a kind of inauthentic existence which is defined as one's situation under the law. This causes one to seek affirmation from others in ethical performance. The law is defined by its effect in such a situation, rather than by an objective and eternal standard of God. There is a kind of authentic existence, then, which is achieved in faith as the work of God. This is an event wherein God creates faith and frees one to live outside of the law in the new aeon, though the sinful nature lives in the old. The human person is not defined as any particular essence which persists over time, but instead through one's relatedness to God and the law. Due to this concept, one's essence is defined by the act of God in faith that brings the new self into existence. It is

---

[554] Ibid., 35.

[555] Ibid., 30.

[556] Ibid., 28.

in this way that, for the Radical Lutheran authors, existence precedes essence. Some of these same ideas, and in particular the prioritization of event over essence, are apparent in the manner in which revelation and truth are described in these writers.

Truth as Event

Within the scholastic tradition, it is understood that truth is a purely objective reality. A true statement is one which corresponds to something that exists outside of itself. This is consistent with Aristotelian logic, wherein the discovery of truth is a theoretical and scientific enterprise.[557] This conception remained throughout the medieval period and at the beginning of the modern era until the birth of modern philosophy. Since that time, there have been different understandings of truth which have been proposed by philosophers and theologians. While some retain a purely objectivist understanding, others have placed truth solely within the realm of the human subject, wherein there is no real verification of true statements outside of the individual ego. Many have adopted a position which transcends both pure subjectivism and the theoretical understanding of truth taught by the Greeks.[558] This is that of both Heidegger and the Radical Lutheran authors.

For Heidegger, true statements about the world are understood not purely through a theoretical explication of the nature of reality. Instead, truth is understood by way of a

---

[557] See Christopher P. Long, *Aristotle on the Nature of Truth*, 2013.

[558] These positions are chronicled in Chase B. Wrenn, *Truth*, 2014.

thing's *use* to Dasein. John Macquarrie states that Heidegger's perspective views the cosmos not as an objective essence whose laws are to be theoretically discovered, but instead as a "workshop" which man uses for various purposes in the world.[559] Objects are understood only as they are needed in one's own experience, and individual things are viewed in the context of the systems in which they are involved insofar as they impact man's existence. Macquarrie gives the example of a fountain pen to describe the nature of Heidegger's understanding of this point.[560] The fountain pen is composed of a number of different parts, including the material which makes it up and the ink it needs to write. When one pulls out a fountain pen, the person does not sit and contemplate the various pieces and materials which make up that object. Instead, the pen is viewed in terms of its function as an instrument of writing. It is also understood within a particular system: that of writing. Its "essence" for the human subject is its ability to function for the purposes of writing, and the individual parts are only considered in light of such a function. One, for example, has an awareness of the ink when it dries up, as the function is then hampered by such a situation. This is further demonstrated in Heidegger's definition of truth.

Heidegger speaks about truth in an essay titled "The Essence of Truth," which defines the concept concisely for the present discussion. As with his examination of being, Heidegger is not attempting to formulate one theory on this topic in the midst of many others. Instead, he seeks to go behind the

---

[559] Macquarrie, *Existentialist Theology*, 49.
[560] Ibid., 49.

basic philosophical questions which have guided philosophers for generations. While older thinkers posited various theories about exactly how truth relates to the human subject, Heidegger desires to get to the much more basic question, what is truth? In his essay, he explains the older common perspective as that of propositional truth, wherein truth consists in the identification between a concept in the intellect and the reality of the thing which the intellect comprehends. In particular, Heidegger is critical of Aquinas in this regard, arguing that he misunderstands Aristotle. Heidegger labels this aspect of truth as *veritas*, which is then distinguished from *aletheia*, which he perceives to be a more fundamental aspect of the nature of truth. This aspect of truth is defined as "unconcealment," which is an encounter between a person and a being or beings. This unconcealment involves Dasein allowing things to be what they are, rather than imposing oneself upon them. The most significant thing about this definition of truth is, as Vladislav Suvak explains, "something that *happens* . . . an event of *being* (*Ereignis*), which is only *revealed* to us."[561] This definition of truth as *event* rather than *proposition* was highly influential upon Neo-orthodox theology, and consequently, Radical Lutheran authors.

John Macquarrie explains the relationship between Heidegger's concept of truth and theology, especially as it is adapted by Rudolph Bultmann. He notes that proper knowledge of God is not simply theoretical or scientific, wherein one makes a series of propositional statements about deity in the abstract. Instead, he argues, it describes "the knowledge

---

[561] Suvak, *Essence of Truth*, 7.

which is implicit in our faith in God."⁵⁶² Personal history and experience are essential aspects of theological explication. Macquarrie cites Paul Tillich on this point, who says regarding existential theology, "If the word 'existential' points to a participation which transcends both subjectivity and objectivity, then man's relation to the gods is rightly called existential."⁵⁶³ This knowledge is not subjective, because it does not consist merely in a description of one's feelings or personal opinion.⁵⁶⁴ It is real knowledge, based upon an encounter with one who is Other. It is not objective, in that one does not explain God as an uninterested observer as one might view the natural world. God cannot be described as a First Cause in the scholastic sense, for example.⁵⁶⁵ This approach to theological knowledge as encounter is clear in Bayer, Forde, Paulson, and other contemporary Lutheran thinkers. Here, Oswald Bayer's definition of the passive way, which demonstrates Heidegger's conception of truth as event, rather than proposition, is critiqued. In Bayer's approach, however, it is not the concept of truth *itself* which is under discussion, but that of *theological* truth.

For Bayer, theology has often suffered from a false dichotomy between theory and practice. This is especially prevalent in the medieval discussions surrounding Mary and Martha as found in Meister Eckhart and other mystics.⁵⁶⁶ This dichotomy has resulted in a radical divide between theology

---

[562] Macquarrie, *Existentialist Theology*, 56.

[563] Ibid., 57.

[564] Ibid., 50.

[565] Ibid., 63.

[566] Bayer, *Theology the Lutheran Way*, 23.

as a speculative enterprise and ethics, which is then viewed as a distinct discipline. This division has its roots in Aristotle and extends throughout the modern period. In opposition to this, Bayer writes that this theological method is rejected by Luther, who adds the third element of faith into the scheme, which then overcomes such a sharp dichotomy. This is done through the *vita receptiva* (receptive life), which stands apart from both the *vita activa* (active life) and the *vita contemplativa* (contemplative life).[567] As in Heidegger's understanding of truth, this particular approach to theology attempts to move beyond the subject-object divide and places understanding within the category of "event"—particularly through the act of law-gospel proclamation. This approach moves beyond a theoretical and abstract manner of objectified scientific theology, as taught in the scholastics, to one which is concrete, individual, and historically grounded.

Bayer frames his discussion around Gabriel Biel's question of whether theology is a theoretical or practical science.[568] This division between theory and praxis, according to Bayer, is due to Aristotle's privileging of contemplation over action. Luther, in contrast to many scholastic thinkers, argues that theology is primarily practical in nature, rather than theoretical.[569] There is thus a clear break between Luther and the scholastic authors who, in Bayer's opinion, dealt with matters which were overly speculative and not relevant to Christian experience. Bayer argues, however, that Luther does not merely differ in that he argues for the priority of practice over

---

[567] Ibid., 22.
[568] Ibid., 21.
[569] Ibid., 22.

theory in the Aristotelian sense of these terms, but instead, "he breaks out of the traditional Aristotelian binary scheme that distinguishes between theory and practice."[570] This is done through Luther's explication of the passive life of faith. Theology, for Luther, is defined within the context of a God-human relationship in which the person is a passive subject and God the actor. It is spoken of not in the third person as a descriptive enterprise wherein one explains the nature of God, but as first- and second-person statements which occur between God and man.[571] Theology is founded, primarily, within the event that occurs through divine speech.

The concept of the *vita passiva* is found in Luther primarily in his early writings. It is most commonly used in his writings on the Psalms (1519–1521), and it echoes themes expressed in the Heidelberg Disputation.[572] As Bayer recognizes, this distinction comes primarily from Tauler, whom Luther cites as a significant influence. In order to understand the background of Luther's conception of passivity, then, it is necessary that some comments be made regarding Tauler's use of the concept which informs the reformer. The idea of passivity is a consistent emphasis in the sermons of Tauler. He often reminds his hearers that righteousness is not to be gained by external works, but instead through the interior union of God and the soul. One receives God's work by opening oneself up to him, rather than by striving for outward things. In one sermon on the holy family's experience in Egypt, Tauler explains the

---

[570] Ibid., 22.

[571] Ibid., 18.

[572] Ibid., 23.

spiritual meaning of the angel's visit to Joseph.[573] Egypt is interpreted by Tauler as spiritual darkness, in accord with its place in the story of Israel. Joseph, in this narrative, remains in Egypt until the precise moment in which God calls him to freedom found in the land of Israel. Tauler argues that Joseph could not have left such darkness without God's direct intervention. Many seek to find salvation within themselves and through their striving for God. They desire to depart from Egypt apart from God's call. Instead, Tauler contends, one must "give up all the running and outward searching," and instead surrender to God, waiting upon *his* action.[574] In another sermon, Tauler describes further the way of life of those who are devoted to God, stating that they live in "self-surrender" and "refuse to cling to anything of their own, be it their works, their special devotions, what they undertake and what they leave aside."[575] Other themes which appear in Tauler that are echoed by Luther include his criticisms of trust in natural reason[576] and the continual recognition of one's own sinfulness before God,[577] along with a privileging of passivity over active works.[578] Tauler also, in one place, argues that true heartfelt repentance results in the immediate forgiveness even of "a hundred or a thousand mortal sins" when receiving the Lord's Supper.[579] Parallels between the

---

[573] Tauler, *Sermons*, 43–45.
[574] Ibid., 43.
[575] Ibid., 47.
[576] Ibid., 70.
[577] Ibid., 71.
[578] Ibid., 72.
[579] Ibid., 110.

two thinkers on these points are clear. While one cannot argue for an exact identification between Tauler and Luther on the concept of passivity, an understanding of Tauler helps to identify the nature of the *vita passiva* as Luther understands it.

The problem with Bayer's approach to passivity in Luther's thought is not in his insistence on Luther's use of the concept, but rather the implications drawn from it. For Bayer, the passive way stands in stark contrast to any notion that theology is a science. Bayer argues that in Luther's approach, faith—as a work in which one is passive—is itself theology.[580] As such, theology is "neither knowledge nor action."[581] This, then, is the basis for Bayer's rejection of theological metaphysics, as he contends that both metaphysics and morality are "radically destroyed" by this passive way.[582] This leads to his dismissal of classical understandings of God as a unifying metaphysic.[583] Bayer's proposal of the *vita passiva* places Luther in a strong contrast to later scholastic thinkers in this regard, who explicate doctrine as a form of knowledge. Bayer cites Gerhard as an example of one who divorced theology and practice, though not to the extent as would occur in later thinkers.[584] The question to be addressed here is whether Luther's passive approach to theology does indeed present an alternative manner of theologizing to that practiced in the age of orthodoxy.

---

[580] Bayer, *Theology the Lutheran Way*, 26.

[581] Ibid., 24.

[582] Ibid., 25.

[583] Ibid., 26.

[584] Ibid., 12.

In the first volume of his *Evangelical Lutheran Dogmatics*, Adolf Hoenecke presents a concise summary of the nature of theology according to Lutheran scholasticism. In describing the essence of theology, he notes that the term is used in a twofold sense. In its most proper manner of speaking—its *original sense*—theology is practical, as an aptitude created in the soul by the Holy Spirit through means of the word and sacraments.[585] It is important that in this definition, theology is defined primarily *not* as knowledge, but as a divine work. It would be accurate to identify such a perspective as an adaptation of Luther's *vita passiva*. Hoenecke further explains that theology is *habitus* rather than *doctrina*, and that the presentation of theology in a scientific and structured form is an accidental, rather than essential, characteristic.[586] Theology is not defined as theory, but its proper end is practice, which includes the application of salvation and the outworking of sanctification. Hoenecke gives further explication to this idea in his contention that theology is possible only for the regenerate person.[587] While an unsaved individual might explain propositional knowledge of God correctly, this is not true theology. Such a person is capable only of *notitia mere litteralis* (merely literal knowledge), rather than *notitia spiritualis* (spiritual knowledge).[588] This is the place, for example, for natural theology, which imparts truths about God without resulting in salvation. True theology is a product of divine illumination, rather than mere reason or observation

---

[585] Hoenecke, *Lutheran Dogmatics*, I:281.

[586] Ibid., I:283.

[587] Ibid., I:286.

[588] Ibid., I:286.

of the natural world. This illumination is twofold. First is the illumination which occurs from the Spirit's indwelling. This is something of which only the regenerate are capable. Second is pedagogical illumination, which is the work of the Spirit from without that may not lead to regeneration due to human resistance.[589] In each of these types of illumination, God is the one who imparts true knowledge about himself which cannot be achieved merely by the rational capacity of human creatures. This all demonstrates that Luther's fundamental conception of theology's rootedness in the passivity of faith was not abandoned in the scholastic era. The implications Bayer draws from such an idea are not present in these authors.

There is, in the Lutheran scholastics, no opposition between the *vita passiva* and the explication of doctrinal content in a systematic manner. Contemplation, faith, and virtue are all bound up as essential aspects of the Christian life, not to be divorced from one another. Contemplation of divine truth and its exposition through systematic categories, which Bayer criticizes as abstract, is described by Hoenecke as theology in a *transferred* sense.[590] It is in this sense that theology can be called something objective, wherein the truth of propositional statements is independent of the human subject explaining such ideas.[591] It is only in this secondary sense that theology can be described as a science, with a recognition of the centrality of the primary definition of the term. With this being said, the scholastics do not reject discussions of metaphysics or of the divine attributes in general, which Bayer sets in

---

[589] Ibid., I:287.

[590] Ibid., I:282.

[591] Ibid., I:282.

opposition to the *vita passiva*. Certainly, the Lutheran orthodox authors do not argue for contemplation as an end in itself, as the aim of theology is always practical in nature. It is described as twofold: the salvation of man (the intermediate purpose), and the glory of God (the ultimate purpose).[592] However, they certainly view God as a unifying element of reality. This is why God is always identified throughout dogmatic topics as both the primary efficient cause and the final end of all things. His own being is the beginning and end of all things, just as the apostle Paul writes: "For in Him, and to Him, and through Him, are all things" (Rom 11:36). In light of such assertions, it is hard to defend Bayer's notion that there is no metaphysical unity in the world.

Bayer's definition of the *vita passiva* places this method in contrast to classical metaphysics. It is under this topic that Bayer rejects the notion that "everything individual and particular has the general as its basis," thus voicing disagreement with both Plato's and Aristotle's essentialism.[593] It is here that understanding Tauler's conception of the *vita passiva* is important. As argued above, Luther's thoughts on this topic are largely drawn from Tauler. What is important about Tauler, however, is that he argues from a distinctively Neoplatonic perspective. For the mystic, there is no inherent divorce between Greek thought and the passive life of faith. In fact, the latter is tied very much to the former. In Tauler's thought, one's passivity before God is part of self-denial, which is the beginning of one's path to unification with God.[594] Sin, in

---

[592] Ibid., I:289.

[593] Bayer, *Theology the Lutheran Way*, 26.

[594] Tauler, *Sermons*, 52.

essence, is selfishness, which alienates one from God, who is the source of life. Salvation, then, is the act of turning away from self, and instead the opening of oneself to God. Tauler describes the goal of the Christian life with these words: "[the soul] will turn into itself to sink down and be immersed and melted into the pure, divine, simple, and innermost core, where the sublime spark of the soul flows back to the source from which it sprang."[595] This demonstrates a perichoretic movement of the soul, wherein God is born in the soul, which then leads one into union with the Father.[596] Like Plotinus, Tauler views God as the source of all being. All things emanate from him, and salvation involves reunification with him, which at times can result in ecstatic experience—though he never describes his own life in such terms.[597] There is no clearer proponent of metaphysical unity in the world than Tauler.

The fact that Tauler held together a passive spirituality and Neoplatonic essentialism is irrelevant to the present thesis if it can be proved that Luther held to the former, but rejected the latter. This is Bayer's assumption. However, such a divide cannot be substantiated. There is no indication whatsoever in Luther's work that he disagreed with the metaphysical unity assumed by Tauler or other German mystics who influenced his thought. It is true, certainly, that such Neoplatonic language was not the aspect of their writings which Luther most admired. However, it is hard to imagine that Luther would have reprinted and given such unrelenting praise to

---

[595] Ibid., 73.
[596] Ibid., 106.
[597] Ibid., 31.

both the *Theologica Germanica* and Tauler's sermons had strong disagreements on these central points been apparent to him. It is also noteworthy that Luther's language of the *vita passiva* appears early in his career, at precisely the time that he was actively promoting Tauler's writings, and after he had *defended* Platonic metaphysics over against Aristotelian scholastic thought at the Heidelberg Disputation. For Bayer's thesis to be demonstrated, it must be proven that Luther moved away from the Platonic leanings of the Heidelberg Disputation in 1518 sometime prior to his 1519 lectures on the Psalms. Until such a departure is proven, it can be assumed that his convictions on such a fundamental matter did not shift within that year.

Bayer uses the *vita passiva* in Luther's theology as a means to dismiss the concept of theology as a science, or an objective study of propositional, supposedly abstract doctrinal statements. Instead, theology is essentially an act which involves both subject and object. The object—God—reveals himself through dialogue with the human person, and this interaction constitutes theology. It is clear that Bayer does not attempt to make theological truth purely subjective, as a description of mere human experience of feeling. However, what Bayer does do, like Heidegger, is shift the focus of truth from propositional statements which correspond to reality outside of the intellect, to an event. While for Heidegger, this event involves the human subject allowing other objects to be as they are unconcealed before him, for Bayer, this event is one in which God, rather than the free decision of the subject, is active. However, despite these important differences, Bayer affirms Heidegger's shift from truth as proposition to event. The scholastics, along with Luther, promote a more balanced perspective, in which revelation is both propositional and practical. The Lutheran orthodox thinkers affirm an objective revelation which consists in propositional content about reality, while also arguing that theology, in its most proper sense, is done solely by the regenerate. Thus, Bayer's attempt to emphasize the passivity of theology in Luther's thought is able to coincide with classical metaphysical convictions, without the apparent contradiction seen by Bayer.

Existentialism: Conclusions

It has been demonstrated that some of the fundamental tenets of existential thought are utilized by Radical Lutheran authors, including Gerhard Forde, Oswald Bayer, and Steven Paulson. Alongside Heidegger, each of these authors attempts to define reality in a historically oriented manner rather than in discussion of abstract essences. As existential philosophers reject the strong essentialism of both Plato and Aristotle, Forde, Bayer, and Paulson argue against the same substantialist convictions as they are taught by Protestant scholasticism. Though these thinkers differ on some particulars, they are unified in their rejection of essence as the starting point of philosophy and the means by which God's nature is to be exposited.

One area in which essentialist language is firmly rejected is in the classical definitions of God common in both Greek antiquity and earlier Christian theology. In particular, divine simplicity and impassibility are dismissed in favor of a God who is himself impacted by the process of history. The cross impacts God's nature itself. Older attempts, such as that of Gerhard, to define God by way of the attributes which are associated with classical theism, are rejected as remnants of a theology of glory. Theology is explained not as theoretical, but as existential, thus putting discussions of God's attributes in a secondary position. It was demonstrated that such rejections are simplistic, and none of the writers engage in any substantial amount of exegetical argumentation or interaction with proponents of classical theistic concepts. They also fail to explain that notions such as divine simplicity are taught within the Augsburg Confession and stand behind the writings of Luther alongside later theologians in the Lutheran tradition.

Alongside the doctrine of God, Radical Lutheran authors identify law and gospel by their existential impacts upon the sinner rather than in view of an objective essence. They differ from the Lutheran scholastics, who affirm the *lex aeterna* as an objective set of divine commandments which retain significance through the eschaton. This Fordean existential approach aligns with Heidegger's distinction between ontical and ontological inquiry, in which the former explains facts, and the latter, the significance of such ideas to the individual. While scholasticism first emphasizes the essence of a doctrine (such as the law, being the eternal will of God) and then explains its function in light of such a definition (the law's three uses, for example), Radical Lutheranism instead defines essence by function. The difficulties of such an approach become clear in the view of the atonement promoted by Gerhard Forde, in which its significance is almost completely in the human subject. There is no objective transfer of human guilt to Christ in his death, and the atonement itself is not necessary for God to grant forgiveness to the sinner. Another problem is that the essential goodness of the divine law is downplayed when it is identified purely with wrath and sin.

The classical approach avoids such problems, which inevitably arise in this schema.

Furthermore, these biases against real-essentialism are apparent in the historical work of thinkers with such convictions. It was demonstrated that Kolb, Arand, and Nestingen often criticize essentialism with the impression that the authors of the Formula of Concord shared such critiques. This claim leads to a belief that the theological errors of Osiander and Flacius were fundamentally philosophical rather than theological. Yet, in the primary sources, there is no trace of a rejection of their chosen philosophical framework. Instead, the Formula of Concord accepts Aristotelian metaphysics as indisputably true. The same bias is clear in Oswald Bayer, who cites classical metaphysics as an example of the supposed "theology of glory." However, in the Heidelberg Disputation itself, Luther affirms Platonic metaphysics, and thus most certainly does not identify such with a theologian of glory. These sources must, instead, be read in view of their own statements regarding classical metaphysics, and when such is done, it is apparent that their evaluation is not as negative as modern commentators assume.

Another area in which Radical Lutheran authors follow existential thinkers is in their discussion of life under sin as a kind of inauthentic existence, and the gospel as leading one to authentic existence. As was demonstrated, Forde uses language directly from Sartre's famous play, stating that the law is a circle which surrounds the individual and declares, "NO EXIT." The law is identical with existential dread rather than an objective set of demands. These same concepts are used by Paulson, who is similarly critical of the *lex aeterna*, and Oswald Bayer, who speaks of a life of self-justification before others as one of non-being in search of validation of existence. In each of these authors, the gospel brings an end to this dilemma and to the law altogether. There is, as in Bultmann, a personalized-eschatological approach to Christian existence, as one lives under the old aeon (law) and the new (gospel) simultaneously. Forde's idea of justification is placed within this framework.

Finally, these thinkers privilege the category of "event" over that of "essence," which mirrors Heidegger's notion of truth in some important ways. This prioritization is clear in Bayer's theological methodology, which he labels the "*vita passiva*." This method, supposedly taken from Luther, gets rid of a strong divide between subject and object, as well as theoretical theology and ethics. This passive way has its center not in abstract propositional truths as in a science, but in the act of law-gospel proclamation, which is an event occurring between God and the sinner. This notion is discussed further in the section on linguistic philosophy below.

While this present work is critical of existential philosophy, it is to be admitted that not all of the elements of existential thinking as used by these thinkers are wrong. Certainly, there is a strong existential element to Christian theology, and Lutheranism in particular. Philosophers have argued that the movement has its root in St. Augustine, Martin Luther, and even Thomas Aquinas. It is no secret that leading up to the Reformation itself was a kind of existential crisis in Luther, which led to his discovery of the Pauline doctrine of justification by faith. From a personal perspective, the law often appears to be identical with wrath, and the gospel certainly does lead to a new kind of existence which is free from concerns of self-justification. However, the fundamental rejection of the priority of essence leads to numerous problems, and the existential system as a whole is inadequate in explaining several theological truths. The first is that in this view, there is no ontological basis for the law as command. Though these authors all defend the goodness of the law, such is hard to affirm while identifying it purely with the experience of wrath. The goodness of God himself is in question if he does not act justly in giving punishment which is proportional to sin, as Paulson argues. Second, one simply must adopt an essentialist metaphysic to have any unified conception of the continually existing subject. If personhood is defined primarily by an act, whether that be a human or divine one, then there is no valid basis by which one can affirm that redemption is a reality at all. Without an ego which survives the transition from wrath to grace, the category of death and resurrection has replaced that of redemption, rather than supplementing it. Third, the notion that theology is not a science in *any* sense has profound implications for the work of the theologian, as well as for one's approach to biblical inspiration. For theological truth to have any objective validity outside of the human ego, it *has* to be scientific and propositional in some sense. In short, without a substance-ontology as its root, these existential ideas are completely inadequate in giving any comprehensive theological system.

5

Implications for Contemporary Issues

Introduction

The major theoretical argument as to the theological superiority of the classical Lutheran scholastic approach over modern methods had now been concluded. Here, the practical implications of the dissonance between these approaches to Christian thought are explained in light of issues facing the church today. In this final chapter, the research and conclusions of the study are summarized and explained. Following this, a final research question is answered with a study of three particular areas in which the modern church is impacted by divergent theological approaches. After this is a section on further areas to be explored regarding this subject, followed by a final conclusion to the work presented here.

The question answered in this chapter is, *What are the implications of the loss of the scholastic method in the contemporary church?* The importance of theological distinctives is never purely theoretical, as these ideas have an impact upon ministry in which the local church is engaged, whether congregants are aware of this or not. An entire monograph could be written on these practical differences, but such a comprehensive discussion is not possible here. Some of these questions will, however, be addressed in more detail in the further volumes of this series. In order to explain the issues adequately, three practical implications of the Radical Lutheran method which are among the most significant have been selected. First, the nature of Lutheran identity is explored, and it is demonstrated that the nature of what Lutheranism is differs fundamentally in these two dissonant approaches. Second, the discipline of apologetics, which is entirely dismissed by some Radical Lutheran authors, but is an important aspect of scholastic theology, is discussed. Third, the contemporary debates surrounding gender in the church are engaged in light of both methods, and it is demonstrated that essentialism is a necessity in defending male and female as distinct genders created by God. Prior to this, however, the insights of the study thus far are summarized.

Major Insights Gleaned from This Study

Throughout this study thus far, the theological and philosophical foundations of both the Lutheran scholastic method and that of Radical Lutheranism have been explained in response to the primary problem posed at the beginning of this study. Following this, three subsidiary questions have been addressed in each chapter, and a final question is answered here. Prior to engaging in the practical implications of the dissonance between these two approaches, the conclusions of each previous chapter are explained in view of each research question, as this study comes to an end.

The first of the subsidiary research questions that was answered was, *What is the current state of scholarship concerning theological methodology within the Lutheran tradition?* It was demonstrated that there are three primary categories into which most contemporary Lutheran work on theological method can be placed: the Radical Lutheran, the confessional with Radical Lutheran influence, and the scholastic. The method of Radical Lutheranism was explained in the works of three primary authors: Gerhard Forde, Oswald Bayer, and Steven Paulson. These authors are not strictly confessional, but instead divorce the theology of Luther from the later tradition, especially from seventeenth-century Protestant scholasticism. These writers function on the basis of certain aspects of both existential and linguistic philosophy, while rejecting several fundamental tenets of essentialism. The second category of authors hold to a strict view of confessional subscription and are thus not as willing to reject the era of Lutheran thought that follows the sixteenth-century Reformation. However, they are still highly critical of several elements of classical Western philosophy. The writers discussed were Robert Kolb, Charles Arand, and William S. Schumacher. The third approach to theological method discussed was that of scholasticism. This approach is not as popular among Lutheran writers in the modern church as are the other two approaches. The most vocal proponent of this perspective within the Lutheran tradition in recent years was Robert Preus, who defended the validity of seventeenth-century categories through his study of the primary sources of that era. It was demonstrated that this method has been revived in broader Protestantism, and especially in the Reformed church through the writings of Richard Muller. This then led to the second question regarding the foundations of scholasticism.

In the following chapter, I asked, *What are the theological and philosophical foundations of the Lutheran scholastic method?* It was demonstrated that Lutheran thinkers adopted many of the metaphysical convictions that were prominent in the medieval church. In particular, the real-essentialist philosophies of both Plato and Aristotle were used to varying degrees in order to explain certain scriptural truths. Both of these philosophical systems were explained in relation to Lutheran authors who used them. Though many Radical Lutheran authors resist this conclusion, Platonism was Luther's own favored philosophy, though he did not explore this extensively. In opposition to certain caricatures of the reformer, Luther was not in opposition to reason or philosophy, but instead to their misuse. The second generation of Lutherans, including Martin Chemnitz and the other authors of the Formula of Concord, utilized some of Aristotle's metaphysical categories. His definition of causation was used by Melanchthon, and the distinction between substance and accidental properties is explicitly taught in the Formula of Concord. Later scholastics, such as Johann Gerhard, followed the Formula here and tended to favor the use of Aristotle's categories, though they also borrowed from elements of Neoplatonism, especially as taught by St. Augustine. These Neoplatonic elements generally are found within devotional writing, though they occasionally appear in dogmatic texts as well. In summary, the answer to the question posed here is that the foundation of the Lutheran scholastic method is a scripturally based theology which accepts a strong metaphysical essentialism and a classical approach to God's nature.

The third question answered was, *What are some of the contemporary challenges to the scholastic method within Lutheranism?* This section also included a response to such challenges. The philosophical underpinnings of the Radical Lutheran method were explained as differing from those of the scholastics. The Radical Lutheran authors draw from a variety of movements, including existentialism, speech-act theory, relational ontology, and Hume's notion of causation. Though they differ on certain points, each of the authors discussed rejects the fundamental nature of essence as a category in which the theologian should be engaged. They argue instead that reality is to be defined by language and relation. Essence is, at most, a secondary category which flows out of the others.

It was demonstrated that these newer foundations are inadequate both scripturally and theologically. While certain insights of these modern thinkers are beneficial, they cannot properly stand without the foundation of classical metaphysics. Particular areas of theology have been addressed wherein the Radical Lutheran method does not allow for a proper understanding of the scriptural data. One is the doctrine of God, in which Forde, Paulson, and Bayer all depart from classical theism. The traditional incommunicable attributes of simplicity, immutability, and impassibility are all either modified or rejected. In scholastic thought, however, these notions are both accepted and defended. The second area in which the Radical Lutheran approach demonstrates its flaws is in anthropology. Due to both the relational and linguistic categories which replace that of essence, these authors adopt a form of Flacianism and have no accounting for the continuance of the human subject from sin unto redemption. The scholastics stand more in line with Article I of the Formula of Concord, noting that each person contains a human essence, as well as accidental attributes. Due to this, they avoid the problems which arise among Radical Lutheran authors. Finally, the rejection of Aristotelian language of causation has allowed Forde, Bayer, and Paulson to reject the *ordo salutis*, and consequently leads to an anemic doctrine of sanctification, wherein the act of renovation is almost synonymous with justification. In contrast, the scholastics account for all of the biblical data regarding the various aspects of salvation, as well as the reality of progress in sanctification. In all of these ways, the Radical Lutheran method has been demonstrated to be inadequate. The theoretical argument has thus concluded as to the veracity of one method over the other. Here, the practical implications of this dissonance are engaged.

The fourth and final research question, which follows the other three, is, *What are the implications of the loss of the scholastic method in the contemporary church?* This question is answered here in connection with three subjects: Lutheran identity, the use of Christian apologetics, and the nature of gender as a created reality. As these issues are discussed, it is clear that the inadequacies of the Radical Lutheran approach have important implications in the practical life and ministry of the church. First is Lutheran identity, which is a foundation for the others.

Lutheran Identity

The question of Lutheran identity has been asked throughout the centuries following the Reformation of Martin Luther. In the sixteenth century, questions were raised about a number of theological issues, which resulted in the writing of the Book of Concord, which, for a time, was broadly understood as the definitive statement of Lutheran identity. In the eighteenth century, strong divisions arose within the Lutheran church in Germany between those who promoted the scholastic theology of the seventeenth-century textbooks, and followers of the Pietist movement begun by Philip Jacob Spener.[598] While the former viewed Lutheran identity primarily in its doctrinal distinctives, the latter concerned itself mostly with matters of the heart and morality. The following century had further divides as Protestant Liberalism arose, and several significant thinkers began to downplay the theology taught in the Lutheran Confessions. In America, Samuel S. Schmucker argued for an "American Lutheranism" which contained a modified version of the Augsburg Confession that conceded to the Reformed view on the Lord's Supper.[599] C. F. W. Walther, Adolph Hoenecke, Charles Krauth, and others argued against Schmucker in favor of a strong confessionalism with roots in the scholastic tradition. Like these previous centuries, the twentieth also had its own questions raised by churches of the Reformation which continue to guide conversations in the twenty-first century about exactly what it means to be a Lutheran.

The twentieth century was a time of theological change and contention for a number of reasons. Protestant Liberalism, which was influential in past generations, became less prominent after both world wars, as Neo-orthodoxy became an influential force within the church. Theologians

---

[598] Shantz, *Introduction to German Pietism*, 15–41.

[599] Gritsch, *History of Lutheranism*, 189–99.

such as Dietrich Bonhoeffer and Gustaf Wingren promoted certain elements of Neo-orthodoxy, while taking the theology of Luther much more seriously than those influenced by Schleiermacher.[600] The last century was one in which Luther studies gained prominence due to the influence of the Luther Renaissance of Karl Holl. Yet, these studies of Luther generally neglected later orthodox writers, and instead sought to define Lutheranism by its originator. Another important factor in Lutheran identity in the twentieth century was the rise of the ecumenical movement.[601] Especially since the Second Vatican Council, interest grew in finding areas of agreement between Lutheranism and Roman Catholicism, especially as both fought the common enemy of secularism in the West. This led to joint discussions on a variety of topics, one result of which was the *Joint Declaration on the Doctrine of Justification,* published in 1999, which claimed agreement on the long-divisive issue. The Finnish approach to Luther has similarly been used to build ecumenical bridges with the Eastern Orthodox tradition.[602] Others have reacted strongly against this trend by emphasizing the distinctive nature of Lutheran thought, rather than its shared heritage with other Christian traditions. The Radical Lutheran authors generally emphasize discontinuity, especially as they reject classical theism and place the law/gospel distinction in a central position. A final division among those who claim the name Lutheran has arisen within the twenty-first century surrounding issues of sexuality and gender identity. Here,

---

[600] Gritsch, *History of Lutheranism*, 228–33.

[601] Ibid., 239–44.

[602] See Mannermaa, *Christ Present in Faith.*

some proposals regarding the identity of the Lutheran church are discussed, and it is demonstrated that the consequences of Radical Lutheran thought on this topic are damaging to Lutheranism's identity in the twenty-first century.

The Radical Lutheran author who speaks most directly about Lutheran identity is Steven Paulson, especially in his book *Lutheran Theology*. Throughout this text, Paulson defines the Lutheran church almost exclusively by its article of justification—particularly his unique understanding of the teaching. The text sets itself up as an attack on all that humans deem to be valuable. In particular, Paulson criticizes the notion of virtue and its centrality in Christian thought in the early centuries. For Paulson, Christianity is not the search for virtue, but the end of it.[603] This position includes a harsh critique of patristic approaches to the Christian life which viewed the lives of Moses and others as exemplars of the path from sin to virtue. Throughout the text, Paulson repeatedly argues against patristic thought on a number of points, such as the *non-assumptus* principle of the Cappadocians, arguing instead that Christ assumes sin.[604] Augustine, he purports, misunderstood the nature of God's law, being guilty of the supposed legal scheme that Paulson rejects.[605] He also criticizes the medieval tradition, arguing that theology is not actually a "collection of doctrines" as the scholastics stated, but instead involves preaching the words of law and gospel.[606] Theology should not include the setting forth of the nature of God first,

---

[603] Paulson, *Lutheran Theology*, 2–3.

[604] Ibid., 103.

[605] Ibid., 71.

[606] Ibid., 61.

but instead should begin with the distinction between law and gospel.[607] A further note is that Paulson engages most topics in a novel manner, rejecting previous interpretations. An example of this is the one cited above regarding the nature of the first sin, which Paulson identifies as an attempt to do metaphysics apart from created objects. The point is that when Paulson engages writers prior to Luther, his approach is generally polemical. The overall tone of his writing is that Lutheran theology is diametrically opposed to other traditions. His view would hardly be labeled an ecumenical one.

This opposition proposed by Paulson is toward not only patristic and medieval writers, but also the seventeenth-century scholastics. Paulson accuses them, likewise, of teaching theology as a set of propositions, rather than as the living words of law and gospel.[608] They were wrong to utilize Aristotle in theological formulations. He identifies, as one example, the notion that faith has a twofold energy: receptive and operative. The two powers of faith correspond to justification and renovation, respectively. For Paulson, this is wrong because the idea relies upon an Aristotelian idea of cause and effect.[609] As demonstrated in the previous chapter, this criticism is based on a complete misunderstanding of what is meant when the scholastics speak of faith as the cause of justification. Another problem that Paulson identifies in post-Reformation Lutheranism is that these writers believed that God's wrath was proportionate to one's sin. They mistakenly argued that the death of Christ was necessary for God to

---

[607] Ibid., 29.

[608] Ibid., 61.

[609] Ibid., 60.

maintain his justice according to the divine law.[610] It is this notion of the eternal law, in particular, which guided the scholastics in their theological formulation, which Paulson rejects. He defines the history of Lutheranism as "attempts to bring the law back into the Christian life."[611] This leads to his definition of Lutheranism.

For Paulson, Lutheranism is at heart a preaching movement.[612] He rejects other proposals for identifying the Lutheran Reformation as one tradition in the church catholic, a theological proposal to the whole church, or a mere ethnic particularity in Western Europe. This preaching movement is identified with the proclamation of law and gospel. In essence, then, Lutheranism is defined by law and gospel. However, what Paulson means by law is not how the idea was understood in earlier authors, as an eternal order which reflects God's nature. Instead, the law is God's voice of accusation.[613] The gospel, similarly, is not a doctrinal statement about God's justice and its satisfaction through the cross. It is the words "I forgive you" as a performative utterance. The manner in which Paulson frames Lutheran identity is problematic at best.

The first place where Paulson's proposal has serious flaws is in its sectarian leanings. The Lutheran Reformers themselves, though certainly offering important differentiating perspectives on law and gospel, the two kingdoms, and other doctrines, were concerned to demonstrate the catholicity

---

[610] Ibid., 11.

[611] Ibid., 4.

[612] Ibid., 5.

[613] Ibid., 2–5.

of the movement. The *Augsburg Confession* begins with a traditional exposition of the attributes of God, including his simplicity. The entire Book of Concord contains citations of the church fathers alongside Scripture to demonstrate the validity of their perspectives. Martin Chemnitz spends his multi-volume criticism of the Council of Trent explaining the views of the church fathers in defense of Luther's reforms. Johann Gerhard frequently cited both patristic and medieval theologians in his *Theological Commonplaces*. While Paulson might protest that he affirms the fathers on certain issues, the tenor of his work is one of discontinuity rather than continuity. If the Lutheran movement is solely concerned with preaching, as Paulson suggests, and if that preaching is connected to Paulson's own particular understanding of law and gospel (which apparently most other Lutherans have gotten wrong), then it is quite a small sampling of individuals in the history of the church who have rightly understood Christian theology. This leads to immense difficulties in building ecumenical relations with people of other Christian traditions, or even within Lutheranism itself.

    The second major problem with Paulson's view is that one singular theologian (Luther) is given an authoritative position in Christian theology. Paulson rejects several elements of the Lutheran Confessions which teach both the third use of the law and the *lex aeterna* and thus does not define the Lutheran movement by its primary documents. His dismissive view of post-Reformation Lutheranism also leads him to define the movement by something other than its entire historical tradition. What Paulson is left with is simply Luther as an isolated figure (and Melanchthon to an extent). While the reformer certainly has a central role in the tradition which bears his name, there is a danger in exalting Luther above all other figures in the history of Christian theology. A confessional approach allows for balance and catholicity.

Another problem with the Radical Lutheran approach to Lutheranism, which extends far beyond Paulson, is the way in which the realities of sanctification or new obedience are downplayed or even rejected altogether.[614] As Gerhard Forde states, "sanctification is thus simply *the art of getting used to justification.*"[615] In general, these authors reject any emphasis upon the Christian's works as either a cooperative effort or something to be preached on. This is not to say that Forde or Paulson denies the reality of good works altogether, as they both confess good works to be the result of the free proclamation of the gospel. Yet this obedience is purely spontaneous. The law functions only in its civil use to prod individuals unto obedience, but there is no guidance for the Christian under God's law in a traditional sense. In some approaches to sermon-writing in this tradition, it is argued that the law is to be preached in its condemnatory sense, followed by a bold act of gospel proclamation.[616] There is no proclamation of law to follow the gospel. This notion flows out of Gerhard Forde's popular essay "Radical Lutheranism," where the movement gets its name.[617] In this article, Forde argues that in light of challenges to the Lutheran doctrine of justification, the church should become more radical in its

---

[614] My books *Lex Aeterna* and *Hands of Faith* both deal extensively with this topic. Also see Biermann, *Case for Character*.

[615] Forde, *Preached God*, 226 (emphasis original).

[616] See Grimenstein, *Lutheran Primer for Preaching*.

[617] Forde, *More Radical Gospel*, 3–16.

exposition of justification apart from works. This radicality includes a neglect of the reality of renovation, progress in faith, and new obedience.

This attack on moral approaches to the Christian life also includes criticisms of the function of reason and philosophy in theology, as discussed extensively in the previous two chapters. One of the criticisms leveled against Lutheranism from the very beginnings of the Reformation up to today is that its theology promotes antinomianism. Alongside this, Lutheran thought is portrayed as anti-rational. The Radical Lutheran view plays into both misconceptions, leading to a Lutheranism which is reductionistic and devoid of central categories and themes within broader Christian thought. A read of Gerhard Forde's essay in the volume *Christian Spirituality* gives the impression that the difference between the Lutheran tradition and others is that those others all believe in sanctification and Lutherans do not! The point here is not to say that the Lutheran tradition should simply capitulate its doctrine to other traditions for the sake of a false ecumenicity. However, it is to say that Luther's unique insights can be placed within a broader doctrinal system in which there is agreement beyond one particular part of the church. While disagreements between traditions on these questions of the relationship between justification and sanctification remain, it should at least be acknowledged that both realities exist and are important. These flaws within the Radical Lutheran view of Lutheran identity as found in both Paulson and Forde are compared here with other proposals, and it is demonstrated that it is the Lutheran scholastic tradition that has a proper balance between both the uniqueness of Luther's Reformation and the catholic temperament of its history and future.

A popular proposal for Lutheran identity that comes from outside the Radical Lutheran movement is contained in Eric Gritsch and Robert Jenson's popular work *Lutheranism: The Theological Movement and Its Confessional Writings*. These authors emphasize the importance of the *Book of Concord* in giving definition to the Lutheran tradition, yet they do not identify the movement as a sectarian one, cutting itself off from previous church tradition. Gritsch and Jenson identify the Lutheran Confessions as a "proposal of dogma" given to the church catholic.[618] Ultimately, then, these doctrines are not identified with any particular territory or denomination, but offer up a proposal of what is true to the entire church.[619] The goal is, then, that these teachings would be spoken to, and eventually accepted by, the entire body of Christians. The center of these doctrines of the Lutheran church is defined as that of justification by faith.[620] All other important Lutheran distinctives flow out of this single truth. However, Gritsch and Jenson do not speak of justification in its scholastic meaning, but like the Radical Lutheran authors, they connect justification to a particular manner of speech. They argue that, instead of being one dogma defined by specific content, justification is "the metalinguistic stipulation of what *kind* of talking . . . can properly be proclamation and word of the church."[621] Whatever teaching is occurring within the church, it is to be done through the giving of an unconditional promise. They then argue, like Bayer, that law and gospel are modes

---

[618] Gritsch and Jenson, *Lutheranism*, 3.

[619] Ibid., 6.

[620] Ibid., 6.

[621] Ibid., 42–43.

of speech.[622] The thesis offered here is that Lutheranism is a proposal to the church catholic of the dogma of justification by faith, which is not a single doctrine, but an unconditional manner of speaking which defines the way in which the church communicates.

There are both benefits and shortcomings of Gritsch and Jenson's argument. Positively, they affirm that Lutheranism is not sectarian, but is a proposal for the whole church. It is this ecumenical spirit which is missing in the definitions offered by Paulson and others. Gritsch and Jenson recognize, as did the scholastics, that the Lutheran tradition is a continuation of, rather than a departure from, previous church history. Second, Gritsch and Jenson both affirm the importance of the Lutheran Confessions in the identity of the church, and thus avoid the mistake of connecting Lutheran thought solely with the reformer. The problem, however, is that Gritsch and Jenson both reject important aspects of classical Christian thought. Robert Jenson, in particular, is highly critical of classical theism, instead defining God by his own future. It is in precisely this area, however, that the Lutheran Confessions and thinkers such as Johann Gerhard and Martin Chemnitz continually emphasized that there is no departure from earlier authors. There is a difficulty in maintaining any kind of ecumenicity when the basic assertions of classical theism, which are inherent in Christian thought in the patristic and medieval eras and in the creeds, are rejected for some other model. Thus, while the outlines of Gritsch and Jenson's identification are correct, Jenson's rejection of classical theism demonstrates that there is difficulty for them in maintaining a truly catholic

---

[622] Ibid., 43.

approach to the Reformation.

Another approach to Lutheran identity, which reflects the Lutheran scholastic tradition, is found in Charles Porterfield Krauth's book *The Conservative Reformation and Its Theology*, first published in 1875. Krauth wrote in the United States at a time when the Lutheran church in America was struggling to identify itself. In the midst of these battles, some Lutherans cut themselves off from any significant theological interaction or even prayer fellowship from those with whom they disagreed. Others thought that Lutheranism must change to accommodate the Reformed tendencies in the American church. In the middle of those positions stood Krauth, who argued for a strong Lutheran identity, while maintaining cordial and productive conversation with those from other Christian traditions. This might be labeled a gentler and more ecumenical form of confessionalism than was found in figures like Abraham Calov, who consigned Reformed Christians to eternal perdition. Krauth stands within the tradition of Johann Gerhard, whom he cites frequently. This approach is that of the conservative Reformation.

In the beginning of this text, Krauth outlines two tendencies within the church: the conservative and the progressive.[623] Conservatism looks toward the past for guidance and truth, while progressivism looks for hope and change in the future. For Krauth, conservatism defines the Roman tradition, with an unwillingness to change at all, clinging to conceptions of the past without any notion of progress. Note that Krauth wrote in the nineteenth century and that the Roman Church today could hardly be described as without progressive tendencies. The

---

[623] Krauth, *Conservative Reformation*, vii.

progressive tendency, if it neglects the conservative, leads to radicalism, which Krauth identifies with the Anabaptist movement along with forms of Protestant Liberalism which were prominent in the nineteenth century. Within each of the Christian traditions, there are tendencies toward one or the other of these principles.[624] Krauth notes that Zwingli is radical, but Calvin mixes both of these progressive and conservative tendencies, though in his view the progressive is more pronounced. It is within this context that Krauth writes of the Lutheran Reformation as containing the proper balance of both of these modes of thinking.[625] Lutheranism clings to the long Christian tradition as it has developed in the West, including its theological categories and liturgical forms. However, it is not beholden purely to the past or to some supposed golden age of Christendom. Instead, the impurities of past doctrine are removed as the church moves into its future. For Krauth, there was hope for a final reunification of the church at some point in the future, and in his view, this would be done through Reformation catholicity, especially as taught in the Lutheran tradition.[626]

This perspective outlined by Krauth can be labeled "Reformational Catholicism," which balances catholicity alongside

---

[624] Ibid., viii.

[625] Ibid., xii.

[626] Ibid., xiv.

the distinctive doctrines of the Reformation.[627] This balance is exemplified in theologians like Chemnitz and Gerhard, along with others who represent the best of the scholastic tradition. These thinkers continually emphasize the connection between their own thought and that of earlier writers, including patristic authors and the ecumenical councils (though the seventh leads to some difficulty). This continuity does not exist only in the patristic era, but these thinkers also use insights from medieval theologians, especially on theology proper. Gerhard cites Aquinas quite extensively in his treatment of the doctrine of God, and he defends classical theism, which includes a strong view of divine simplicity and immutability. It is this approach which is a productive and historic view of Lutheran identity.

It is clear that both the Lutheran scholastic tradition and the Radical Lutheran approach have differing proposals for what constitutes Lutheran identity. For the Radical Lutheran authors, Lutheranism is defined by preaching, and particularly the preaching of law and gospel. Emphasis lies on discontinuity between this and other Christian traditions, and there is a strong divide between the pre- and post-Reformation church. It is also the contention of these authors that Martin Luther is the single theological authority for the tradition that bears his name. The Lutheran Confessions are used to

---

[627] Presbyterian theologian Peter Leithart has recently argued for such a notion in his book *The End of Protestantism* (2016). Though differences exist between his own theological perspective and that of the Lutheran tradition, the general tenor of these theologies is the same—unity is to be sought in the church within the broader catholic tradition, but with strong Reformational emphasis. This is the mediation spoken of by Krauth between the conservative and progressive tendencies.

an extent, but it is purported that they stray from Luther's purer theology on a number of points, especially as related to God's law. The scholastic tradition retains a place between progressivism and conservatism, both in using the theology of the past—especially classical approaches to the doctrine of God—and in moving forward in proposing important reforms as they accord with Scripture. Unlike Radical Lutheranism, this allows for a stronger maintenance of the past Christian identity as well as ecumenical relations with other Christian traditions. Additionally, the Lutheran orthodox approach avoids the complete open ecumenism of documents like the *Joint Declaration on the Doctrine of Justification* which simplify the significant differences that remain between the Lutheran and Roman Catholic churches. It is this scholastic approach to Lutheran identity which is most beneficial in both the present and the future of the church of the Augsburg Confession.

Apologetics

The divergences on Lutheran identity are further displayed in the different attitudes toward apologetics in Lutheran scholasticism and Radical Lutheranism. Christians have, from the first days of the church's existence, been involved in the apologetic task. The apostles debated Jesus' messianic status in the synagogues, and Paul used the philosophy and poetry of the Greeks to explain the nature of the God of Israel on Mars Hill. In the decades following the death of the apostles, Justin Martyr, Athenagoras, and others took up this task in declaring and defending the truths of Christianity through a study of both history and philosophy. Even as Christianity gained prominence in the Western world, Christian thinkers continued to formulate philosophical proofs for the existence of God and engaged in apologetics against Jewish and Islamic theology. The contemporary world is one which, perhaps even more than past centuries, needs a rigorous philosophical and historical defense of the Christian faith. Yet the Radical Lutheran authors either dismiss apologetics altogether or argue against traditional attributes of God which have historically been a central part of the defense of Christian theism. On this point, the broad chasm between the Lutheran scholastic approach of the seventeenth century and contemporary Radical Lutheran authors is immense. This section begins with a discussion of the necessity for apologetics in the current society. Second, the Radical Lutheran approach is discussed in relation to the questions raised in apologetics, and the scholastic method is defended. It is demonstrated that contemporary questions are answered not by the Radical Lutheran authors, but by scholastic thought.

Though challenges to theism have been popular since the Enlightenment, this opposition has heightened since the Radical Islamic terror attacks in New York on September 11, 2001. This event began much public discourse about the harm of religion upon society, and it led to the rise of the movement known as the "New Atheism," which is a term first used by Gary Wolf and has since become standard phraseology. The first book engaged in these discussions was Sam Harris's work *The End of Faith: Religion, Terror, and the Future of Reason*, published in 2004. Though this work gained some popularity, it was Richard Dawkins's 2006 work *The God Delusion* which brought these ideas mainstream attention. The prominent figures within this loosely affiliated movement were given the title "the Four Horsemen" of the New

Atheism: Sam Harris, Richard Dawkins, Christopher Hitchens, and Daniel Dennett. Challenges offered by these thinkers included a criticism of the morality of the Old Testament, a contention that war and violence have been the result of religious convictions, the notion that Darwinism is incompatible with the supernatural elements of religion, and (ill-informed) philosophical arguments against God's existence. Responses from Christian apologists and theologians to these books have been numerous. Many have been successful in demonstrating the theological and philosophical ignorance of these writers, though it is to be acknowledged that some responses were perhaps not so beneficial. Despite the fact that many of the arguments of the New Atheists barely merit any serious philosophical interaction (due to the often poor understandings of both philosophy and theology present in them), this movement has positively pushed many Christian thinkers into the area of apologetics, which was seen as a necessity in answering these criticisms. Though it has been well over a decade since this atheist movement began, and Richard Dawkins has not been receiving the media attention that he did at one time, the criticisms continue, and thus still deserve a response.

As has been established by a number of sociological studies, Western civilization is becoming increasingly less religious—at least in any traditional sense. Even the United States, which has not been influenced as thoroughly by secularism as most Western European nations, is facing strong challenges to traditional Christianity. The Barna Group, which specializes in statistical research about religion in the United States, released some significant numbers regarding the religious convictions of those in Generation Z. This generation, for the purposes of the study, includes individuals born between the years 1999 and 2015. For those who are presently in their teenage years, these statistics demonstrate the loss of religious conviction. Barna labels Generation Z the first "post-Christian" generation.[628] What is particularly noteworthy is not just that evangelical Christianity is in decline, but that religious beliefs as a whole are becoming less common. It is reported that 13 percent of individuals in Generation Z classify themselves as atheists, which is more than double that of the average population. The trend, at the present time, is that each generation identifies less with Christianity and more with no faith at all. When participants in this survey were asked why they rejected Christianity, the most common answer was the problem of evil in the world, which they view as incompatible with the existence of benevolent deity. Other common responses were that Christians are hypocrites, and that science and religion are incompatible. Along with this, 46 percent of those surveyed stated that they will not believe without factual evidence.[629] These statistics demonstrate the present reality: religion is in decline, and the challenges to religion are largely intellectual. In particular, it is the question of evil and the limits of science which are used to dispute the truth-claims of Christianity. In such an environment, the apologetic task is a necessity and will continue to be, especially if this trend continues.

With these statistics, it is clear that a large part of any position in ministry wherein one engages with younger generations is the task of apologetics. This is no longer a field

---

[628] Barna, "Atheism Doubles."

[629] Ibid.

merely for experts, but pastors and other ministry leaders are to be equipped with answers in order to engage in any meaningful way with the atheists and agnostics who now populate a significant portion of the Western world. The Radical Lutheran authors, however, with their rejection of traditional metaphysics and the doctrine of God, do not have sufficient responses to these challenges. What they engage in is more of a retreat from apologetics than giving intellectually sufficient answers to the questions raised by skeptics. The scholastic method, however, offers a robust approach to philosophy and theology which aids in the apologetic task.

While Radical Lutherans authors do not spend an extensive amount of space discussing apologetics, the comments that are made are almost entirely negative. An example can be found in Paulson's work, wherein he states blatantly that "Lutherans do not spend time on proofs of God's existence."[630] Such a statement is simply untrue if one regards the scholastic Lutheran tradition at all, wherein manifold proofs of God's existence are offered. For Paulson, however, apologetics are not merely unnecessary, but un-Lutheran. Again, this demonstrates the failure of his approach to Lutheran identity to take the majority of the Lutheran tradition itself into account. The reason proofs are to be rejected, according to Paulson, is that the humans have an inherent knowledge that God exists, and such knowledge is suppressed, as St. Paul writes to the Romans (Rom 1:20). It is here that Paulson goes on to reject metaphysics altogether, again using the broad statement that "Abstraction from created life has always been the problem Lutheran theology has with 'metaphysics,' or

---

[630] Paulson, *Lutheran Theology*, 71.

'ontology.'"[631] For Paulson, Lutheran theology rejects any notion of God as he is in himself, including the classical characterization of theology proper both in older medieval thought and in Protestant scholasticism. One should not engage in proofs of God's existence, in discussions of the divine attributes, or in metaphysics whatsoever. Such an approach is hardly helpful in the current age of skepticism, which merits a more rigorous philosophical approach, rather than a retreat from the discipline altogether.

The argument that Paulson presents is based upon a misunderstanding of the function of apologetics in much Christian thought. The fact that the knowledge of God's existence is inherent within each individual does not then negate the usefulness of arguments which demonstrate God's existence. In his treatment of the proofs, Conrad Lindberg notes that God's existence is an absolute certainty, as clear as the existence of the self.[632] This knowledge is inherent, though suppressed by the unbeliever. Lindberg does not then, as does Paulson, simply dismiss arguments for God's existence altogether, but instead states that they have a "relative value" for the Christian in giving hope in times of doubt and struggle, and that they are necessary in apologetics.[633] He then follows with four arguments for God's existence. Gerhard approaches the subject in a similar manner. He begins his discussion by noting Paul's contention in Romans 1 that inherent knowledge of God exists, and then asks whether proofs are necessary in light of

---

[631] Ibid., 72.

[632] Lindberg, *Christian Dogmatics*, 19–20.

[633] Ibid., 20–21.

this knowledge. He answers in the affirmative.[634] He gives three distinct reasons such proofs are beneficial. First, they are used to refute the claims of skeptics. Second, they strengthen the faith of believers in times of doubt. Third, they strengthen one's natural knowledge of God.[635] Gerhard contends that a twofold knowledge of God exists: inherent and acquired.[636] The former is connected primarily to the conscience, while the latter refers to observation of the natural world. Paulson affirms the former while apparently rejecting the latter completely. Interestingly, the passage that Paulson cites in Romans itself testifies to these external proofs, speaking of the divine attributes as those which are seen "by the things that are made" (Rom 1:20). The classical proofs of God's existence are simply expositions of this statement, explaining in exactly what ways God and his attributes are proven by nature and reason. Contemporary Lutheran apologists also speak about the proofs in a manner similar to that of the older scholastic thinkers.

An example of contemporary apologetics from a Lutheran perspective is found in the volume *Making the Case for Christianity: Responding to Modern Objections*, edited by Korey Maas and Adam Francisco. This text presents a series of essays on a variety of apologetic topics, giving responses from a uniquely Lutheran point of view. In his introduction to the volume, Maas explains the necessity and purpose of apologetics, noting the increasingly pluralistic culture in which Western Christians find themselves. As objections

---

[634] Gerhard, *Nature of God*, 56.

[635] Ibid., 57.

[636] Ibid., 59.

continue to be raised against the faith, Christians are to heed St. Peter's admonition to make a defense (1 Pet 3:15). Maas is clear to state that these arguments do not in themselves make anyone a Christian through persuasive rhetoric or logic alone.[637] It is to be remembered that faith is a gift of the Holy Spirit, rather than an act of the will or intellect. The purpose of such arguments is mostly in countering objections sinners raise in order to dismiss the claims of the gospel.[638] Maas argues that apologetics is a tool to bring people under the recognition of their guilt, that the Holy Spirit may then open their ears to hear the gospel.[639] This introduction is followed by an essay by Joshua Pagan in which God's existence is defended through the popular Kalam argument.[640] He engages throughout in the discipline of metaphysics which Paulson is similarly dismissive of. Clearly, the claim of Paulson that Lutherans "do not spend time on proofs for God's existence" is false for the authors of this volume, who contend that God's existence is rationally demonstrable.[641] The either-or scenario posited by Paulson between innate and acquired knowledge of God's existence is not reflective of historic Lutheranism, nor of the many contemporary Lutheran apologists who contend for a rational demonstration of the truth claims of Christianity. It is the historic view which has an answer to challenges of skepticism that is absent in Paulson and other Radical Lutheran authors.

---

[637] Maas and Francisco, *Making the Case*, 3.

[638] Ibid., 3.

[639] Ibid., 7.

[640] Ibid., 11-32.

[641] Paulson, *Lutheran Theology*, 71.

As is evident in the Barna study cited above, the most common objection to the Christian faith in Generation Z is the question of the existence of a benevolent God in a world which is full of evil and suffering. This is commonly referred to as the problem of evil. A number of philosophical answers to this dilemma have emerged throughout the centuries, and in recent years, Alvin Plantinga's free will defense has been especially prominent.[642] Plantinga argues that free will necessitates that creatures can use that will to make bad decisions and thus bring evil and suffering into the world. It is a greater good to allow freedom in creatures, even with the resultant suffering, than to force morally good actions upon creatures. Therefore, a benevolent God and suffering can coexist. William Lane Craig offers a further development of this notion in a Molinist approach, wherein the current world of suffering is one of a number of possible worlds in which humans have free agency.[643] It is this actualized world which has significantly less evils than the others, and thus God's goodness is defended. Clark Pinnock and other open theists argue that God has limited his omnipotence and foreknowledge, and thus cannot control evil in the manner that others assume.[644] Calvinists contend that God has predestined all events, but that the greatest good is God's glory.[645] Evil exists, but its existence serves God's glory, which is a greater good, and thus it also does not negate God's benevolence. Jürgen Moltmann purports that God suffers in his own essence along

---

[642] Plantinga, *God, Freedom, and Evil*.

[643] Craig, *Only Wise God*.

[644] Pinnock, *Openness of God*.

[645] Piper and Taylor, *Suffering and Sovereignty*.

with creation, thus giving comfort to the bereaved in God's immanence in suffering.[646] These are only a small number of contemporary approaches to theodicy, but what is clear is that such a question is to be taken seriously, and that it is an apologetic necessity to give some defense regarding this issue. The Radical Lutheran authors do address suffering, but they do not give an answer to the philosophical question regarding the connection between evil and the benevolence of God.

Gerhard Forde addresses the question of suffering in *On Being a Theologian of the Cross*, specifically in his explanation of thesis 21 of the Heidelberg Disputation. Forde is highly critical of the theology of those thinkers who address suffering by denying divine impassibility. Though he himself is not a strong proponent of classical theism, Forde notes that theologies of divine suffering do not give a sufficient answer to the problem.[647] In another place, Forde speaks about this with the analogy of a butcher who weeps each time he kills an animal. The weeping would change absolutely nothing about the reality itself, and would not bring any more "comfort" to the animal about to be slaughtered.[648] Forde similarly dismisses other efforts to solve the problem of suffering by separating God from evil acts as attempts to "absolve" God of suffering, when scripturally God is very much involved in it.[649] Part of the problem, he argues, is in the contemporary conflation of suffering and evil.[650] For Luther, however,

---

[646] Moltmann, *Crucified God*.
[647] Forde, *Theologian of the Cross*, 82.
[648] Forde, *Preached God*, 40.
[649] Forde, *Theologian of the Cross*, 84–85.
[650] Ibid., 84.

suffering itself is not inherently evil. Instead, it is often good. It is, after all, the suffering of Christ which brings salvation. Forde then shifts the entire question away from the theoretical to the concrete realities of suffering in one's own life. Personal suffering brings about conflict with God.[651] The only release from this suffering, then, is God-preached. This is the proclamation of the gospel through primary discourse. The question of suffering is not one to be debated, but to be resolved through absolution.[652] In his approach to the issue, Forde addresses the concrete and personal nature of suffering, and the centrality of gospel proclamation in response to it. However, he does not address the underlying philosophical concerns in these discussions.

Because of the rejection of theoretical or scientific approaches to theology for the concrete, Radical Lutheran authors do not have a place for theodicy in their writings. There is some benefit in this, as the majority of theoretical attempts to construct a theodicy are highly problematic from a theological perspective. Open theists, for example, neuter the doctrine of God so that he is unable to see the future or control events in the manner that historic Christian orthodoxy has always contended. The free will defense can lead to a view of pure libertarianism regarding the will and thus negate God's involvement in the world. Forde outlines feminist theologies which, in their attempt to divorce God from violence and suffering, refer to the cross as "divine child abuse."[653] Others deny divine impassibility by connecting suffering with God's

---

[651] Ibid., 88.

[652] Forde, *Preached God*, 43.

[653] Forde, *Theologian of the Cross*, 85.

own nature, or posit a form of process theism. With all of these flaws, Forde is right to negate the usefulness of such attempts to explain suffering. However, this does not mean that a theoretical answer to the question should be negated altogether. While the gospel is certainly a comfort in times of trial and suffering, there remain genuine philosophical questions posed by skeptics which warrant some sort of response.

Angus Menuge presents a solution to the problem which both addresses these important questions and emphasizes gospel proclamation, as does Forde. He begins by discussing Plantinga's free will response to the problem of evil, wherein God allows evil because of the value of human freedom in making decisions.[654] In response to some criticisms of the argument, Menuge argues that consequences to bad decisions must be serious ones in order for people to actually face the immorality of their choices.[655] He argues that this is consistent with Lutheran theology, as humans do have the free ability to resist God's grace (while faith itself remains a divine gift).[656] In honesty, however, he acknowledges that the reasons particular events of suffering are somehow leading toward a greater good are difficult to ascertain. Menuge contends that this is to be expected due to the limitations of the human person in relation to God. He uses an analogy from Stephen Wykstra, who likens the difference between God and man to that of an infant and a human adult. The infant has absolutely no comprehension whatsoever of why the pain

---

[654] Maas and Francisco, *Making the Case*, 145.

[655] Ibid., 146.

[656] Ibid., 147.

of shots or other necessities occur, nor is that child able to understand, due to its limited cognitive faculties. In the same manner, then, the human is likely simply unable to understand the exact function of suffering, or the greater purpose which it serves.[657] This solution that Menuge offers to the problem of evil gives a reasonable response to the contention that God and suffering cannot coexist. Whether the free will defense is entirely accurate or not, what it does demonstrate is that suffering and evil can logically coexist simultaneously with a benevolent God if there is a greater good under which they exist. Rather than trying to explain too much and thus negate important biblical teachings, Menuge also reminds his readers of human limitations. Following this philosophical argument, he then points to the cross as the solution to human suffering.

Borrowing from Jeffrey Mallinson, Menuge argues for an "epistemology of the cross" in relation to these issues of suffering, in opposition to an epistemology of glory.[658] Rather than beginning with a broad conception of theism which is then discussed with regard to the existence of evil, he argues that one should begin with the cross of Jesus Christ, where the Son of God takes suffering upon himself.[659] The question of evil cannot be debated in the same manner as a scientific hypothesis or mathematical formula, since it is primarily one of personal experience.[660] Therefore, it must be addressed specifically within that context. Within this argument, Menuge summarizes his approach, confessing

---

[657] Ibid., 151.
[658] Ibid., 161.
[659] Ibid., 162.
[660] Ibid., 63.

that "*Christ* is God's answer to the problem of evil."[661] Ultimately, Jesus' own sufferings are the place in which evil is overcome. It is here that any Christian apologetic about evil and suffering must begin. In this manner, Menuge affirms Forde's emphasis on preaching the gospel as the central need for the one facing suffering. However, he does this while simultaneously acknowledging the usefulness of these other philosophical approaches to theodicy, demonstrating that the existence of evil and a benevolent God are logically consistent propositions.[662] Menuge then affirms the use of philosophy in apologetics as do the scholastics, while also holding a distinctively Christocentric approach.

Regarding the practice of apologetics, the Radical Lutheran tradition and the scholastic method have vastly different approaches, just as has been seen in other areas. This is apparent in regard to two particular apologetic discussions: the existence of God and the problem of evil. The Lutheran scholastics argue that the existence of God is both written on the heart and rationally demonstrable. Two examples cited here were the writings of Conrad Lindberg and Johann Gerhard. The former provides four arguments for God's existence, and the latter describes five, largely reiterating proofs from Augustine, Anselm, and Aquinas. In contrast to this, Paulson argues that there is no need whatsoever to provide arguments for God's existence, since such knowledge is already existent and suppressed. Further, many of the arguments for the existence of God proposed by philosophers rely on divine attributes associated with classical theism,

---

[661] Ibid., 63.

[662] Ibid., 164.

which is rejected by Radical Lutherans as a *theologia gloriae*.[663] The second question addressed in apologetics is that of God and the existence of suffering and evil, which, according to contemporary surveys, is the most common objection to Christianity today. Gerhard Forde rightly and helpfully points those suffering to the solution to this problem in the gospel of Christ, but fails to provide any intellectually satisfying resolution to the proposed dilemma between the existence of both God and suffering. In light of affirmations of apologetics in scholasticism, many modern apologists, such as Angus Menuge, are able to give both intellectually and pastorally satisfying explanations to these questions. As criticisms of the Christian faith continue in the future, there will be a growing need for philosophically informed defenses of the Christian tradition. The Radical Lutheran approach is simply inadequate to do this, whereas the scholastic method aids in answering contemporary questions satisfactorily.

Gender Issues

The final practical implication of the dissonance between these two approaches to theology discussed here is in regard to contemporary debates surrounding gender which impact the church and society at large. There are two opposed perspectives debated in philosophy regarding this topic: gender essentialism, and gender as a social construct which is divorced from sex. The latter perspective has gained prominence in the academy, and is currently guiding conversations at seminaries and in congregations across the world. This

---

[663] See Feser, *Five Proofs*, and Hart, *Experience of God*.

perspective relates to the ethical validity of transgenderism, the nature of heterosexuality and homosexuality, and personal identity. While these questions are not at the forefront of the debates surrounding Radical Lutheranism, they are prominent concerns in the modern church which all Christian traditions must answer. The answers given surrounding the nature of humanity and personal identity in these conversations depend upon how one approaches the human essence, and in particular, the essence of the male and female genders. The approach to humanity taken by many modern Lutherans, as discussed throughout this work, rejects the category of substance or essence in favor of a relational or word-centric approach. In order to defend gender essentialism, however, one *must* adopt an essentialist metaphysic to some extent. In this way, the Radical Lutheran method is incapable of addressing these concerns adequately, while the traditional essentialist categories as used by the scholastics give a strong grounding to the traditional Christian approach to gender differences and identity. Here, the basis of contemporary views of gender is explained, followed by a discussion of the impact of these concepts in the church. Following this, it is demonstrated that an essentialist metaphysic is an absolute necessity in answering these current challenges.

The roots of modern gender theory are found in both existentialism and postmodernism. The work which is most often cited as the foundation of gender fluidity is Simone de Beauvoir's book *The Second Sex*, which began the second wave of feminism. Beauvoir was a French existential philosopher and lifelong partner of Jean Paul Sartre. Like Sartre, she accepted the notion that existence precedes essence, meaning that the self is created by free actions, as Sartre defines in *Being and Nothingness*. In her popular treatment of gender, and of the suppression of women in particular, Beauvoir writes her best-known statement, "One is not born, but rather becomes, woman."[664] This phrase appears at the beginning of the second volume of her work, defining the female gender in childhood years. Though classical philosophy ties gender to a distinct essence with which one is born, Beauvoir argues that there is no biological necessity for one to be a woman in the sense that this is understood by society at large.[665] Apart from societal expectations, she argues that the individual would not even "grasp himself as sexually differentiated."[666] As one ages, however, and experiences life in society as a whole, these gender differences are enforced, and the superiority of the male sex is instilled upon growing children. She cites, for example, the male portrait of God within the Christian tradition as an agent of oppression of the female sex.[667] Through these learned characteristics, both men and women take on their respective roles as society requires, and thus become their gender. Males have the dominant and superior roles, and women the submissive and inferior. As is typical in existential thought, the self as gendered is created by one's actions. Seemingly, then, there is no tie whatsoever between biology and gender.

Since the original publication of Beauvoir's work in 1949, gender theory has become a significant field in philosophy and sociology, along with theology. The ideas present in

---

[664] Beauvoir, *Second Sex*, 283.

[665] Ibid., 283.

[666] Ibid., 283.

[667] Ibid., 303–4.

that work were further expanded through the philosophy of postmodernism—particularly through Derrida's deconstruction and Foucalt's writings on sexuality. One of the most influential texts on the subject in recent decades is Judith Butler's book *Gender Trouble*, published in 1990, with some later revisions (2006). This text displays some of the most common assumptions in modern gender debates. What is particularly influential is Butler's insistence that gender is performative in nature, rather than substantial. Throughout this text, Butler is highly critical of classical philosophy that defends what is often labeled "gender essentialism." This is the idea that there is any inherent essence of either male or female in which one partakes, which would be the ontological foundation for one's various actions or attributes.

For Butler, many previous feminist approaches have been mistaken. Though they rightly fight against patriarchy, they have wrongly assumed that there is some generally understood meaning of "woman."[668] For her, there is no female essence, but for male-dominated society, women are defined by the politics of privilege and submission.[669] It is this approach which has driven much of feminism, which defines femininity by its opposition to masculinity.[670] Butler argues, instead, that feminism must take up the task of "a radical rethinking of the ontological constructions of identity."[671] She contends that there is no inherent continuity between one's biological makeup and gender, which is societally constructed.

---

[668] Butler, *Gender Trouble*, 5.

[669] Ibid., 5–6.

[670] Ibid., 13.

[671] Ibid., 7.

Therefore, both masculinity and femininity are divorced from sex.[672] As there is no inherent substance that is male or female, these categories themselves are simply societally and contextually determined, rather than inherent.[673] This leads to her strong rejection of essentialist metaphysics in favor of a view of identity which denies the persistence of the subject.

For Butler, the idea of a persistent identity is a mere societal construct used in order to make reality intelligible.[674] This attempt at intelligibility leads to the construction of these artificial gender categories that limit the possibilities of the female, while the male is understood as the "general" gender, thus giving men superiority and freedom at the expense of others.[675] The solution offered to this problem is to deny that the self is a substantive thing at all. Instead, Butler argues, following Michel Haar, the individual is to be understood linguistically,[676] as one interacts within various social constructions. In relation to gender, male and female are not to be spoken of as nouns (which implies substance), but instead as verbs. Gender is an expression, or a doing, rather than an underlying essence which precedes expression.[677] Butler argues that rather than an identity performing certain acts, those acts actually constitute identity itself.[678] Butler further

---

[672] Ibid., 9.
[673] Ibid., 14.
[674] Ibid., 23.
[675] Ibid., 25.
[676] Ibid., 27.
[677] Ibid., 34.
[678] Ibid., 34.

notes that gender, along with a "doing," is a "becoming."⁶⁷⁹ There is no beginning point for femininity, nor is there a goal for which one is striving. It is a doing and becoming which are constantly and forever in process as society itself understands such constructs. This approach, for Butler, places gender in a category beyond truth and falsehood,⁶⁸⁰ and instead she purports that whatever one does, one is.⁶⁸¹ To summarize the points here, Butler rejects essentialist metaphysics, and instead adopts both postmodernism and existential thought by arguing that the individual is self-constituted. This theory is applied, in particular, to the notion of gender, which she argues is defined by repeated actions that are societally constructed. There is therefore no essential male or female gender at all, but mere performative acts, and no identity which persists underneath such actions.

Some have followed Butler's argument in even more radical directions. In a popular-level introduction to these concepts titled *Queer Theory, Gender Theory: An Instant Primer*, Riki Wilchins further explores the ideas present in Beauvoir and Butler. It is argued that gender is itself a language, and like other interactions, it is determined by principles of power.⁶⁸² Wilchins follows Derrida in rejecting earlier Western conceptions of reality, arguing that there is no real transcendent truth at all, but only socially constructed concepts.⁶⁸³ Attempts at affirming any single transcendental truth, along with

---

⁶⁷⁹ Ibid., 45.

⁶⁸⁰ Ibid., 186.

⁶⁸¹ Ibid., 192.

⁶⁸² Wilchins, *Gender Theory*, 40.

⁶⁸³ Ibid., 50–52.

the formulation of binaries (the male/female being most important here), are acts of power and oppression.[684] These oppressive acts include assigning genders to infants, which negates the existence of the queer, and one's own subjectivity in creating self-identity.[685] Since language itself is that which constitutes the self, in order for further gender identities to be recognized, words must change.[686] This radical rejection of traditional gender categories is also applied, by Wilchins, to sex. This position, then, goes beyond many of the other views that divorce gender from sex, by arguing that neither is biologically founded, and both are mere constructions. Wilchins argues that this can be demonstrated by the fact that similarities between individuals are downplayed, and the evidence is skewed in order to promote differentiation between two opposed sexes.[687] This argument by Wilchins demonstrates the extremes to which these ideologies go without any grounding in classical essentialist metaphysical convictions. In modern gender theory, the category of substance is rejected altogether, resulting in a relativist approach to sex, gender, and personal identity as a whole. It is incumbent on the church to answer these challenges, and to do so, it must acknowledge real-essentialism.

That these understandings of gender which arise in modern thought have impacted the church is clear, as anyone who is attentive to contemporary ecclesiological trends knows. Discussions on these points have been ongoing in nearly

---

[684] Ibid., 47.
[685] Ibid., 68.
[686] Ibid., 70.
[687] Ibid., 88–89.

every Christian tradition, including Lutheranism. An example of such conversations is in the Evangelical Lutheran Church in America. In 2009, following extensive debate, the ELCA approved of same-sex relationships within the church, though acknowledging that various perspectives on the issue remained within the church body. Since that time, ordinations of openly homosexual clergy, including both pastors and bishops, have occurred. This has similarly happened with transgendered individuals. This decision caused many congregations to split from the ELCA, forming the North American Lutheran Church, Lutheran Congregations in Mission for Christ, and joining various other more traditionally minded church bodies. Since that decision, the ELCA has issued statements addressing gender that adopt the modern social construction theory addressed above.

In 2015, the ELCA adopted a document titled "Gender-Based Violence," which condemns the violence perpetrated by males (generally) toward the female sex. This, in itself, is not particularly noteworthy, as conservative denominations such as the LCMS have also rightly released statements which condemn physical and sexual abuse. However, the document released by the ELCA includes some important caveats which extend beyond a simple condemnation of abuse. The beginning of the text has a note next to the word "gender," which reads as follows:

> *Gender refers to categories into which culture/societies separate behaviors and characteristics that are usually considered masculine or feminine. The most common gender identities are woman and man, but other identities exist and are becoming more widely used and*

*understood.*⁶⁸⁸

In this endnote, the primary aspects of postmodern gender theory are all confirmed. First, gender itself is identified not with sex or any creational intent at all, but with societally conditioned behaviors. Second, the notions of masculinity and femininity are also identified as mere cultural identifiers with no inherent content. Third, male and female are identified as only two of a large number of gender identities, which are also culturally created and conditioned. By affirming such statements, the ELCA has rejected the creational differences between male and female as mere societal norms. As these ideas become more popular, theologians are forced to defend their traditional views with more rigor than in previous generations. Though many of those within the Radical Lutheran movement are in opposition to the recent decisions within the ELCA, their own ontological system does not have a proper grounding to defend traditional gender roles, which are founded upon an essentialist metaphysic.

The reason the Radical Lutheran method is inadequate in this area is in its adoption of both linguistic and relational ontologies. Theories of gender fluidity largely depend upon an approach to the person which defines one's gender in terms of one's place within the linguistic structure of society. To be a male is not to be one in any essential sense, but to perform the linguistic and societal acts which one associates with maleness. This is Butler's idea of gender performativity, in which doing determines being. The Radical Lutheran authors have a similar linguistic approach to the human essence.

---

[688] ELCA, *Gender-Based Violence*, 17.

Rather than mere societal structures, however, the language which determines humanity is the word of God—particularly, his words of law and gospel. While gender theorists function from a position of postmodern subjectivity which Forde, Paulson, and other Lutheran writers would strongly reject, the Radical Lutheran authors agree on their fundamental critique of classical ontologies. If one is constituted purely by speech, and there is no essence that stands behind such speech, then one could argue that perhaps God's speech can change an individual from one gender to another as in a "renaming ceremony" which occurred in January of 2018 at a Lutheran congregation in New Jersey.[689] The notion of a performative speech-act could apply to the establishment of a new gender identity in the same manner that it does for the Radical Lutherans in the creation of the regenerate identity. In order to defend against such uses of speech performativity, an essentialist view of gender must serve as the functional basis under which any linguistic or relational ideas of ontology must function.

The relational conception of being is similarly problematic in dealing with modern gender theory. As discussed above in critique of Schumacher's argument that human relations constitute the essence of the nature of the person, this idea cannot account for the stability of identity in view of the change which often happens in human relationships. If relations really do constitute human essence in the purest sense, then essence is able to change as do those social relationships. From Butler's approach, gender is constituted by the acts one performs in social relationships, thereby

---

[689] Richardson, "Naming Ceremony."

constituting identity. A pure relational ontology has no ground by which Butler can be genuinely criticized, as any criticism leveled entails that there is an inherent male or female essence that underlies relation, thereby acknowledging the essentialist claim. As mentioned above, when pressed, Schumacher does basically acknowledge as much himself. Again, the relational ontological notions that Schumacher, Bayer, and others propose are beneficial as far as they go, but they cannot stand apart from ontological essentialism without devolving into the ideas of identity as defended by Butler.

This leads to the final problem that Radical Lutheranism has in combatting radical gender theorists: the continuity of the self. As evidenced in various places above, Gerhard Forde denies that there is any continuously existing subject, as the word of absolution recreates the human person. This same problem appears in Paulson's writing, as well as in the inherent Flacianism of Bayer's view. If, as Bayer says, sin is of the human essence, then redemption from sin changes the human essence itself, and thereby changes human identity. Relating to gender questions, one must then ask by what standard one actually must remain either male or female. If the self is completely discontinuous, then it is not unreasonable to assume that the gender of a person is similarly discontinuous. There must be a persistent self, along with a persistent identity of the individual, including an essential gender, in which one partakes if the creational nature of humanity in the first chapters of Genesis is to have any inherent meaning whatsoever. Forde is simply wrong in his contention that no continuous subject exists. The fact that this leads him to be ill-equipped in giving a strong answer to proponents of social construction gender theories is one evidence of this.

Modern approaches to gender that deny the fundamental reality of an essence which constitutes both male and female rely upon an ontology which is influenced by existentialism and postmodernism, in rejection of classical essentialist ontologies. Though the Radical Lutheran authors are not as strongly existential or postmodern, they utilize some of these same criticisms of classical metaphysics. In doing so, they have no strong arguments against these modern developments. As these problems continue to confront the church, responses which are philosophically robust and convincing can only come from those who are committed to essentialism, by which it is demonstrated that the human person is not linguistically, relationally, or societally constructed, but persists within God-given categories of nature and gender.

Conclusion

As this study concludes, the findings can be summarized. It is clear that the scholastic method is a viable method of doing theology in the modern world, and is superior to alternative approaches. The Radical Lutheran method is flawed in its approach to metaphysics, which rejects classical essentialist thought in favor of categories taken from existentialism, linguistic philosophy, and relational ontology. While each of these philosophical movements has value to an extent in aiding the theologian in explaining particular aspects of Christian theology, none of them is an adequate replacement for essentialism. Without a grounding in real-essentialism, each of these philosophical conceptions leads to numerous theological problems. Rather than rejecting Plato and Aristotle, modern developments are wise to instead use the basis of these older ontologies, while allowing for modification and development in light of modern research. It is the scholastic method which is equipped to give intellectually sufficient answers to the questions of both theologians and modern society. To approach theology from a scholastic perspective is not purely to repristinate the past, but instead to use the same foundational methods at work in Gerhard, Quenstedt, and other Protestant scholastics, which can be developed and modified in each era. In this final chapter, the superiority of the scholastic approach over the Radical Lutheran approach has been demonstrated in relation to the practical issues which face the church in the twenty-first century.

This section began with the question, *What are the implications of the loss of the scholastic method in the contemporary church?* These implications have been explained in three particular areas: the nature of Lutheran identity, the function of apologetics, and contemporary debates about the nature of gender and identity. In each of these areas, Radical Lutheranism and scholasticism have vastly different answers. When viewing these particular questions, it is apparent that Radical Lutheranism gives insufficient responses, and the dissonance between these perspectives has immense practical value for the Christian church.

Regarding Lutheran identity, Radical Lutheran writers contend primarily for discontinuity. As the name itself implies, Luther's Reformation is viewed as a radical departure from previous Christian thought. For some, the Lutheran Reformation seems to be identical with the doctrine of justification, and particularly as that doctrine is understood as a performative speech-act. Sanctification in its traditional sense is either ignored or denied outright. The scholastics, in contrast to this, balance both catholicity and progress. It is this idea that Krauth identifies as the conservative Reformation. The Lutheran movement is to be viewed as a development of the theology of the church catholic, accepting the theological convictions of the early and medieval church, such as the basic assumptions of classical theism, which also includes certain essentialist metaphysical notions. This approach to Lutheranism has immense ecumenical value, though without negating the remaining important differences among various Christian traditions. The scholastic view of the Lutheran church is to be preferred for both theological and practical reasons which are apparent above.

The second practical area addressed demonstrates a similar strong division between these schools of thought. The Radical Lutheran authors often dismiss apologetics, while the scholastics emphasize its importance and the rational demonstrability of the Christian faith. Paulson argues that arguments for the existence of God are not part of Lutheranism at all. They are unnecessary, as God's existence is already known in the heart, but suppressed due to sin. The scholastics, in opposition to this, provide numerous arguments for the existence of God. Like Paulson, they acknowledge that there is an inherent knowledge of God that exists in all creatures, but they further assert that there is also an acquired knowledge which can be gained through reason and experience. This acquired knowledge allows for the formulation of philosophical arguments for the existence of God. These arguments are to be used both for the conviction of unbelief and for the strengthening of Christians within their own faith. Modern Lutheran apologists have continued to use several of the scholastic arguments and should continue to do so, as opposition to Christianity has statistically risen in recent years.

Among those current challenges to the Christian faith, it was noted that the most common is that of the existence of God alongside suffering in the world. Radical Lutheran authors, such as Gerhard Forde, do not ignore this issue, but instead point to the cross of Christ as the solution to suffering. While this approach is beneficial, there do remain intellectual challenges to the logical coherence of divine benevolence and suffering in God's creation. Forde does not answer these questions, especially due to his general distaste for metaphysical and broader philosophical questions surrounding God's nature. The scholastic approach can both ground itself in Christ's sufferings and also give logical demonstration that the existence of a benevolent God and suffering are not inherently incompatible, as has been shown in Plantinga's free will argument, for example. Regarding these issues, Radical Lutheranism is simply unable to provide sufficient answers, while the scholastic method engages in philosophical criticisms in an academically and logically rigorous manner, and thus will continue to defend Christian theism against whatever opposition arises in the future.

The final practical issue addressed here was the development of critical gender theory and its adoption in certain parts of the church, including the ELCA. Radical Lutheranism and gender theorists have similar criticisms of classical approaches to the human person which identify them with a particular unchanging essence. As these problems continue to impact churches, it is incumbent upon theologians to answer these issues in a thorough and sufficient manner.

The Radical Lutheran method is unable to do this, as it has already conceded much of the necessary grounding of gender essentialism in favor of an anthropology which is based upon language and relation. If the church is to defend itself against these modern movements in gender theory, it can do so only through a thorough grounding in real-essentialism.

The world is in a process of change, both culturally and ideologically. In a situation such as this, the church must decide what it will stand for and how it will find its identity moving forward in a post-Christian world. Radical Lutheranism and Lutheran scholasticism present two very different paths forward. The first emphasizes both philosophical discontinuity with past Western culture and theological divergence from patristic theology, the Middle Ages, and post-Reformation Protestantism. It denies the necessity of defending the Christian faith in an age of strong skepticism, and provides little to no defense against problematic modern cultural movements. The latter connects the Lutheran church to its history, both in the Western philosophical tradition and within the church catholic. It provides a strong emphasis for ecumenical dialogue without conceding ground on necessary issues. Scholasticism also provides for a robust apologetic in a skeptical age, providing logically coherent and convincing answers to difficult challenges that arise. This tradition also provides strong resources to engage with postmodern ideologies in the modern era, without retreating from such discussions altogether. If the Lutheran church is to survive in the modern era with an impact in both the world and the broader church, there is only one real option: the scholastic method must be revived and defended. There is simply no other option.

Bibliography

Allen, Diogenes. *Philosophy for Understanding Theology.* Atlanta: John Knox, 1985.

The Ante-Nicene Fathers: Translations of the Writings of the Fathers Down to A.D. 325. Edited by Alexander Roberts and James Donaldson. 10 vols. 1885–1887.

Aquinas, Thomas. *Introduction to St. Thomas Aquinas. The Summa Theologica, The Summa Contra Gentiles.* Edited by AC Pegis. New York: Random House, 1945.

_____. *An Introduction to the Metaphysics of St. Thomas Aquinas.* Translated by JF Anderson. Washington D.C.: Regnery, 1953.

_____. *On the Truth of the Catholic Faith.* Translated by AC Pegis. Garden City, NY: Hanover House, 1955.

Arand, Charles P. "Two Kinds of Righteousness as a Framework for Law and Gospel in the Apology" *Lutheran Quarterly.* XV (2001): 417-439.

Arand, Charles, Robert Kolb and James A Nestingen. *The Lutheran Confessions: History and Theology of The Book of*

Concord. Minneapolis: Fortress, 2012.

Aristotle. *The Metaphysics*. Translated by HL Tancred. London: Penguin, 1998.

Arndt, Johann. *True Christianity*. Translated by Paul Erb. New York: Paulist, 1979.

Asselt, W.J.V. *Introduction to Reformed Scholasticism*. Grand Rapids: Reformation Heritage, 2011.

_____. *Reformation and Scholasticism: An Ecumenical Enterprise*. Grand Rapids: Baker, 2001.

Austin, John L. *How to Do Things with Words*. Cambridge: Harvard, 1975.

Baines, Ronald S. (editor). *Confessing the Impossible God: The Biblical, Classical, & Confessional Doctrine of Divine Impassibility*. Palmdale, CA: RBAP, 2016.

Barna, George, "Atheism Doubles Among Generation Z," *Barna*.
http://www.barna.com/research/atheism-doubles-among-generation-z/

Barnard, Leslie W. *Justin Martyr: His Life and Thought*. Cambridge: Cambridge University Press, 2008.

Barrett, William. *Irrational Man: A Study in Existential Philosophy*. New York: Doubleday, 1962.

Barrett, William and Henry D. Aiken (eds), *Philosophy in the Twentieth Century: An Anthology*. New York: Random House, 1962.

Barth, Karl. *Protestant Theology in the Nineteenth Century*. Grand Rapids: Eerdmans, 2002.

Bayer, Oswald. *Theology the Lutheran Way*. Edited and Translated by JG Silcock and MC Mattes. Grand Rapids: Eerdmans, 2007.

_____. *Martin Luther's Theology: A Contemporary Interpretation*. Translated by TH Trapp. Grand Rapids: Eerdmans, 2008.

_____. *Living by Faith: Justification and Sanctification*. Lutheran Quarterly Books. Grand Rapids: Eerdmans, 2003.

Beardsley, Monroe (ed.) *The European Philosophers from Descartes to Nietzsche*. Modern Library Classics. New York: Modern Library, 2002.

Biermann, Joel D. *A Case for Character: Towards a Lutheran Virtue Ethics*. Minneapolis: Fortress, 2015.

_____. *Wholly Citizens: God's Two Realms and Christian Engagement with the World*. Minneapolis: Fortress, 2017.

Braaten, Carl E. (ed.) *Union with Christ: The New Finnish Interpretation of Luther*. Grand Rapids: Eerdmans, 1998.

Bradley, James E. and Richard A. Muller. *Church History: An Introduction to Research, Reference Works, and Methods*. Grand Rapids: Eerdmans, 1995.

Bretall, Robert (editor). *A Kierkegaard Anthology*. New York: Modern Library, 1936.

Bultmann, Rudolph. *The Presence of Eternity: History and Eschatology*. Edinburgh: Edinburgh University Press, 1975.

Butler, Judith. *Gender Trouble*. New York: Routledge, 2006.

Carry, Phillip "*Sola Fide*: Luther and Calvin," *Concordia Theological Quarterly*. 71 (2009):265-281.

Chemnitz, Martin. *The Two Natures in Christ*. Translated by J.A.O. Preus. St. Louis: Concordia, 1971.

_____. *Loci Theologici*. Translated by JAO Preus. St. Louis: Concordia, 1989.

Churchland, Patricia S. *Neurophilosophy: Toward a Unified Science of the Mind-Brain*. Cambridge, MA: Bradford, 1989.

Clark, James M. *The Great German Mystics: Eckhart, Tauler, and Suso*. London: Basil Blackwell, 1949.

Cooper, Jordan B. *Christification: A Lutheran Approach to Theosis*. Eugene, OR: Wipf and Stock, 2014.

_____. *Hands of Faith: A Historical and Theological Study of the*

Two Kinds of Righteousness in Lutheran Thought. Eugene, OR: Wipf and Stock, 2016.

_____. *Lex Aeterna: A Defense of the Orthodox Lutheran Doctrine of God's Law and Critique of Gerhard Forde*. Eugene, OR: Wipf and Stock, 2017.

Copleston, Frederick. *Greece and Rome: From the Pre-Socratics to Plotinus. A History of Philosophy*. New York Doubleday, 1962.

_____. *Medieval Philosophy: From Augustine to Duns Scotus. A History of Philosophy*. New York: Doubleday, 1962.

Craig, William Lane. *The Only Wise God: The Compatibility of Divine Foreknowledge and Human Freedom*. Eugene, OR: Wipf and Stock, 2017.

Dawkins, Richard. *The God Delusion*. Wilmington, MA: Mariner, 2008.

De Beauvoir, Simone. *The Second Sex: A New Translation of the Landmark Classic*. Translated by Constance Borde and Sheila Malovany-Chevallier, 2011.

Descartes, Renes. *Key Philosophical Writings*. Edited by T. Griffith. Hertfordshire: Wordsworth, 1997.

Dionysius the Areopogite. *On the Divine Names and the Mystical Theology*. Translated by C.E. Rolt. London: Macmillan, 1920.

Dolezal, James. *God Without Parts: Divine Simplicity and the*

Metaphysics of God's Absoluteness. Eugene, OR: Wipf and Stock, 2011.

Doolan, Gregory. *Aquinas on Divine Ideas as Exemplar Causes*. Washington, DC: Catholic University of America, 2014.

ELCA. *Gender-based Violence*. Chicago: Evangelical Lutheran Church in America, 2015.

Ellis, Brian. *The Philosophy of Nature: A Guide to the New Essentialism*. Montreal: McGill-Queen's University Press, 2002.

Evans G.R. *Philosophy and Theology in the Middle Ages*. London: Routledge, 1993.

Fairweather, Eugene. *A Scholastic Miscellany: From Anselm to Ockham*. Library of Christian Classics Volume X. Philadelphia, Westminster: 1956.

Feser, Edward. *The Last Superstition: A Refutation of the New Atheism*. South Bend, IN: St. Augustine's, 2008.

_____. *Aquinas: A Beginner's Guide*. London: Oneworld, 2009.

_____. *Locke*. Oneworld Thinkers. London: Oneworld, 2013.

_____. *Scholastic Metaphysics: A Contemporary Introduction*. Piscataway, NJ: Transaction, 2014.

_____. *Five Proofs of the Existence of God*. San Francisco: Ignatius, 2017.

Flynn, Thomas R. *Existentialism: A Very Short Introduction*. Oxford: Oxford University, 2006.

Forde, Gerhard O. *The Law-Gospel Debate: An Interpretation of Its Historical Development*. Minneapolis: Fortress, 1969.

_____. *Where God Meets Man: Luther's Down to Earth Approach to the Gospel*. Minneapolis: Augsburg, 1972.

_____. *Justification by Faith: A Matter of Life and Death*. Mifflintown, PA: Sigler, 1990.

_____. *Theology is for Proclamation*. Fortress: Minneapolis, 1990.

_____. *On Being a Theologian of the Cross: Reflections on Luther's Heidelberg Disputation, 1518*. Grand Rapids: Eerdmans, 1997.

_____. *A More Radical Gospel: Essays on Eschatology, Authority, Atonement, and Ecumenism*. Edited by MC Mattes and SD Paulson. Grand Rapids: Eerdmans, 2004.

_____. *The Captivation of the Will: Luther V. Erasmus on Freedom and Bondage*. Grand Rapids: Eerdmans, 2005.

_____. *The Preached God: Proclamation in Word and Sacrament*. Edited by Mark C. Mattes and Steven D. Paulson. Grand

Rapids: Eerdmans, 2007.

Friedman, Maurice (editor). *The Worlds of Existentialism: A Critical Reader*. New York: Random House, 1964.

Gardner, Sebastian. *Kant and the Critique of Pure Reason*. London: Routledge, 1999.

Gerhard, Johann. *On the Nature of God and On the Trinity*. Translated by Richard J. Dinda. St. Louis: Concordia, 2007.

_____. *On the Nature of Theology and On the Scripture*. Translated by Richard J. Dinda. St. Louis: Concordia, 2009.

_____. *Sacred Meditations*. Translated by Wade R. Johnston. Saginaw, MI: Magdeburg, 2011.

Gilson, Etienne. *Being and Some Philosophers*. Ontario: Pontifical Institute, 1949.

Grimenstein, Edward O. *A Lutheran Primer for Preaching: A Theological and Practical Approach to Sermon Writing*. St. Louis: Concordia, 2015.

Gritsch, Erick W. *A History of Lutheranism*. Minneapolis: Fortress, 2002.

Gritsch, Erick W. and Robert W. Jenson. *Lutheranism: The Theological Movement and Its Confessional Writings*. Philadelphia: Fortress, 1976.

Hagglund, Bengt 1980. "Melanchthon Versus Luther: The Contemporary Struggle," *Concordia Theological Quarterly* 44/2-3 (1980): 123-133.

Harris, Samuel. *The End of Faith: Religion, Terror, and the Future of Reason.* New York: W.W. Norton, 2004.

Hart, David Bentley. *The Experience of God: Being, Consciousness, Bliss.* New Haven: Yale, 2013.

Hayward, John F. *Existentialism and Religious Liberalism.* Boston: Beacon, 1962.

Hein, Steven A. "Reason and the Two Kingdoms: An Essay in Luther's Thought" *The Springfielder* 36/2 (1972): 138-148.

Hinlicky, Paul R. *Divine Simplicity: Christ the Crisis of Metaphysics.* Minneapolis: Fortress, 2016.

Hoenecke, Adolph. *Evangelical Lutheran Dogmatics.* Translated by J Langebartels and H Vogel. Milwaukee: Northwester, 1999-2009.

Hoffman, Bengt R. *Theology of the Heart: The Role of Mysticism in the Theology of Martin Luther.* Minneapolis: Kirkhouse, 1998.

Holl, Karl. *What Did Luther Understand by Religion?* Minneapolis: Fortress, 1977.

Howsare, Rodney A. *Balthasar and Protestantism: The Ecumenical Implications of His Theological Style.* London: Bloomsbury,

2005.

Hume, David. *A Treatise on Human Nature.* Edited by DGC Macnabb. London: Collins Sons, 1962.

Janz, Denis R. *Luther and Late Medieval Thomism: A Study in Theological Anthropology.* Ontario: Wilfrid Laurier, 1983.

_____. *Luther on Thomas Aquinas.* Havertown, PA: Zabern, 1989.

_____. "Syllogism or Paradox: Aquinas and Luther on Theological Method. *Theological Studies* 59 (1998): 3-21.

Jenson, Robert W. *Systematic Theology Volume 1: The Triune God.* New York: Oxford, 1997.

Junius, Francis. *A Treatise on True Theology.* Translated by DC Noe. Grand Rapids: Reformation Heritage, 2014.

Kendall, R.T. *Calvin and English Calvinism to 1649.* Eugene, OR: Wipf and Stock, 2011.

Kenney, John Peter. *The Mysticism of Augustine: Rereading the Confessions.* Abingdon: Routledge, 2005.

_____. "'None Come Closer to Us than These:' Augustine and the Platonists." *Religions.* 114/7 (2016): 1-16.

Kolb, Robert and Charles P. Arand. *The Genius of Luther's Theology: A Wittenberg Way of Thinking for the Contemporary Church.* Grand Rapids: Baker, 2008.

Kolb, Robert and Timothy J. Wengert (editors). *The Book of Concord: The Confessions of the Evangelical Lutheran Church.* Translated by Charles Arand, et. al. Minneapolis: Fortress, 2000.

Koterski, J.W. "The Doctrine of Participation in Thomistic Metaphysics." *The Future of Thomism.* Edited by DW Hudson and DW Moran. Notre Dame, IN: Notre Dame, 185-196.

Krauth, Charles Porterfield. *The Conservative Reformation and Its Theology.* Philadelphia: United Lutheran, 1913.

Kripke, Saul A. *Naming and Necessity.* Cambridge: Harvard, 1980.

Leinsle, Ulrich G. *Introduction to Scholastic Theology.* Translated by M.J. Miller. Washington D.C.: Catholic University of America, 2010.

Leithart, Peter. *The End of Proestantism: Pursuing Unity in a Fragmented Church.* Grand Rapids: Brazos, 2016.

Lewis, Gordon R. and Bruce A. Demarest. *Integrative Theology: Volume 1, Knowing Ultimate Reality: The Living God.* Grand Rapids: Zondervan, 2014.

Lindberg, Carl E. *Christian Dogmatics and Notes on the History of Dogma.* Translated by C.E. Hoffsten. Rock Island, IL: Augustana, 1922.

Livingston, James C. *Modern Christian Thought: From the*

Enlightenment to Vatican II. New York: Macmillan, 1971.

Lossky, Vladimir. *The Mystical Theology of the Eastern Church.* Crestwood, NY: St. Vladimir's Seminary Press, 1957.

Lotz, David W. *Ritschl & Luther: A Fresh Perspective on Albrecht Ritschl's Theology in Light of His Luther Study.* New York: Abingdon, 1974.

Luther, Martin. *Early Theological Works.* Edited and Translated by James Atkinson. Philadelphia: Westminster, 1962.

MacQuarrie, John. *An Existentialist Theology: A Comparison of Heidegger and Bultmann.* London: SCM, 1955.

Mannermaa, Tuomo. *Christ Present in Faith: Luther's View of Justification.* Minneapolis: Fortress, 2005.

Maas, Korey D. and Adam S. Francisco (editors) *Making the Case for Christianity: Responding to Modern Objections.* St. Louis: Concordia, 2014.

Moltmann, Jurgen. *The Crucified God: The Cross of Christ as the Foundation and Criticism of Christian Theology.* Minneapolis: Fortress, 1993.

Muller, Richard A. *Post-Reformation Reformed Dogmatics: The Rise and Development of Reformed Orthodoxy, ca. 1520 to ca. 1725.* Vol. 1. Grand Rapids: Baker, 2003.

Murphy L.F., "Gabriel Biel as Transmitter of Aquinas to

Luther." *Renaissance and Reformation* 7/1 (1983): 26-41.

Murray, Scott R. *Law, Life, and the Living God: The Third Use of the Law in Modern American Lutheranism.* St. Louis: Concordia, 2001.

Nahm, Milton C. *Selections from Early Greek Philosophy.* New York: Meredith, 1964.

Nieuwenhove, Rik Van. *An Introduction to Medieval Theology.* Cambridge: Cambridge, 2012.

Oberman, Heiko A. *The Harvest of Medieval Theology.* Baker: Grand Rapids, 1963.

———. *The Dawn of the Reformation: Essays in Late Medieval and Early Reformation Thought.* Grand Rapids: Eerdmans, 1992.

Ockham, William of. *Philosophical Writings.* Translated by Philotheus Boehner. Indianapolis: Hackett, 1990.

Oderberg, David S. *Real Essentialism.* London: Routledge, 2007.

Olson, Robert G. *An Introduction to Existentialism.* Mineola, NY: Dover, 1962.

Osborne, Thomas. "Faith, Philosophy, and the Nominalist Background to Luther's Defense of the Real Presence." *Journal of the History of Ideas* 63/1 (63-82): 2002.

Owens, Joseph. *An Elementary Christian Metaphysic.* Milwaukee: Bruce, 1963.

Parker, Eric. "The Platonism of Martin Luther" *Calvinist International.* http://www.calvinistinternational.com/2013/05/20/the-platonism-of-martin-luther/

Paulson, Steven D. *Lutheran Theology.* New York: T&T Clark, 2011.

Pieper, Francis. *Christian Dogmatics.* St. Louis: Concordia, 1950-1957.

Pinnock, Clark H. *The Openness of God: A Biblical Challenge to the Traditional Understanding of God.* Downers Grove, IL: IVP Academic, 1994.

Piper, John and Justin Taylor. *Suffering and the Sovereignty of God.* Wheaton, IL: Crossway, 2006.

Plantinga, Alvin. *God, Freedom, and Evil.* Grand Rapids: Eerdmans, 1989.

Plato. *Selected Dialogues.* Translated by B. Jowett. Franklin Center, PA: Franklin, 1983.

Plotinus. *The Six Enneads.* Translated by Stephen MacKenna and B.S. Page. Chicago: William Benton, 1952.

Preus, Robert D. *The Theology of Post-Reformation Lutheranism: A Study of Theological Prolegomena.* Vol. 1. St. Louis: Concordia, 1970.

Preus, Robert D. and Wilbert H. Rosin (eds.) *A Contemporary Look at the Formula of Concord.* St. Louis: Concordia, 2001.

Puchniak, James "Augustine's Conception of Deification, Revisited," in *Theosis: Deification in Christian Theology.* Eugene, OR: Pickwick, 2006: 122-133.

Quenstedt, Johannes A. *The Nature and Character of Theology: An Introduction to the Thought of J.A. Quenstedt from Theologia Didactio-Polemica Sive Systema Theologicum.* Translated by Luther Poellot. St. Louis: Concordia, 1986.

Quine, W.V.O. *Word and Object.* Cambridge: MIT, 1960.

Quirk M.J. "Martin Heidegger: Being, Beings and Truth" *Sophia Project*, 2000. http://www.sophia-project.org.

Reed, Antony C. "Melanchthon's 1521 *Loci Communes*: The First Protestant Apology" *Churchman*. 85/3 (1971).

Richardson, Bradford. "New Jersey Church Celebrates Transgender Pastor's Transition with Naming Ceremony," *Washington Times*, 2018.
  http://www.washingtontimes.com/news/2018/feb/13/new-jersey-church-celebrates-transgender-pastors-t/

Ritschl, Albrecht. *The Christian Doctrine of Justification and Reconciliation.* Edited and Translated by HR Mackintosh and AB Macaulay. Edinburgh: T&T Clark, 1900.

_____. *Three Essays: Theology and Metaphysics,* "Prolegomena" to the History of Pietism, Instruction in the Christian Religion. Translated by P Hefner. Minneapolis: Fortress, 1972.

Robbins, Jerry K. "Luther on Reason: A Reappraisal." *Word and World* 13/2 (1993): 191-202.

Rosin, Wilbert H. "The Importance of Epistemology for Luther's and Melanchthon's Theology." *Concordia Theological Quarterly* 44/2-3 (1980): 134-140.

Saint Augustine, *The Confessions*. Translated by Maria Boulding. Works of Saint Augustine. Hyde Park, NY: New City Press, 2002.

_____. *The Trinity: De Trinitate*. Translated by Edmund Hill. Works of Saint Augustine. Hyde Park, NY: New City Press, 2012.

Sasse, Hermann. *We Confess the Sacraments*. Translated by Norman Nagel. St. Louis: Concordia, 1985.

Saussure, Ferdinand. *Course in General Linguistics*. Translated by W Baskin. New York: Columbia, 1959.

Scaer, David P. 1980. "Did Luther and Melanchthon Agree on the Real Presence?" *Concordia Theological Quarterly* 44/2-3 (1980): 141-147.

Schaff, Philip. *A History of the Christian Church*. 8 vols. 1858-1890.

Schmid, Heinrich. *The Doctrinal Theology of the Evangelical Lutheran Church.* Translated by C.A. Hay and Henry E. Jacobs. Minneapolis: Augsburg, 1899.

Schmidt, Alvin J. *Hallmarks of Lutheran Identity.* St. Louis: Concordia, 2017.

Schumacher, William W. *Who Do I Say That You Are? Anthropology and the Theology of Theosis in the Finnish School of Tuomo Mannermaa.* Eugene, OR: Wipf and Stock, 2010.

Scotus, Duns. *Philosophical Writings.* Translated by A. Wolter. Indianapolis: Hackett, 1987.

Shantz, Douglas H. *An Introduction to German Pietism: Protestant Renewal at the Dawn of Modern Europe.* Baltimore: Johns Hopkins, 2013.

Smith, Kevin G. *Academic Writing and Theological Research: A Guide for Students.* Johannesburg: South African Theological Seminary, 2008.

Staniloea, Dumitru. *The Experience of God: Revelation and Knowledge of the Triune God.* Brookline, MA: Holy Cross, 1998.

Suvak, Vladislav. "The Essence of Truth (Aletheia) and the Western Tradition in the Thought of Heidegger and Patocka," *Thinking Fundamentals, IWM Junior Visiting Fellows Conference* IX/4 (2000).

Tauler, John. *Sermons.* Translated by M Shrady. New York:

Paulist, 1985.

Theologia Germanica. Translated by Bengt Hoffman. New York: Paulist, 1980.

Trueman, Carl R. and R. Scott Clark. *Protestant Scholasticism: Essays in Reassessment.* Eugene, OR: Wipf and Stock, 2005.

Wassmer, T.A. 1960. "The Trinitarian Theology of Augustine and His Debt to Plotinus." *Harvard Theological Review.* 53/4 (1960): 261-268.

Weidner, Revere Franklin. *Pneumatology, Or the Doctrine of the Work of the Holy Spirit.* Chicago: Wartburg, 1915.

Weinandy, Thomas. *Does God Change?* Studies in Historical Theology Volume 4. Still River, MA: St. Bede's, 2002.

Westerholm, Stephen. *Perspectives Old and New on Paul: The "Lutheran" Paul and His Critics.* Grand Rapids: Eerdmans, 2004.

Wilchins, Richie. *Queer Theory, Gender Theory: An Instant Primer.* Bronx, NY: Magnus, 2014.

Wolfson, Harry Austryn. *The Philosophy of the Church Fathers: Faith, Trinity, Incarnation.* Cambridge: Harvard, 1956.

Yaghjian, Lucretia B. *Writing Theology Well: A Rhetoric for Theological and Biblical Writers.* New York: Continuum, 2006.

Printed in Poland
by Amazon Fulfillment
Poland Sp. z o.o., Wrocław